"WHAT A MARVELOUS BOOK!"
John Bradshaw

"A splendid book. It speaks to us of the essential need of our time—the rebirth of the long-despised feminine values of caring, nurturing, waiting, and trust."

Helen M. Luke
Author of *Women: Earth and Spirit*

"Reasoned and compassionate . . . Thought-provoking . . . Nelson examines every detail of each of these stories, the male roles as well as the female, the archetypes, the imagery and the metaphors, and shows that the condition (and conditioning) of women today is not dissimilar to the long ago and far away."

National Catholic Reporter

"Nelson retells the tales and then analyzes each part of the story to show how it applies to many women today who are falling into the same inner traps in which the women in the stories are caught. She brings to bear insights gained from her studies at the C. G. Jung Institute in Zurich . . . and from ten years of running women's groups. . . . The stories are charmingly told and the explanations are lucid and enlightening."

The Philosopher's Stone

"A rich and balanced discussion. First class."

Praying

OTHER BOOKS BY GERTRUD MUELLER NELSON

Clip-Art for Feasts and Seasons
Clip-Art for Celebrations and Service
To Dance with God:
Family Ritual and Community Celebration

HERE ALL DWELL FREE

Stories to Heal the Wounded Feminine

Gertrud Mueller Nelson
With illustrations by the author

Fawcett Columbine • New York

A Fawcett Columbine Book
Published by Ballantine Books

Library of Congress Catalog Card Number: 92-90395

ISBN: 0-449-90789-9

Cover design by Georgia Morrissey
Cover painting by Joyce Patti

Manufactured in the United States of America
First Ballantine Books Edition: February 1993
10 9 8 7 6 5 4 3 2

for
Annika Maria
Sara Kirsten
and
Peter Ansgar
and
Jerry

CONTENTS

Part I The Handless Maiden

Part II   Briar Rose

Part III   A New Creation

Part IV   Related Stories

PREFACE:
HOW THIS BOOK
CAME TO BE

A long time ago, before TV, before the drip-dry shirt, perhaps even before the automatic washer and dryer, I was a little girl and I looked forward to Tuesdays. At that time Tuesday was also known as ironing day. And on Tuesdays my mother, one or another of my sisters or brothers and I would go down to the basement with a great basket of fresh-smelling linens to iron. Did my mother like to iron? I don't know. I only know that I liked it when my mother ironed because, if we children quietly handed her the next item to be pressed and put what was freshly ironed into its appropriate pile, we might gently coax to life the mood she slipped into on an ironing day. It was a storytelling mood—one that we carefully prompted and encouraged with little suggestions, hoping that she'd soon begin. In due time, as the rhythm of ironing set in, she would indeed feel a story coming on.

My mother was—and still is—a very good storyteller and her repertoire never ceases to astonish. Most of her stories she knew by heart and, though Tuesdays were not the only occasions when we could coax a story from her, I rather suspect that telling stories while ironing was a way to transform a task and tap the dreamy, reflective place the mind retreats to during routine tasks, looking for the gifts of another world.

It was also clear that, on some level, my mother believed deeply in the truth and power of myths and fairy tales, because they were a rich part of our heritage as we grew. From her we learned the Greek myths, a sizable collection of fairy tales from all the world, the legends of the saints, stories from Hebrew Scripture, Gospel stories as they occurred in their seasons, and a bonus smattering of holy legends that never quite made it as far as the Gospels. And as well as this oral tradition, it was from her, and from my father with his nose for good books, that I received, at a young age, my very own volume of the complete Grimms and a fat, handsome volume of Greek myths.

I never outgrew these stories or these two books but rather steadily grew into them. They were nourishing fare in my childhood and adolescence, the pure, unobstructed view into mystery. I drew from these books as a primary source in my teaching and used my students as an excuse to reenter that world with them. They were exactly the stories I told and the books that I read to my own children and which they read and continue to read in their young adulthood.

But there comes a time when we are no longer simple enough to see our visions with a clear eye. And it was then that I found the mediation of Carl Gustav Jung's psychology a useful lens through which to peer into the visions once more.

After some work at the Jung Institute in Zurich, I was asked by our local Jung Society to talk on myths and fairy tales. What began rather formally as a four-part presentation grew into more than a decade of women's gatherings in my living room. I drew a great deal of help from Jung's insight and most especially from his student, a seminal analyst of myths and fairy tales, Marie-Louise von Franz.

We began, on those Wednesday mornings, with tea and talk during which time we became acquainted and warmed as a group. Then we gathered in the living room in a circle. We listened to a story. I followed with an "oral essay" on what I had learned from the story from my readings and more especially from my personal experience. The presentation was followed by discussion—and sometimes simply by long periods of silence. How surprised we often were, deeply touched, amazed—but mostly greatly comforted—that the heroic lives described in these stories grappled with the issues we faced in our own lives. So none of us, living lives of unspoken questions in our kitchens and work cubicles, were really so alone. Our struggles were uniquely ours, but they were also the struggles that belonged to the development of the feminine. Women everywhere shared our wounds, failed their trials, but behold, they also were given the means to heal and transform.

The fairy tales carried us through our relationships, lent meaning to our loves and our losses, shed light on our sexual confusion, helped us to mother and raise our daughters and sons. We grew clearer about the nature and meaning of the feminine and about our own natures as women. And we discovered that conflicting styles of living out our femininity and the wounds of fate have always been part of the human condition. We felt curiously joined to those who peopled our stories, to each other, to all women, and to the feminine wherever we found it.

Speaking for myself, I came to realize that the variations and details of my personal life formed a journey no less heroic than those described in our stories—inimitable, unique, astonishing.

Though our search began with a woman's focus, we soon learned that the development of the feminine was also part of a man's unfolding of his inner feminine side. And there were stories to help us understand the heroic journeys of the men in our lives.

From Wednesday to Wednesday at ten in the morning and year after year, these men saw us grow braver and more understanding of them. Certainly some of them, hearing the stories that especially moved us, also found them useful in understanding us better. What's more, we all learned that it was not just women who were wounded and in need of healing; the feminine values in men and in our masculine society were also in danger and in need of healing. And so it was that many men were also introduced to the neglected feminine side of their own selves.

For just as yin and yang spin and tumble into one another and are never static, and just as each is inoculated with a spot

of its opposite, so men and women are inoculated with a bit
of their opposite side. Men, though they may be assertive, active
and dynamic, are also touched with a "feminine" element inside
them, where they find their qualities of feeling and relatedness,
their imagination or their gifts for empathy. And women,
though they may be more comfortable with an interiority, with
their intuitive knowledge, with receptivity and interpersonal
relationships, are touched with the "masculine" energies that
allow them to create order, make decisions, take the initiative
or function practically in the outside world. In a right relationship between men and women each of them has a right relationship to his or her inner soul—he to his inner feminine side
and she to her inner masculine side. These qualities will be their
guides and not dominants in the creation of whole and healthy
personalities. The words "masculine" and "feminine," then,
are to be understood as qualities found within women and men
in turn, but are not to be mistaken as descriptive of "males"
or "females."

The wisdom we gleaned from these tales, like a pebble
dropped in a pond, sent waves out in circles and touched people
far beyond the Wednesday experience. We had scratched something powerful, useful and attractive to people of both sexes
and all ages. I suspected as much when our group—now jam-
ming the living room, filling the dining room and spilling over
into the kitchen—included my daughter with some of her

friends crouched on the floor between feet and folding chairs, quiet as mice. They claimed a bad case of "senioritis" as their excuse for needing to play hooky and sneak back to the house to be with us. Their senioritis recurred magically on a number of those Wednesday mornings, though now with the blessing of their curious English teacher, who only asked for their oral reports on what they learned there. The Wednesday group finally outgrew its space and the luxury of free weekdays was curtailed by economic realities. My own work continued with fairy tales and grew into workshops and seminars.

I found, in the sharing of fairy tales with people around the country, a great interest in an extended unfolding of the truth these stories told. They found that the issues of our feminine revolution needed redefinition as a feminine *evolution* with the promise of healing. Now, because of the continued encouragement of friends, I have tried here to capture a little of what we learned about the truth of just two of our favorite fairy tales.

IN APPRECIATION

This book emerges from a long-held personal belief in the truth of fairy tales. I am indebted to my parents, and to all those tellers of tales who came before them, who followed some instinctual wisdom and passed along the stories that keep on needing to be retold and reheard. I thank warmly the many women and men who shared my stories with me and who, in turn, shared the stories of their own journeys with such touching honesty. There are among my friends many who have been everything from my teachers to a cheering section and some who have rolled up sleeves to be readers as the manuscript evolved.

I owe special thanks to Marie-Louise von Franz, whose seminars I attended in Zurich, and for her several excellent pioneer books on the understanding of mythic truth. Her work has been my primary source for this book. Nancy Gregg Hatch, who was a most gentle and supportive midwife to my last book, *To Dance with God*, has been at my side again, encouraging this one. She was a member of the original living-room gatherings and since then her enthusiasm and faithfulness have been unflagging. My friend Patricia Schaefer collaborated with me on a workshop, adding solid, practical material that has also enriched this work. Betty Ann Backus, Bea Burch, Larry Connelly, CSP, Fanny Howe, Cynthia R. Hibbs, Howard and Hildegard Mueller Kerney, Rosemarie Kohn, Judy and Richard Madsen, Grace McCormack, Mary Virginia Micka, CSJ, Patricia Mittendorff, Arline Paa, Marky Reynolds, Irene Russell, Ann Silber, Olga Snow, Kathy Smith, Susan Tobias, Christopher Witt, CSP, the members of my worshiping community—and all who have either read the manuscript or somehow offered their wisdom to the work: I thank you.

A good editor and good friend is Thomas Cahill. To have someone at the other end of the kingdom believe in you and in your process makes all the difference in the world. Thank you.

My own family has always lived and breathed fairy tales. My thanks to Peter, our eldest, who at a tender age dressed as Achilles with a shield made, alas, not of seven ox hides, but merely of the next best stuff, and wearing a colander festooned with pheasant feathers as his helmet, he wielded his sword, the battered trophy of a hero's journey. He is still slaying dragons and saving the seas and oceans of the earth. He reminds me that a young man's heroic quest is active and adventuresome and wishes I'd get on with telling you his favorite tale, "The Two Brothers." Sara, as a mother's daughter, has long shared from her vantage point the experiences of her blooming autonomy. As a nature writer of considerable grace, she devotes her talent to honoring our mother the earth—and helps her earthly mother with some editorial wisdom. To Annika, our youngest, I owe the finest definition of myth I will ever hear or ever share. I see the artist in her working to bring what is true on the outside and what is true on the inside to a place where they overlap. And to my husband, Jerry Nelson, my thanks for the famous stories he scooped out of his deepest self and shared to the delight of his family. I am indebted to the insights of his profession which he shares with me, to his patience, encouragement and great, good grace as my work unfolded and this book was being written. But mostly I am glad that he wove his own hero's journey into mine and has become my very good friend.

Here All Dwell Free

INTRODUCTION:
TOWARD AN UNDERSTANDING
OF FAIRY TALES

Once Upon a Time

Once upon a time there was a certain miller . . . Once upon a time, in a far-off castle, there lived a King and a Queen . . . Once upon a time fairy tales were told not just to children but were shared among people of all ages, because the wisdom in fairy tales is ageless and their age is timeless. That is why they so often begin with those words "Once upon a time"—which is to say in a time-out-of-time, or in timeless eternity, *in illo tempore*, in a time beyond history. "Once upon a time" heads us off to a realm of archetypal truth and mythic reality.

In our rationality and logic we often find it difficult to enter into mythic reality. As adults, we have cultivated our intellects to deal mainly with the rational world. We rather like to think that mystery or magic is so much childish nonsense. But leave it to a child to come up with a way to understand the validity of mythic reality. This is a definition for myth that I learned from my youngest daughter when she was about five. She was being tested by a school psychologist to see if she was ready to attend kindergarten. He had asked her some questions to determine something about her verbal skills and that evening he phoned us to tell us of their conversation. He had asked her:

"Annika, do your parents read you stories?"

"Stories? Oh yes. My papa tells us Piggle-Wiggle stories and my mama reads us Greek myths."

"Greek myths! Really? What are myths?"

"Oh, you know. Mythology? Those are stories"—and she paused—"stories that aren't true on the outside. But they *are* true on the inside!"

This definition seems a useful tool. It indicates that there is an inner truth just as much as there is an outer truth. It indicates that inner truth and outer truth are probably equal in value though one lives in the dark and the other in the light. Each truth speaks its own language and must be understood in its own realm.

But isn't it the fate of the human condition that the very process of becoming adult is to work so long at making sense of outer truth and its reality that we often give it a greater value? We certainly give it more time. This is the realm where we take things literally. We place these realities into historical context. We hand them over to science to measure and test. Preoccupied with outer realities, we may forget the inner world altogether—forget its mythic language and how to understand it. Out of sight, out of mind. But, for all that, still alive and well.

For our mythic, inner reality never gives up pursuing us. Now it just has to try harder. Aiming to get our attention, it pops out in "slips of the tongue." It dresses up in the clothes of the people we passionately admire and wears the disguise of those we fear, mistrust or reject. It enriches our creativity or petrifies our growth. It rides heavily on our shoulders and whispers in our ear, begging to be made conscious and to be taken seriously by influencing our habits or burdening us with symptoms, fears and gnawing guilts. It fills us with longing and haunts us with the desire to search for "something more." All night it spins out wonderful and horrible tales fashioned only for us, producing fantastic images, offering useful insight, never giving up.

But since dream language—or mythic language—tells us a truth which is not literal but inner and since we have lost touch with our inner world, we cannot receive our messages. We fail to take its wisdom to heart until we can hear that symbolic language, know the level on which it speaks and can translate its meaning.

Mythic language, then, for us complicated adults (*never for children*), may need translation and pondering if its wisdom is to soak through our guarded hearts and hand up nourishment to our outer lives. If we ignore our inside truth, we will keep on honoring and blaming our inner heroes and our inner enemies by projecting them onto persons or countries or races of the outside world. We will be riddled with neurotic symptoms and plagued with anxieties. We will wrongly interpret what is inner and personal to be true as outer and literal and will consume compulsively, only to wonder why our hunger is never stilled. Finally we will have rejected the gift whose purpose is to lead us to healing and wholeness. Mythic language is a thread we can follow to our very transformation and redemption.

A Collective Dream, a Religious Search

In the old days the spinning of stories—by open fires, while husking the corn, while knitting socks—was a kind of spiritual occupation or a form of religious search. Just as we might follow a thread through our dreams and learn to unravel meaning there and gain enlightenment, we can also follow the threads that are spun out in the great collective dreams of myth and fairy tale. For a fairy tale is the dream language of a whole culture. Fairy tales are our own big dreams. The heroes and villains who have paraded across pillows everywhere and who have taken up residence in the secret corners of our waking dreams, to live out untold dramas, rise to the surface in the fairy tale. There these dream folk, now distilled of personal distortions, become the truths and symbols which belong to us all. In fairy tales they speak the colorful language of the soul of a people. They teach us about our culture and they return to us essential psychic facts about ourselves.

Unlike allegories, fables or cautionary tales which may have been created to form a culture, fairy tales, then, are more like rumblings from a deep, unconscious source within the culture. They often show the culture for what it is or forewarn and predict. They also contain a wisdom about the human condition. Devoid of self-consciousness, fairy tales focus on the realm we live in most but give us a perspective from the bottom up.

Fairy tales often begin on the surface: they make some ordinary comment on what is going on in the ordinary, surface world. Then, suddenly, the surface gives way and we are plunged down the well into the inner world. With the abandon of a child we tumble, unable to brace ourselves, and find ourselves in a mysterious place. Now we are in an enchanted forest, or we walk on the bottom of the sea, or animals speak to us and we can understand. In this place are revealed to us our heroic duties and the dreadful trials we must endure so that change can be effected and a deliverance set in motion. From the bottom up or from the inside out, we have a new view of our conscious world by encountering the grand projected images of the unconscious.

Just as in the interpretation of our dreams, we take to heart all the characters who people the drama. For we carry traits of both the hero *and* the villain, the kind mother *and* the witch, the princess *and* the prince, the fool *and* the wise one, the frog *and* the king. We become more human and more whole as we meet ourselves in every character portrayed and own them as aspects of ourselves—crowns, warts and all.

Because fairy tales contain powerful truths about the human condition, many of them, with tenacity and uncanny persistence, turn up, theme and variation, in vastly different cultures. The stories seem to say that certain truths are everyone's reality, no matter where you live. We are all sisters and brothers in our journey toward wholeness, and the stories breathe new life into the mysteries of our shared condition to make it comprehensible and to lend us the courage to lift up our eyes and see one another as fellow pilgrims on a holy road.

So we crack open our stories and enter "a fairy tale world" but quickly discover that this world offers no "retreat from reality," nor does it invite us to a world of shining bliss. Rather, anguish and darkness are the fairy tale's prevailing tone—the anguish of a lost paradisiacal happiness and the inevitable darkness that enters every life. In darkness and anguish we stumble upon the fevers of the soul or the fevers of the culture. More often than not, there is an enchantment which is not a positive transformation—not enchanting at all, as we like to use that word—but a stunting or maiming of the hero or the culture.

In the darkness and pain of the story we engage our own "stuck" places, the blocks, the wounds, the fears, the passions, the possibilities. We learn that only anguish and a *dis*enchantment can transform us. Disguises are pulled away: the kind mother is also a witch, the generous man is a devil, the frog is a prince, the scullery maid a princess. Only in disenchantment and in lowliness will the hero become real. In engaging the frogginess of ourselves, transformation is made possible. Dressed in our scullery rags and not in our ball gowns, we will come to recognize who we are. Seated in ashes, we can be connected to our noble nature. In fairy tales the hero is transformed to what he or she was always meant to be—but was unable to become until hard work and heroic deeds had been accomplished.

After sorrow and heroic deeds we arrive in that paradoxical place that lies between illusion and disillusionment, between enchantment and disenchantment, a place of tension that points toward wholeness—which also means health, holiness—and the promise of redemption.

Happily Ever After

Fairy tales, for all their economy of language and symbolic form, often reveal a kind of symmetry. They diagnose the problem for us. They plunge us into the crisis, often filled with chaos and darkness, and the mandate to perform daring tasks or suffer a deep wound. But in the midst of the dark predicament there is revealed a prescription for healing. In suffering, the hero works toward this healing. And when the story ends with the symbolism of a marriage and of perfect love, this can be understood as something profound: the dualism of masculine and feminine have transcended polarization and have come to a place where opposites no longer elude each other or work against each other or misunderstand each other. Rather, the crisis of opposites is resolved and the conflict is healed. What has been incompatible now merges in loving empathy. Such a marriage is the ultimate place of wholeness and the story uses the biological differences between male and female to speak symbolically about psychic and spiritual opposites or polarities. This is a mythic marriage, not necessarily literal—a union beyond gender. This is the overlapping of any and all opposites to create a single, new reality—the hope of every human soul—where opposites, though separate, become equal, balanced, shared and fruitful.

It seems a mighty final chord—a neat wrap-up, a comforting resolution. And a story in symbols can do that, only to return us to the fray of our own lives and to that disordered chorus of those who have lost their gods and think they can invent themselves. We go back to the struggle between parents and children, between old values and new, between village and city, inside and outside, masculine and feminine—to learn again and again that neither is valid if it excludes the other. Both realities are at once a constriction and a ticket to freedom. Only in their marriage, in perfect love and community, with massive infusions of grace, can we work for the true Kingdom: that third way, the unitive vision that accepts all contradictions, aware of everything, judgmental of no one.

These are the issues which enter every life. The theologian John Shea says it so well:

> When we reach our limits, when our ordered worlds collapse, when we cannot enact our moral ideals, when we are disenchanted, we are inescapably related to this Mystery which is immanent and transcendent, which issues invitations we must respond to, which is ambiguous about its intentions, and which is real and important beyond all else . . . Our dwelling with Mystery is both menacing and promising, a relationship of exceeding darkness and undeserved light. In this situation with this awareness we do a distinctively human thing. We gather together and tell stories . . . to calm our terror and hold our hope on high. (*Stories of God* [Chicago: The Thomas More Press, 1978].)

About These Stories

Of the many stories that do indeed "calm our terror and hold our hope on high" I have chosen two rich fairy tales for this book.

- I chose these two because we all suffer and struggle to make sense of our developmental crises. These stories talk exactly to that struggle.
- What the world wants of us and what our deepest self wants seem to be in terrible conflict. Here we may find some solace.
- Men may find meaning in these stories because they have been struggling to recognize and value the feeling, tender, patient, relational aspects of their full personalities—almost at the risk of their masculine identity—and so often find that element in themselves broken and in need of healing.
- When women feel pressured to "do it all"—often at the risk of their deepest feminine values—or when they find their feminine identity held in question or lacerated by experience, they may find these stories speak to them.
- Many children today seem to fall between the cracks because the adults who raise them are preoccupied with a massive cultural confusion about what is expected of them. Parents and teachers may find clarification here.
- I chose these two stories because two thirds of the people in the United States suffer from depression, too often a depression that only deepens in some neurotic quagmire of a low-grade and inefficient religious searching. These stories tell of our religious search.
- Because our liberation depends on the dark realm of an unconventional inner life, we can learn something of the nature of that realm in these stories.
- These two stories may speak to the fever of our time, which is to regard masculine and feminine traits as purely culturally defined, thereby robbing those traits of what is poetic and not at all literal.
- I hope these two stories will address all of these situations, not in the hard light of reason, but in the moon's light that defies purely rational explication.

- I selected these two stories because they make a useful study in contrasts.
- Our two heroes, the Handless Maiden and Briar Rose, may lead us to wisdom about our personal and collective stuck places.
- Their stories, like our own, are beset with challenges and tests, with powers and destinies they have not designed but which are yet their own and in which they find the stuff of their transformation.
- These stories may offer some clues to our development as women. They may teach us something about the healing, nurturance, evolution and liberating of feminine values, whether found in the psychic structure of men or in the identity of women. And they may return to us the concept of feminine value wherever it is found in our culture.

I hope these stories and their discussion will only whet your appetites. You will find much more to uncover, material not limited to these pages or by my imagination. You will find, I hope, the inspiration to track down other stories nearly like these (I have included a few at the back of the book) and will apply the paradigms you have learned here to them, to many classic tales and, above all, to the mythic journey which you call your own.

Part I

THE HANDLESS MAIDEN

Chapter 1

THE STORY OF
THE HANDLESS MAIDEN

Once upon a time
there was a certain miller who
bit by bit had fallen into poverty.
He had nothing left but his mill
and a large apple tree which grew behind it.

One day when he had gone into the forest to cut wood,
an old man whom he had never seen before
stepped up to him and said:

"Why do you slave away at cutting wood?
I can make you wealthy beyond your dreams.
All you have to do is promise me
what is standing behind your mill."

"Well," thought the miller,
"indeed, that must be my apple tree."
So he agreed, gave a written promise to the strange man
and was pleased with what seemed to be
a very good bargain.

The stranger, however,
laughed with a sound of evil cunning and said:
"Remember, in three years' time I will come to your mill
and carry away what belongs to me."

Then he went.

When the miller got home,
his wife came running to meet him
and she called out:
"Tell me, miller, whatever happened while you were gone?
All at once every box and chest in the house,
every purse and cupboard is filled
and we have become rich!
No one came here to bring it in
and I can't imagine how this has happened."

To this he answered:
"All this comes from a stranger who met me in the forest.
He promised me great treasure
if I would hand over to him what stands behind the mill.
We can easily spare that old apple tree
in return for all these riches."

"Oh, husband," said the wife, trembling with terror.
"That could only have been the Devil!
He surely didn't mean the apple tree,
but rather our daughter, who was standing behind the mill
sweeping the yard today!"

Their daughter, a beautiful and devout girl,
lived through the three years without blame.
And when the day came that the Devil was to fetch her,
she washed herself clean,
and around herself
she drew a chalk circle.

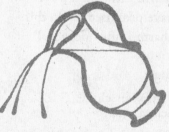

The Devil appeared quite early,
but he could not get near her.

Angrily, he told the miller:
"Take all water away from her
that she may no longer wash,
for otherwise I have no power over her."

The miller was afraid, so he did what he was told.
The next day the Devil came again,
but the girl had wept so on her hands,
that they were quite clean.

Then again the Devil could not get near her
so he raged at the miller and said:
"Cut off her hands!
Or else I will have no power over her."

The miller was shocked and said:
"How could I cut off the hands of my own child?"

But the Devil threatened him and said:
"Either I take her or it is you I carry off."

The miller was filled with alarm,
so he went to his daughter and said:
"My child, I must cut off both your hands
or else the Devil will carry me away.
In my terror I have promised to do this.
Forgive me the harm I must do you."

And she answered:
"Dear Father, I am your child,
do with me what you will."
And she laid down both her hands
and let them be cut off.

Now the Devil came for the third time,
but the maiden had wept so long and so much
on her poor stumps that they, too,
were washed quite clean with her tears.

With that, the Devil had to give in,
for he had lost all right over her.

Then the miller said to her:
"Because of you, my daughter,
we have received great wealth.
Now I will keep you handsomely as long as you live."

But the girl replied:
"No, Father. Here I cannot stay.
I must go forth into the world.
Bind my arms to my back
and compassionate people
will give me what I need."

At sunrise she set out on her way.
She walked the whole day until night fell.
Then she came to a royal garden
and by the shimmering of the moonlight
she saw that trees laden with beautiful fruits grew in it.
But she could not enter the garden,
for it was surrounded by water.

Now the maiden was very hungry, having not eaten a bite,
and hunger tormented her.
She thought, "Oh, if only I could get inside this garden to eat
some fruit before I die of hunger!"

Then she knelt down,
called on the Lord God
and prayed.

With that, an angel suddenly came toward her
and the angel caused the water in the moat to part
so that she could walk through it on a dry path.

So the maiden entered the garden
and the angel went with her.

She saw a tree heavy with beautiful pears,
but the pears were all counted.
To quiet her terrible hunger,
the maiden ate one—just one—off with her mouth.

Now there was hidden in the trees a gardener watching;
but because he was frightened by the presence of the angel
and because he thought the maiden was a spirit,
he remained silent
and did not dare to cry out or speak to them.

When the maiden had eaten the pear,
she was satisfied
and she went to hide herself among the bushes.

The next morning the King, to whom the garden belonged,
came down to it
and, in counting his pears, discovered that one was missing.
He questioned the gardener and the gardener said:

"Last night, a spirit came into this garden,
a spirit with no hands,
and it proceeded to eat off one of the pears with its mouth."

The King said:
"But however did this spirit get over the water
and where did it go after it had eaten the pear?"

The gardener answered:
"Someone came in a snow-white garment from heaven
who caused a dry path to appear in the moat
for the spirit to walk through.
And because that must have been an angel, I was too afraid
and neither asked any questions nor cried out.
When the spirit had finished eating the pear, it went away."

So the King decided to keep watch with his gardener
the next night.

As it grew dark, he returned to the garden
and brought with him a priest
who was to speak to the spirit.
Together they waited beneath the tree and watched.

At midnight the maiden came creeping out of the bushes,
went to the tree
and again ate one pear off
with her mouth.
All the while, the angel stood by her.

The priest went out to them and said:
"Are you from heaven or from earth?
Are you a spirit or a human?"

The maiden answered:
"I am no spirit, but an unhappy mortal deserted by all but
the grace of God."

The King said:
"And if you are forsaken by all the world,
yet will I not forsake you."

He took the maiden with him into his royal palace
and because she was so beautiful and good
he loved her with his whole heart
and made her his wife.

And he saw to it that she was fashioned
a pair of silver hands.

After a year, the King had to go on a journey,
so he gave his young Queen
into the care of his mother and said:
"If my wife should happen to bring forth a child,
take the very best care of her,
nurse her well
and tell me of the birth at once in a letter."

And it so happened
that the young Queen did indeed give birth
to a fine boy.

Promptly the old mother
hurried to announce the joyful news
in a letter to her son.

She gave the letter to a messenger
to hurry away and deliver.
But the messenger, weary with the long distance,
rested by a brook
and was in fact so tired
that he fell asleep.

Now the Devil, who it happened was indeed
still and always looking for an opportunity
to bring harm to the young Queen,
exchanged the joyful letter for another
and said that the Queen had
given birth to a terrible monster.

When the King read the letter,
he was shocked and troubled,
but he wrote an answer directly, saying
that they were to take great care of the Queen and nurse
her well until his arrival.

The messenger hurried back with the letter
but rested in the same place
and again fell asleep.
The Devil came once more
and replaced the letter in his pocket,
with a letter ordering them to put the Queen and her little
child to death.

The old mother, on receiving the letter,
was terribly shocked and could not believe what she read.
She wrote back again to the King
but each time a letter was sent
the Devil substituted a false letter,
and in the last letter it was written that the old mother was

to preserve the young Queen's tongue and eyes as a token
that she had indeed been put to death.

Now the old mother wept
to think such innocent blood was to be shed,
and she caused a hind to be brought her by night
and had her tongue and eyes cut out.
And these she kept.

Then she told the young Queen:
"I cannot bring myself to have you killed
as the King commands,
but here you may no longer stay.
Go forth into the wide world. Take your child
and never come back to this kingdom again!"

The poor woman tied her child to her back
and went away weeping.
Day and night, she walked and walked
until she arrived in the middle of a deep and wild wood.

She fell on her knees and begged God for help,
and with that an angel of the Lord appeared before her
and led her to a little house.

Over its door was written:

HERE ALL DWELL FREE

A snow-white maiden came out of the little house and said:
"Welcome, Lady Queen," and brought her inside.
She unbound the little boy from her back
and held him to her breast that he might drink
and laid him to sleep in a beautiful little bed.

Then the poor woman asked:
"How did you know that I was a queen?"
And the white creature answered:
"I am an angel sent to watch over you and your child."

Now the Queen stayed in the little house for seven years
and was well cared for there.
Then, by God's grace and because of her faith,
her hands, which had been cut off,
grew once more.

At last the King returned home from his journey
and his first wish was to see his wife and the child.
Then his old mother began to weep and said:
"You wicked man! Why did you write to me ordering that I
take those two dear innocent lives?"

And she showed him the letters which the Devil had forged.
"I did as you commanded," she told him.
Then she brought forth the tokens: the eyes and the tongue.

With that the King began to weep so bitterly
for his poor wife and his little son
that the old mother had compassion on him and said:
"Be at peace, your wife still lives.
It was a hind I caused to be killed, secretly,
and I took these tokens from it.
But your wife I sent forth into the wide world
with the child bound to her back.
I made her promise
never to return to this kingdom again,
because you were so angry with her."

Then the King spoke:
"I will search as far as the sky is blue,
and neither will I eat or drink
until I have found my dear wife again and my child—

if in the meanwhile they have not died of hunger
or been killed.''

With that the King traveled everywhere
for seven long years
and looked for her in every cleft in the rocks,
in every cave,
in every valley,
on every mountaintop,
but he could not find her
and he thought surely she had died of want.

During all this time he neither ate nor drank
but God's grace was his support.

Finally he came into a great dark forest
and he walked and he walked
until he came upon the little house
whose sign said:

HERE ALL DWELL FREE.

From out of the house, the angel came forth,
took him gently by the hand

and led him inside, saying:
"Welcome, Lord King. From where did you come?"

He answered:
"I will soon have wandered about
for the space of seven long years.
It is my wife and her child I seek,
but I cannot find them anywhere."

The angel then offered him meat and drink,
but he did not take anything
and only wished to rest a little.
He lay down to sleep
and put a napkin over his face.

With that, the angel went into the chamber
where the Queen was with her son—
the boy whom she usually called "Sorrowful"—
and said to her:
"Come out with your child; your husband is here."

So she went out to the place where the King rested
and the napkin slipped from his face.
Then she said:
"Sorrowful, pick up your father's napkin
and cover his face again."
And this the child did.

The King in his sleep heard what passed,
and it pleased him to
let the napkin fall once more.

But the child grew impatient and said:
"Dear Mother, how can I cover 'my father's face'

when I have no father in this world?
I have learned to say the prayer,
'Our Father who art in heaven.'
You have taught me that my father was in heaven's kingdom,
and was the good God,
so how can I know this wild man
to be my father? He is not my father."

When the King heard that,
he got up and asked who they were.

Then she said:
"I am your wife,
and this is your son, Sorrowful."

And the King noticed her living hands and said:
"My wife had silver hands."

She answered:
"By God's grace
have my natural hands grown back again."
And the angel went into the inner room,
and brought forth the silver hands,
and showed them to him.

With that the King knew most certainly
that she was indeed his dear wife and this
his own dear child,
and he kissed them and was glad and said:
"A heavy stone has fallen from my heart."

Then the angel of God ate with them once again.

And after that they returned home
to the King's old mother.

There was great rejoicing throughout the whole kingdom,
and the King and Queen were married again
and lived contentedly to their happy end.

Chapter 2

HEALING THE
HANDLESS MAIDEN

An Overview

There is power in this story. It grips us in deep places—
prods into corners we didn't know we had. We become
flooded with the blooming daughter's struggle, aware that
she is fatefully forced to choose between passivity and activity, between dependence and independence. We recognize that the miller's daughter is so dedicated to her father
that she loses her hands—in fact, she loses her grip on her
own development. Her development is made difficult and
convoluted because of her devotion to the "masculine principle," that is, to ideas and opinions or values—here sym-
bolized by her father.

Bit by bit, she loses hold of her life, further and further
she withdraws from it, and she cannot be healed until she
retreats entirely to the quiet, deep, removed place that the
world knows so little about. In painful loneliness and isolation she must go into the dark woods, or remove herself
for a time from an active participation in life.

This developmental pattern seems a frequent theme in feminine psychology. It is also the crucial choice in masculine development, when a man's inner feminine place of feeling, value and relatedness has been wounded, abused or neglected. That fateful choice between an active and a passive life spins itself into an even deeper choice: the miller's daughter faces a crucial choice between surrendering to a fruitless depression that rides on her shoulders and whispers in her ears, rendering her incapable of movement, and embracing a conscious choice to withdraw from life where she will face her woundedness and enter it to its very depth. For unconscious depression does not heal, it only contaminates life with its poison. But conscious depression or conscious suffering will finally bring about healing.

This chosen "withdrawal" from life and engagement of woundedness is recognized by many religious systems as both necessary and valuable. They provide a period of reconciliation or atonement (at-one-ment) during which the faithful face their brokenness and by feeling their misery hope to be mended once more. Jews, for instance, have the Day of Atonement, Yom Kippur. At the start of the Jewish New Year there is that somber day of introspection: an examination of the past year and a personal "housecleaning" for the new year at hand. One asks forgiveness of all those one has wronged and then asks God's forgiveness. Christians celebrate a period of penance and reconciliation—the season of Lent—for this very purpose. The Lenten season and the sacrament of reconciliation are designed for believers to face their woundedness, make restitution for or repent of their failings and accept their suffering as a personal cross. They die finally to an old life and are transformed and made new in the mystery of healing and resurrection.

An acknowledged and well-suffered depression rarely receives recognition and validation from the outside world, a world that measures itself against the masculine principles of action and production, competition and power. The outside world sees any depression as stagnation—a blockage. But stagnation, when it is freely accepted and suffered through, can be in reality an incubation. The incubation period, as von Franz called it, is unhurried, an unseen growth prefatory to an initiation. This initiation is an introduction to a new and conscious way of living life—fully and passionately.

The quiet withdrawal into inactivity illustrated in this story appears over and over again in stories in which the woman is the hero. Often her way of healing is in direct contrast to the active, male, questing principle found in masculine tales. In many fairy tales the male hero, before he can become whole, has to travel, search, wield the sword, battle the dragon, find the treasure and win the bride. Even though the King in our story plays a considerably lesser role, it could well be that he is off on the journey of questing, searching, conquering (some versions say he is away at war), building his art or his career, all of which seem to precede, if not be prerequisite to, his full union with his bride, with indeed his inner feminine side.

Chapter 3

THE MILLER
AND THE MILL

Once upon a time there was a certain miller who bit by bit had fallen into poverty. He had nothing left but his mill and a large apple tree which grew behind it. One day the miller went into the forest to cut wood.

The First Line as Diagnosis

We look especially at the first line of a fairy tale because it tells us the state of affairs. It pronounces the diagnosis of the culture as much as it describes the condition in the story. Here the story opens to find a miller in a state of bankruptcy. His profession as a miller seems to have ground to a halt and now he has fallen to the humblest possible profession: being a woodcutter. Perhaps he has spoiled his relationship to his clients, or the land has suffered a drought and no longer produces grain, or his creativity has run out of steam, and now the culture, in fact, has gone bankrupt.

When we are "bankrupt" or have no defenses left to shield us from our reality, we are confronted by the possibility of a dramatic change, of, indeed, being transformed. Like the rich man who cannot fit through the proverbial eye of the needle for all his lumpy baggage, we cannot enter into the new possibility, into our very salvation, as long as we drag our defenses with us. Too much money, too much comfort, power, good looks, charm, outward success—all can mask the impoverishment of the spirit, and we may need to lose one defense after another, bit by bit, before we come down to size. We know we are close to that point when we hear ourselves say: "I have come to the end of my rope."

Here, the miller has come to the end of his rope. At the end of your rope is a holy place to be: you have a kind of ultimate decision to make and the decision is always a moral one. This is the miller's chance to become a holy man. Here he is, collecting firewood. He is about as "down to earth" as he can be. Even so humble a task (perhaps especially so humble a task!) is an opportunity for him to do the ordinary and simple action well.

> He holds the handle of his ax
> but his hands are empty.
> He loads the wood high on his back
> but it is not enough.

I found this quotation in my notebooks and no longer know where it came from. If it is the wisdom of Zen, then it might describe the woodcutter's labor as so simple and direct, so holy and fulfilling, that he feels none of its weight. But curiously, if it is a Western observation, we might read the same lines as a description of this miller's poverty. When we carry out the ordinary action and berate it as not enough, we become poorer and poorer. Every action is leached of its poetry or its religion. Nothing is seen for its real value, its absolute value. Certainly this miller, who perhaps isn't used to applying much elbow grease to his job—he let water or wind grind his mill wheels —is a candidate for the easy way out, here at the end of his rope.

The Prognosis

And as is often the case when we find ourselves in a very serious situation, dark and negative shadow qualities hang about ready to trick us into an easy and quick solution to that deep problem. We are always tempted to look for the painless way out. We let ourselves think that we can get out of paying the price for our choices—that we can get something for nothing. There's always the hope that we might win the lottery. And the miller, we can guess, is at just this point.

We can further guess that his economic or professional values have always been more important than his relational values. As the mill stands before the tree, so his business has come before his concern and love for his blossoming daughter—the tree and the daughter are here aspects of each other. He would rather "lay up treasures for himself on earth." He has put his heart in economic treasure and has no heart for his daughter or for the nature of things. He has sunk to a "what the hell?" attitude. "The Devil take her."

The Machine

The miller, as an early mechanic, may have developed a mechanical attitude toward his work which contributes to his state of affairs. His attitude is echoed in our own phrase: "Well, back to the old grind." To view work as an "old grind" saps meaning from our existence. For the miller, a calling that might have offered him a "regular" life, a regulated life that has its seasons of work and rest, has ground down to boring routine, a dull flat life. His work has become "run-of-the-mill"—ordinary to the point of boredom. Much as the cogs fit into the wheels without any seeming incentive, the mill goes on day and night; it knows no rest and the work has lost purpose. It's not a job which has a nighttime or a Sabbath. He has done this work—grinding out an existence—in order to survive. But he has never learned to *make* a living. He does not know the satisfaction of the art of living. His mechanical attitude—or science itself—has not made "all things new"; rather, now all things are the same. That would certainly bankrupt him—he has bankrupted his spirit.

And the machine—and this mill—to be efficient, must grind without stopping. Like all mechanical devices, it too goes against nature, it defies nature. Mechanics and a mechanical attitude also tempt us to grind faster and faster and to produce without stopping, looking for some economic reward in exchange for the boredom and not stopping to see where and by whom the price must be paid.

I know a man who sells giant cleaning devices that fit into industrial chimneys and are designed to filter and clean the wastes and exhausts that the industry produces. He tells me that they do their job perfectly. But when they need to be repaired or replaced, the industry management refuses to take notice. They are willing to go with the initial requirement to install the devices but refuse to shut down their machines for repairs or replacements because they lose huge amounts of money just shutting down and restarting them. Naturally, they lose more money if they allow the machines to lie idle during the repairs. So they end up befouling the atmosphere after all. And inside, machinists are chained to the task of keeping the system fired up without stopping.

Technology, or even the mechanical attitude, then, often works against nature and against human nature as well. The great promise of the machine, of course, has always been freedom, the deliverance of humanity from the necessity to struggle against the forces of nature, flood, famine, disease, death and the necessity for onerous work.

But even as we try to break the bonds of natural necessity we lose nature and have not gained freedom, but rather enter a new level of necessity: "technological necessity." Life comes to a screeching halt when the "computer is down" or the automatic washer breaks down with a load of soggy clothes. Conversely, the man battling the freeways with a car phone to his ear must now keep in touch with every branch of his business and keep all his systems fired up. Now, even while racing down freeways, he has lost his moment to dream.

Caught in the Middle

Some early children's jeers and nursery rhymes indicate that the miller was not always a popular figure in the community. It seemed, as a middleman, that he took more than his share and became wealthy at other people's expense and hard work:

> *Wie machens denn die Müller?*
> *Sie betens Vaterunser:*
> *Das halbe Korn is unser.*

> How do the millers do it?
> They pray their Our Fathers:
> Half the grain is ours.

> *Es ist—ein Dieb—in der Mühle.*
> *Wer ist er? Wer ist er? Wer ist er?*
> *Der Müller! Der Müller! Der Müller!*

> There is—a thief—in the mill.
> Who is he? Who is he? Who is he?
> The miller! The miller! The miller!

The miller with this early machine, run not by his sweat but by wind or water, has withdrawn from planting, tilling, harvesting or even transforming the flour by baking the bread—all direct experiences of the holy through ordinary contact with nature. He allows the farmers and the bakers to continue their work but skims a price from them, even as he cheats himself of a direct connection with a holy work.

When we pay our fee to the physician for the arts of healing, we pay as well the legal system and the insurance agency that reach in between us. And the healing arts of the physician have become less a laying on of hands and more the manipulation of technological devices. We all feel caught in the middle.

It seems that the mechanical attitude itself becomes the "middleman" between us and a direct experience and we miss the numinous in matter which is mystery and our introduction to the transcendent. When we get to spinning our wheels, we make it hard for ourselves to experience the sacramentality of ordinary nature and human relationships. We choose the efficient or practical way and the practical is the enemy of the numinous. We say that we cannot cope without a microwave oven, because these days we only *cope*, we no longer have the time for a *craft*: for a meal well prepared and shared—for communion.

So too the miller's mechanical attitude has entrapped him and he has lost touch with the dimension of mystery. We might say that the cause of this loss is the technological spirit which encourages endless manipulation of the surface of reality but is insensitive to its depth. And when we neglect mystery and a sensibility to the wonder of things, the possibility of being fully human is stunted.

Konrad Lorenz, the well-known animal behaviorist, said in his last book, *The Waning of Humaneness*, that mechanics and the sciences, because they use language, allow the sort of progress that outstrips the slower unfolding of the soul, which has an inner or symbolic or poetic language—certainly not the language of the technical world. Hence we are making hurried decisions on a scientific level that are to the detriment of the slower-developing soul.

This doesn't have to be. Science can just as well open the universe even wider for us and actually lead us into mystery. I think of the picture of our own planet earth that science gave

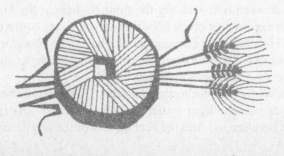

us from outer space. That vision of a vulnerable, blue-green marbled bubble can inspire wonder and a new respect for what lies directly under our feet. What is sacred in science is its ability to lead us to a truth and a sense of wonder.

For our concern is not to rid the world of technology but to see that awareness is our primary and greatest responsibility. To be aware is not to be lulled by ideologies into worshiping the idol we call progress. An enlightened, conscious miller might have used this mill wheel, the symbol of the creative, a mandala, to feed society and to store food for times of need. The mill wheels of his profession may be seen as symbols of a consciousness which he could have chosen to use in a transformative fashion. He might have redefined his profession and benefited the culture that surrounded him. He could even have discovered a new attitude toward gathering wood.

The miller as a middleman, then, can exploit the society he works in or he can use his central position as a point of vision for the benefit of his society. The acceptance and conscious awareness of social responsibility for all our actions, at work or play, define us as adults and signify that ability to make sacred and social that which is otherwise common and private. Some cultures and religions often prescribe how that transformation might take place, and mark the transformation with rituals or sacrament, but our own secular system leaves to chance and individual will that crucial moment of becoming adult. We think, instead, that instant gratification (the pursuit of happiness as a private goal) is a constitutional right. And instant gratification belongs to the dark side of this miller. He gets paid into his right hand but has no idea what he pays out with his left.

Chapter 4

THE PRICE

One day when he had gone into the forest to cut wood, an old man whom he had never seen before stepped up to him and said: "Why do you slave away at cutting wood? I can make you wealthy beyond your dreams. All you have to do is promise me what is standing behind your mill."

"Well," thought the miller, "indeed, that must be my apple tree." So he agreed, gave a written promise to the strange man and was pleased with what seemed to be a very good bargain.

The stranger, however, laughed with a sound of evil cunning and said: "Remember, in three years' time I will come to your mill and carry away what belongs to me."

Then he went.

Rather than engage this poverty into which he has fallen and then wonder what the other possibilities in life might be, the miller strains for a way out. He refuses to regret the wasted hours, the broken promises, the shattered dreams —whatever it was that brought him to this crisis. He does not examine his situation and upgrade his philosophy of life. He misses his chance to become creative and renewed by this experience of impoverishment. He misses the op-

portunity to look past his mill, to discover his own tree and his own daughter in his own backyard. He sells out to the Devil for an easy solution and unwittingly bargains away his daughter—his own daughter who is about to bloom or his own inner feminine side, his soul, which may be about to bloom into something new and promising.

Nature

"Well," thought the miller, "indeed, that must be my apple tree."

This miller thinks that the price he will pay is just a corner of nature, just a tree. It's an old tree. It's just one of those fixtures at the mill that one has grown used to. Why, it's an expendable resource. It is with the same desire for large and instant profit that we all devour our "expendable resources" faster than they can be replenished—if indeed they can ever be replenished.

This attitude toward nature seems to run parallel to our miller's values as a mechanic. We spoke of how industrial technology threatens our connection to nature. Now let us look more deeply at our relationship to nature.

The life of the soul belongs to and is connected to and sustained by the whole pattern of nature. But in our culture we have learned over time to give greater value to everything that separates us from a primary experience of nature. We carry our babies in complicated plastic carriers, expensive devices that separate the little bodies from our own—though we just mean to be practical. We use electric lights to fool the night, to fool the hen into laying through an eternal day. We use electric blankets to circumvent the chill of night. We can wash our dishes or our cars or our clothes and never get wet or soapy. We can eat strawberries in the dead of winter. Summer and winter, night and day, dark and light, heat and cold, wet and dry are canceled out through the tricks of our technology. Nor does the energy come from our own elbow grease. It comes from something outside our immediate experience; hence we don't even know, when we flick the switch or eat the strawberries, where the price is being paid or by whom.

Konrad Lorenz, again, speaking of what he calls "the irreversible vicious-circularity of some aspects of technical and economic development," holds out this bit of hope that must become part of the education of young people for the future. He says the predicament of young people today is especially critical. If we don't destroy the world first, their perceptions of value, their sensibilities to the beautiful and worthwhile must be awakened, the very values most suppressed "by scientism and technomorphic thinking." He urges that we must educate our young people in these perceptions as the only means of developing a sensitivity to harmonies. "The closest possible contact with the living natural world at the earliest possible age is the most promising way to achieve this proper function."

Our story seems to affirm that when the natural order is tampered with we risk selling the "feminine" feeling value to the Devil. Certainly we sell Mother Nature and Mother Earth to devilish destruction.

The Soul

The "feminine" feeling value was also being ground down at the mill. Simply fearing or condemning science and technology is not a deep enough understanding of the mill symbol, because it is also true that we rightly appreciate many of the conveniences that modern technology provides.

With equal concern, we have to guard against a personal "mechanical attitude" which can permeate our very human-ness—when we resort to mechanical tricks, living life and performing our daily tasks in a bored and routine way. To function with a mechanical attitude can cause us to lose purpose. Meaning is drained from our work. It tampers with the spirit and kills what is sensitive, feeling or relational. Work becomes a "millstone around the neck" when we use one talent over and over again. It causes our other talents to lie neglected where they cannot refresh or nourish us. There is no time to stop or take notice or reassess this life we are living.

We become mechanical in our politeness to one another when our smiles are painted on and graciousness is simply a technique we are paid to enact as part of our jobs.

The teacher, the nurse, the therapist, the homilist, the parent, the waitress, the flight attendant, anyone who deals person to person and who has been running on automatic, using only techniques or mental tricks, knows this "grinding it out" and has often ground to a halt: feeling and creativity finally run out. We are reduced to a state we have come to call "burnout."

Sometimes it is choice, sometimes seduction and sometimes economic necessity that calls us to "grind it out" without stopping in order to pay back the bank that owns us. We feed ourselves into political mills for their catchy slogans or political ideologies, ourselves the sacrifice on the holy altar of a false god.

When we lose our God and think that we can invent ourselves, the price we pay is large. A vital and vitalizing feeling, a sense of value, has gone dead.

And perhaps, indeed, it must die as the grain of wheat itself must die if anything new is to bud forth in the ordinary person, living an ordinary life, but alienated from any higher power, and turned in on itself. On one level or the other there's hell to pay.

The Challenge of Middle Years

We know that the "political crisis" or the "technological accident" or the "energy crisis" is ultimately also a challenge to the style of living we have grown used to and now consider our right. "Crisis" is the way that the unconscious of a whole culture breaks through to the surface, fairly screaming to be heard and insisting on a change of heart or attitude or old patterns of living.

The miller's crisis, being at the end of his rope, makes him vulnerable to the Devil. He, in fact, falls victim to his own darkness and his fear of further loss, and in his panic he chooses what is inferior, negative and, indeed, the Devil within himself. His dreadful and understandable fear of further loss just fuels his greed for an instant solution and for riches. His greed is so powerful that his consciousness freezes up. He is paralyzed. He fails to make the developmental leap to which the crisis is invitation. He fails to develop in a positive, healthy way and turns his back on the challenge of his middle years. We can say that he fails his midlife crisis. With that, the cost of his failure is passed on to the people around him, to his family and to the generations to come.

The Daughter

When the father puts his business or career first (the mill stands before the tree), the daughter grows up with a father who is, perhaps, a success in the eyes of the world—he makes a lot of money, he invents a lot of devices, he impresses the academic world or is head of a corporation—but his soul is withered. He, may have no human, feeling heart. At home he is exhausted or cold or withdrawn or present only as a sort of dictator or director of activities, or he's a constant critic. Perhaps his home is just a locker room where he changes and showers between business plays. His marriage relationship may be incidental. He turns his back on his daughter or, more certainly, on his own relational, psychological and spiritual possibilities.

He fails his daughter in her own budding, feeling, feminine side by failing to appreciate her—laughing and talking and rejoicing in how lovely a daughter she is. He fails to give his daughter's femininity any value or dignity or affirmation. A daughter receives much of her affirmation as a woman—a kind of permission to become a woman—from her father's delight and approval of her and from his respect for her sexuality. She learns much about how a man should love her and relate to her by seeing how her father relates to her mother. From her mother she learns *how* to be a woman. (The reverse is true also for a son who receives permission to become manly from his mother because she's not afraid of or disgusted by his masculinity but respects him and approves of him. The boy's father, largely, teaches him how to be a man.) But when the father is predominantly critical of his daughter or largely unaware, uncaring or demeaning of her femininity, he sells that blooming possibility to the Devil.

The Feminine Value

A man very likely treats his women on the outside just as he treats his inner feminine: his feelings, his care and respect, his sensibilities, his muses, his soul. If our culture, with its largely masculine value system, remains unaware of the value and qualities of the "feminine" *wherever* it is found, it too sells itself down the river to the Devil. For we are suffering from a vast cultural chauvinism that runs deeper and wider than a mere chauvinism against women.

The culture's attitude to feminine value, though it may reveal something of itself in how the sexes relate, is deeper and broader than sexual difference. For there is a feminine quality found inside men and a masculine quality found within women. I use the terminology "masculine" and "feminine," then, as qualities found within both men and women but not synonymous with "male" and "female."

As in the balance of yin to yang, women and men are inoculated with a bit of their opposites and do not complete one another in a clean, straight division of halves but rather tumble and flow into one another in a spiraling, perpetual motion. (For a wonderful description of the masculine and the feminine and their specific attributes and contributions, look at the first two chapters of the ancient Chinese book, the *I Ching*.)

The right relationship of a woman to her inner masculine and the right relationship of a man to his inner feminine has everything to say about balance and a healthy personality. Such a personal balance is an asset to, if not a determinant of, healthy relationships between men and women.

But the value and nurturance given to the inner feminine in our whole culture are the greatest victims of "chauvinism" and seem as misunderstood by women as they are by men.

That may be because our Western culture has been founded on the belief that masculine value, the yang side of our reality, without doubt vital to the building of our culture, is "better than" its feminine counterpart. We all tend to attribute great value to what is active, dynamic, direct, productive, sportive, achieving, focused, single-minded, logical, competitive, intellectual, tangible, practical, clear, discriminating, structured, linear, flamboyant, spiritual. . . . We value the summer, the sun and daytime. We reach for the light. We love the word "yes." Indeed, all those words sound good to us.

How quick we are to confer a pejorative value on what we deem "different" or "impractical." We are uncomfortable with stillness, waiting, being, contemplation, yielding, receiving, with ambiguity, the intangible, the hidden, the secret, the absorbing. We think of roundness, softness, the circular, the earthy, nurture, patience, cooperation, incubation, wisdom, the poetic, as too intangible, or as something belonging only to women, or as merely unimportant. While we notice whether the sun is up or down, we don't much notice the moon and her phases. We sleep away the nighttime, sometimes even thinking sleep is a waste of time and our dreaming meaningless. We avoid the word "no." We fear the darkness. We flee the ambiguous. We see waiting as wasting. Even words seem too hard edged here to describe the nature of the "feminine." But these qualities are the yin in the construct of wholeness and belong to us all.

And that is what is at stake here. The price paid in our fairy story is every value the "feminine" stands for. These are qualities, attitudes or positions which not only men must find and nurture within themselves; all of us, women or men in the grip of a male-dominated society, must name the feminine qualities that we are so quick to undermine and recognize them as equal in value, though different in nature. To recognize feminine values (waiting, the interior, receptivity, the ambiguous, the poetic) as being equal to masculine values (the active, exterior, productive, goal-oriented) is most certainly not to be taken as either a directive or an excuse for women themselves to become weak, ineffectual or subservient.

It seems to me that we women, in dread of being rendered passive and weak, and often with a knee-jerk response, fear that, if feminine values of the soul and the psyche are stressed, these will be relegated only to us. We are afraid, and rightly so, that women, literally, must be the sole bearers of interior, feminine values—and, with them, their corresponding negative connotations. A woman will be easily weakened or rendered ineffectual or made subservient, I think, only if she remains unaware of her primary value—unaware or unappreciative of the particular power and dignity of her feminine nature and ignorant of the feminine value in every aspect of life around her. Our story implies that not just the individual but an entire society suffers when it ignores its own wisdom or refuses to be patient, cooperative, compassionate and reverent to the nature of things. The result of such ignorance, it would seem, is a society that manipulates, exploits or oppresses that which it does not understand or value.

Something of this imbalance is already afoot when the miller strikes his bargain with the Devil: he does not consult his wife. He does not consult what is wise or moral within himself. His feminine side is overruled. When he returns home, his wife runs to meet him with the news of their sudden wealth. She does not announce this news with enthusiasm, but rather with suspicion and mistrust. The intuitive feminine knows that something is rotten here and that there will certainly be a price to pay. She knows that the miller has not "read the fine print" where the Devil extracts his due.

> *"Oh, husband," said the wife, trembling with terror. "That could only have been the Devil! He surely didn't mean the apple tree, but rather our daughter, who was standing behind the mill sweeping the yard today!"*

Chapter 5

THE DAUGHTER'S CHOICE

To Go Off with the Devil

When the daughter is not nourished and affirmed by her father's feeling—his caring, his love and relatedness—that vacancy in her is left open for a devilish possession to take over. The daughter can become coldly intellectual or very opinionated and calculating. She seeks to compete in a masculine way in the masculine world. Or she can become, as von Franz says, driven by ambition in the same way her father was driven to worldly success.

Sometimes you see a girl just at adolescence (or a boy, trying to guard against his feminine side) experiment with such a choice—to become coldly intellectual, ruthless, power driven, or functioning without heart. She experiments with limited judgments which are not the caring, feeling values concerned with relationship that are more natural to her as a girl.* Rather she is calculating or simply, coldly, justice-oriented. One of her favorite lines is, "It's

---

* See Carol Gilligan, *In a Different Voice* (Cambridge: Harvard University Press, 1982). Gilligan demonstrates through controlled studies how the voices of genders differ in moral strength and the ethic of care in relationship.

the principle of the thing," and that moral code dominates her decisions and fuels her causes. Justice is not clothed with mercy. Rules and laws push past her femininity and lead her with a kind of driven, possessed attitude. Intellectual pursuits may be taken up—and with a mania that destroys relationships and is destructive of everything around her. She is ruled by her masculine side, not guided by it.

When a woman is possessed by her masculine side she will be no more advanced than the most unevolved man. She will be but a poor imitation of a very unconscious man. African Americans have an old saying: "I'd rather a man be anything than a woman be mean." Eve went off with the Devil when she took the gift of knowledge in hopes of making herself great by it. Powers left in the unconscious, powers with unexamined motives, become evil when we succumb to them out of greed, pride, fear or ambition. Eve surrendered to a power that was evil. But when we accept our gifts of knowledge as a basis for better, more humane decisions, that knowledge is transformed into wisdom. So young women often make this choice at a crucial moment of their development, hooking elbows with the Devil and walking off on a power trip—assenting to and joining in the cultural chauvinism that rejects or mutilates feminine values and the unique power of the feminine.

Or perhaps they become vaguely aware that there is grave danger in such a choice. Perhaps it is better to avoid a "possession" that is manifested in a driven, calculating, merciless, aggressive, power-hungry, loud, bossy, opinionated attitude. Guided by this intuition, the young woman may go another route.

To Become Overly Feminine

The heroine of our story has chosen that other route, and it is a reactive one. She becomes *overly* feminine. Her choice carries an energy of its own—the sort of energy we all use to pull ourselves violently away from what we fear might be our fate. In no way does she want to be carried off by a possession! And what is more, walking off with the Devil would jeopardize her chances of relationships, especially a loving relationship with a man. This kind of intuition has probably played a role in more than one period of women's history. Certainly it informed the cultural bias of recent history, which indicated that a woman had better remain somewhat underdeveloped intellectually if she wanted to get married. And where it continues to play an unconscious role in the development of a young woman, she may choose to refrain from doing too well in her studies. She may have been bright and curious as a little girl in grade school but now, as an adolescent, she may refuse to develop her mind, or she may hide her intelligence, because she intuits that she might become possessed by some negative intellectuality. In the extreme, she thinks it better to be a "dumb blonde" or an "airhead" and spend her time teasing the boys.

Now we watch the young girl in our fairy tale also grapple with that choice. She is in a terrible dilemma. Because of the severity of the situation (and because fairy tales often overstate the issue to make their point) she finds herself having to choose between exaggerated opposites of each other. To keep her hands would be a heroic and autonomous act! But to keep her hands would also mean to fall into the Devil's hands. Her autonomous

act would only exchange her father's problem for the problem
of taking on the Devil herself. That would be as good as having
the Devil for a father!

> *The Devil threatened him and said: "Either I take her or it is you
> I carry off."*

If, however, she relinquishes her sensibilities and power to
her father and allows him to take her hands away she will have
kept the Devil at bay and saved her father as well. It seems
wiser to her to make a god of her father and so also of masculine
values and of men. She gives away her hands and relinquishes
any possible control that she may have had over her own life.
Henceforth her life is out of her hands.

She chooses to be powerless. She chooses to be too painfully
feminine. She chooses to be passive. She almost chooses not to
choose by saying:

> *"Dear Father, I am your child, do with me what you will."*

How close her comment sounds to the Virgin Mary's response to the angel Gabriel when she is asked if she will be the
mother of God. Mary answers: "Behold the handmaid of the
Lord; be it done to me according to thy word." But Mary's
response has a magnificently positive tone to it. Having first
asked this angel how he figures this is going to be done, and
comprehending, she needs no other authority for advice. Mary
chooses, in an autonomous act, to become open—*receptive*—to
the work of the Spirit. In partnership with the Spirit, she is
handmaid of—in the service of—this partnership. To be "in
the service of" has nothing to do with "servitude" or
oppression.

But our story's blooming maiden has chosen the dark side
of receptivity and becomes passive. Like earth, when it is not
turned up and scratched open to receive seed and rain and becomes unresponsive, unaffected or even harshly eroded by the
rain and the seed washed away, so the Handless Maiden becomes helplessly passive. The feminine quality of receptivity
opens itself and receives the gift offered to give it a place of

nourishment, a place where it can take root. But to be passive is the destructive aspect of that feminine quality.

And she laid down both her hands and let them be cut off.

The maiden gives up her feminine power and her living hands and is now destined to use men or be used by them, while Mary raises up and opens her living hands, not to use, but rather to receive and to give forth.

On the side of hope, we know that the maiden is reverent —good and "devout," the fairy tale says. This could mean that she also has a deep, basic integrity and a connection with the Spirit. As the story unfolds, that seems to be true and her spiritual piety stands her in good stead.

On the other hand, we see that the maiden is dutiful to the father and the masculine principle. In her duty she is "good" and clean and blameless and beyond reproach. Her deeds are perhaps so dispassionate as to lack soul. Perhaps there is, in fact, no soul for the Devil to fetch away? Such a maiden may, in fact, get fine grades in school—but simply by being the teacher's pet, by getting all her reports neatly written and dutifully turned in on time. She gets those good grades without risk or messy creativity. She simply obeys. The chalk circle is "a right way of doing things" which, it cannot be refuted, staves off a Devil-possession.

> Now the Devil came for the third time, but the maiden had wept so long and so much on her poor stumps that they, too, were washed quite clean with her tears. With that, the Devil had to give in, for he had lost all right over her.

The message is clear: if you are in grave danger and don't know what else to do—just do the right thing! Follow all the rules. Keep your hands clean.

The Neurotic as Parody of the Religious

The right thing may not always be the best thing, however. Defensive behavior, bodily symptoms and neurotic habits give us something—anything—to do and we often do these things with a compulsiveness that is religious in nature. But because it is unconscious religiosity it can only stave off the danger and not resolve it. Here, the maiden becomes a compulsive cleaner: her purification ceremonies, her magical rituals and rites and her chalk circle do actually prevent the Devil from carrying her off, so habits and defenses have their efficacy. But she staves him off by allowing him to take her hands and throw her into a temporary state of helplessness.

The father and the father-world show no genuine mercy. In a world of cold justice—an eye-for-an-eye justice—the Devil is paid his due and the maiden will be paid hers, that is, if she'd now like to hang about home and be dependent on her father for the rest of her days.

> Because of you, my daughter, we have received great wealth. Now I will keep you handsomely as long as you live."

In the father's offer there is gratitude for his daughter's having saved his skin, but there is no mercy or compassion for her unhappiness or grief. Grief is what we feel in our woundedness and grief is what we suffer with those so much a part of ourselves. But the maiden is left to her grief. She weeps and weeps. She is handicapped and unable to do anything that is effective. But it is to her credit and her courage that she does not take her father's offer to be eternally dependent on him.

Whatever was once simple or paradisiacal in her family home has long since been spoiled. No, she will leave this place and take an important step which is both progressive and regressive. Now she can no longer feed herself or know the world by touch, so she must regress to an earlier way of knowing things and that is a feeling and feeding by mouth. Helpless as an infant now, she must be fed by others. She starts all over again, but this time on her own.

Von Franz points out that in fairy tales the hero's dilemma

is often resolved by "virtue, work, blundering or trickery." Blundering and trickery more often seem to be the way out of a dilemma for masculine heroes. In our story, because the hero is a "good girl" she neither tricks nor blunders, but rather is virtuous and works hard. She also has to suffer much.

Her father, on the other hand, appears to get away with his behavior—he betrays his conscience but actually gains outward success, leaving his daughter to suffer deeply. A passage in Scripture says: "The fathers have eaten sour grapes and the teeth of their children are set on edge." That well describes the sort of psychological inheritance that goes from parent to offspring. Culturally, the story seems to warn us: we, too, have made great strides which we call progress and we have gained great outward success, but at the same time much of what we have gained has been earned at the cost of the deep and unacceptable suffering of minorities, of women, of children, the exploitation of third-world countries, and the destruction of the environment for our future children.

The Maiden's Challenge

While the father of this story, symbolic of masculine-dominated society, may not be at the end of his rope anymore, the forgotten daughter now is. Even as women suffered diminishment and lack of appreciation, even as they gave up their hands and retreated from life, their real strength has not yet been fully tapped or tested or even quite named for what it is. The feminine and feminine values are still being discovered, named and finally being honored. The community of women may find that being at the end of their collective rope is also a holy place to be. It necessitates change.

> But she replied: "No, Father. Here I cannot stay. I must go forth into the world."

On the good side of all this disaster, the evil and the cruelty that the father has inflicted on the daughter, ironically and paradoxically, begin to break the great dependent bond that she had with her father and with a patriarchy. She chooses to risk a new way—to go forward onto the unknown path which may bring her to the road of healing and independence. In fact, the story seems to tell us that something has to be wounded for a new consciousness to emerge. Even now in our own day, how often is a young woman, dependent and wounded, sent from home—"given away!"—by the father or the patriarchal community to be turned over to the arms of the King. For better or for worse remains to be seen.

Chapter 6

THE NEED FOR
A GREAT LOVE

At the heart and center of most fairy tales seem to lie crisis and a conflict of balances between the masculine and the feminine, or the hero and the heroine. Their stories take us on these heartrending searches for one another. They meet, they part, they lose track of each other, they suffer terrible fates. How critical their fates. How impossible that they should ever meet, not to mention remeet. But to be alive is to know that their fate is not all that different from our fate, their adventure from our adventure. And on some level their solution points to our solution.

Identities, and How We Men and Women Form These

The stories also point us to one of those curious and painful mysteries of the human condition: the way the male psyche evolves and develops and the way the female psyche evolves and develops. In fact, it seems a very strange oversight on God's part to have arranged that a young man, bent on discovering who he is and while developing the very critical issue of identity, should come to know himself by *what he does* and by the males he hangs around with or imitates.

And a young woman, also bent on developing that crucial sense of identity and despite all the pressures of the modern bias that she should not be dependent on males, does in fact develop her sense of who she is by whom she relates to—or by *whom she loves*.

That most impractical reversal of how boys and girls, or young men and women, develop identity does help somewhat to explain why the boy is so ambivalent about his girl friend. He still doesn't know quite who he is and so he can't really love her until he *is* somebody. And the girl is in anguish or at least suffers deep pain, because this boy she loves is always fading in and out of her life—depending on whether or not he and his buddies got his car fixed, on whether he was able to satisfy himself, at least this afternoon, that he is a pretty sharp mechanic. His withdrawal confuses her; she doesn't deeply feel she *is* anybody until she loves and is loved by somebody. His greasing his car on a good day for picnics, she feels, just puts their relationship in question. But right now he *needs* to grease the car. He doesn't even want to see her. She makes him uncomfortable and her phone calls that pull him out from under the car, away from the grunting and sweating he wants to do with his friends over his machine, increase his discomfort.

All cleaned up and his car purring, he's now ready to take her out to the movies. But she's in a funk. She wanted to spend the *afternoon* with him and feels upstaged by his stupid friends and his infernal car, and by evening she's too confused to be good company and thinks she'd better stay home and finish her homework. If it isn't being a good grease monkey, then it will be graduate school or the promotion that seems necessary to the man's identity before he feels confident enough to make a deepening commitment to his relationship.

When young men and young women finally do get together long enough for both to fall in love at the same time, each feels that the other partner carries his or her other half. Now they feel complete and perhaps even ready for a committed relationship. They think that they can live happily ever after! At least for a few weeks.

It does seem rather crucial to understand this difference in how men and women develop identity. And even while it manages, against certain odds, to get people to loving one another enough to commit to a marriage, we already know that identities and individuation will continue to unfold and reveal new layers and require greater tests. Certainly our first story attests to this and invites us to follow this developmental progression of identity as it struggles and grows. Then, as soon as each identity seems to have gotten clear and strong, it rolls over to its opposite. But this, if it hasn't already become clear through experience or history, will certainly come true in this fairy tale as it continues to reveal itself.

Chapter 7

THE KING AND
THE MOONLIT GARDEN

From the Chalk Circle
to the Moated Garden

"I must go forth into the world. Bind my arms to my back and compassionate people will give me what I need."

With her arms tied to her back—the heavy fate of dependency she inherited from home—the Handless Maiden makes that major transition which we all have to make: she leaves her family circle and heads into the world. She leaves the chalk circle, that holding tank of training and proper behavior, and knows that she has no place there any longer. Although it has lessened somewhat today, there is still a certain social and personal pressure on women to marry young and have children.

I would say that women who were young before our recent feminist revolution were most especially confronted with that pressure. It makes biological sense—when procreation is the goal of a species. So, at home, we may have learned skills that would make good housekeepers of us, the sweeping, hand-washing, circle-drawing skills that the Handless Maiden learned in her home. If we went on to college, we trained in pretty much one of three professions: as teachers, nurses or secretaries, all helping professions that would also prove useful later in family life. All this we were willing to do until our kings came along.

A college education was, for many, a kind of holding tank until it was time to marry. It was said in those days that "being engaged is the most glamorous time in your life." In senior year, many a classmate returned to school from the holiday flashing her engagement ring to the squeals and cheers of her friends. She was the lucky one whose future was no longer uncertain. She loved and was loved—so she knew who she was. She was a bejeweled princess. She could leave her family and begin a new circle of her own. Certainly she was now an adult.

At sunrise she set out on her way. She walked the whole day until night fell. Then she came to a royal garden and by the shimmering of the moonlight she saw that trees laden with beautiful fruits grew in it. But she could not enter the garden, for it was surrounded by water.

Now the maiden was very hungry, having not eaten a bite, and hunger tormented her. She thought, "Oh, if only I could get inside this garden to eat some fruit before I die of hunger!"

Then she knelt down, called on the Lord God and prayed.

An angel comes toward her, parts the waters and leads her into the garden of a King. Directly, the maiden chooses to eat of the King's rare and counted pears. Being handless, she does not pick the fruit—as Eve did—but she does eat it. Both she and Eve found themselves in a paradisiacal garden and both were drawn to a forbidden fruit. But we can also say that the Handless Maiden has a craving for the highest feminine value that the garden has to offer. The story seems to say that the greatest value is in short supply. But the fact that she has managed to cross the water and choose the best fruit gets the King's attention and even, perhaps, his respect. Perhaps he knows he is dealing with a creature who has "good taste" and who must also have special spiritual strength. One rather wonders if these pears are not even a kind of lure to attract a worthy feminine creature into his realm. He does not, after all, instruct his gardener to destroy any thief who may enter the garden. His gardener, the King's natural, instinctual side, knows in an undifferentiated way that this young woman is extraordinary. He sees her as some sort of handless, pear-eating spirit. He is certainly in awe of her and of the angel who appears out of heaven. The King adds his royal, educated, conscious viewpoint to the gardener's natural insight and resolves to keep watch himself. He joins his gardener and brings a priest. The priest is a mediator between heaven and earth and is a religious aspect of the King, necessary to relate to the religious aspect of the maiden. The priest asks some either/or questions of the maiden:

> "Are you from heaven or from earth? Are you a spirit or a human?" The maiden answered: "I am no spirit, but an unhappy mortal deserted by all but the grace of God." The King said: "And if you are forsaken by all the world, yet will I not forsake you."
>
> He took the maiden with him into his royal palace and because she was so beautiful and good he loved her with his whole heart and made her his wife.

The maiden moves through the spiritual, watery moat—a kind of baptism of social approval, a journey through the Red Sea toward a land of promise—into the circle of the accepted cultural solution: here, a marriage. The King of the garden also represents the collective consciousness of a culture as we understand it. He is not just the man about to become her husband,

but as a King he carries the collective attitude of the culture.
The maiden has left her chalk circle to enter this new circle
where, because she is a good girl, she adopts all the culturally
dictated requirements concerning her wifely and familial duties,
her civic responsibilities, her church duties and the manners
proper to her position in the community. She is quite willing
to carry out the stiffly proper behaviors expected of her—"the
done thing"—here, in the realm of her accepting King.

When we arrive at this part in the story, I've noticed how
often in an audience of listeners there is a general sigh of relief.
With a shuffle, some folks—mostly men—straighten up, look
around and smile. How good that the young woman's agony
is finally over. The King has rescued her and the silver hands
are certainly a neat touch. People think that the story is finished.
I suppose that many a lesser story may stop at this point. Many
do. But that we would settle for a royal rescue and the promise
of silver hands may say something about us. The vision in this
fairy tale and what makes it so rich a story is that life really
asks so much more of us.

For the Handless Maiden still has little identity and no autonomy. This maiden, any vestige of personal identity taken
out of her hands, seeks out meaning and identity in the man
she marries. She says: I'm the wife of the King—of an
attorney—of a physician. She is a princess, but it is only in
relation to being dominated by a King. Her identity comes from
being someone's lover or bride or wife or devotee or assistant.
How can she help but be in love with love? She is nothing and
a nobody outside a relationship.

And yet it is only the *idea* of relationship that gives her hope.
Being painfully, literally, out of touch, she does not yet know
the persons who are members of this relationship. Instead of
two individuals joining up as separate persons to build up a
relationship and enter a partnership, she wants to see them as
two halves that make a single whole—and finds them matching
ski sweaters to wear so that the world will know them to be
such. She depends on domination by the King, or on the prevailing social attitudes, or on the requirements of her husband,
and in that way avoids freedom—a freedom she simply cannot

yet handle. Right now she just *needs* this man and entrusts him with magical qualities which only make her the more dependent.

We spin out the flaws and the weakness of the maiden's emerging situation until it seems that we've run out of hope! But then there glimmer in the darkness some signs that the situation may not be without merit after all. On the positive side, there shines through the mists this wonderful image of the moonlit orchard. The garden is moated with a ring of shimmering water and the maiden, seeing trees laden with most excellent fruit, is desperate with hunger and prays. So sincere is her prayer and so worthy her need that an angel just spills out of nowhere, parts the watery moat, leads her dry shod into the garden and stays with her.

Her acceptance by a loving, uncritical, generous King is surely another step toward her healing. The enclosed royal orchard, a shimmering mandala, is a hint at that. This circular garden as a form—and marriage as sacramental formation—is a wonderfully viable and nourishing place in which to work out her salvation.

Romantic love is not an aberration, it is the heady stuff that launches ships and makes the world go around. It is a powerful taste of the divine as we experience it in one another. It is also the necessary vision that allows one to be crazy and daring enough to make a commitment. She makes a commitment. And so does he. As a friend told me once, it takes a certain maturity to make a commitment, but making a commitment brings a certain maturity.

The moonlight is the gentler feminine illumination of feminine values. Pears seem so feminine a fruit. Traveling through the watery moat into a relationship and through the rites of a marriage can also be understood as an initiation into the value of her own feminine self and those feminine aspects of life that were ignored or trivialized or maimed by her father-world.

In her father's house, in the old chalk circle of the patriarchy, she may have been comfortable, as he was, with ritualistic acts that were carried on in a way that forgot about the always changing, strenuous demands of living creatively. Ritual can easily degenerate into systems that neglect mercy and faithful-

ness, which are responses to a higher order, incarnate in those
who live around us—a response to social justice and a commitment to growth in relationship. Chalk-circle observances
may simply be the acts performed to secure a guaranteed, safe
future. Formulas. Magic. Her chalk-circle rituals did, after all,
hold the Devil at bay.

But following rules and being obedient to a system may
ignore the feminine values of caring and mercy, of "good acts"
done in the name of justice and human dignity. "Being good"
to save your own skin is superstition. Superstition is hoping
that some magic will bail you out in the end.

Isaiah knew all about the superstitious ways of people which
ignore the fact that God cannot be worshiped outside our social
responsibility.

> What are your endless sacrifices to me?
> says Yahweh.
> I am sick of holocausts, of rams
> and the fat of calves.
> The blood of bulls and of goats revolts me.
>
> Your hands are covered with blood,
> wash, make yourselves clean.
> Cease to do evil.
> Learn to do good,
> search for justice,
> help the oppressed,
> be just to the orphan,
> plead for the widow. (Isaiah 1:11,16,17.)

The mystical orchard encircled by a moat is a more evolved
and permanent circle than the chalk one. It supersedes formulas
and provides form and formation. It offers hope and promises
another evolution in the young woman's growth and motives.
The goods and the graces delivered within this next ring point
not to fearful or magical acts but to the beginnings of adulthood
and altruism. The healing promise of this mystical orchard,
however, does not deliver promptly or all at once. She carries
the baggage of her father's house on her back, and, after all,
"her hands are tied." She cannot feed herself. And he? His pears
are counted.

Chapter 8

THE THIEF IN
THE NIGHT

She saw a tree heavy with beautiful pears, but the pears were all counted. To quiet her terrible hunger, the maiden ate one—just one—off with her mouth.

How do we understand that the Handless Maiden must begin her life in the mystical garden by having to steal? It seems right to spend a little time on that detail. For this thieving or the often demanding need of the injured feminine is the personification of an unconscious complex that saps the energy and passion from the conscious world. When you are depressed and the victim of a dark mood, von Franz says, something is stealing your energy and interest and you feel that life is passing you by. Or when you suffer from "writer's block," feeling that nothing new will come to fruit in you, your energy has been diverted. Some "thought" that you don't want to engage and enter and suffer out will stand in your way and dam the flow of creativity. A complex is under the surface, draining away your vitality.

This garden, however, and this relationship—this form

called marriage—these carry promise, if not salvation, for the Handless Maiden. She gnaws hungrily at the fruits of such a possibility. But marriage will prove not to be the whole solution, much as she would wish it to be. Marriage will require her continued development and her personal growth in autonomy, necessary to a deepening relationship. As yet, she cannot know that, and she will first shift over from her father dependency only to become wholly dependent on a husband to take care of her. Small wonder that his resources are limited.

Counted Pears

A man can suffer when his precious pears are nibbled at by the feminine—the "woman who is true on the inside"—of his psyche. If her needs are neglected or she has been wounded, she functions just under the surface of his consciousness and takes from his energy. He becomes sullen and moody. Something is eating him. And even if it isn't his flesh-and-blood wife who is feeling neglected and needy, it is that neglected, feeling, caring, creative side within that gnaws at him for attention and validation. He has lost his balance by living so busy and driven a life. His outer world and the masculine approach have only so much to offer, and his soul has been left behind—perhaps even mutilated, handless.

Sometimes the needs of his feminine soul may become so intense as to deplete his store. The neediness of an inner feminine value may cause it to become unseated. His anima (as Jung called this feminine guide within a man) may become dislodged from her proper position as inner guide and inspiration, as the inner muse who gently nudges him along from behind and urges him to consider the creative challenges of work and relationship. Dislodged from her place and angry at having been ignored, she may leap out in front of his masculine nature and rule him. She puts a spell on him, if you will, that causes him to make a public display of moodiness, of petty nastiness, of hurt feelings, of righteous judgmentalism, or of withdrawal and passivity that is truly worthy only of some unevolved, unconscious fishmonger. He does the poorest possible imitation of the feminine in all its darkest aspects. His inner woman no longer acts as inspiration and guide, living a role that is "true to his inside," but has leaped from a position of guidance to an exteriorized and inappropriate position to lead him around by the nose in a very undignified fashion. He is literally beside himself. And he may further displace the wretched feelings that belong to his inner life, and kick the dog or place blame on his secretary or, better yet, on the one person who could really be his ally, his wife. He forgets that his mood tells him something is wrong on the inside and wants to blame some flesh-and-blood woman for these feelings. Probably his wife has burned the toast or misplaced the checkbook and now "deserves" his wrathful criticism, according to his current way of feeling.

Not only can he make an ogress of the woman in his life, he can, for all the same reasons, become utterly inflated and infatuated with her and make her like some dazzling goddess—someone equally unreal.

I remember standing in front of Botticelli's marvelous *Birth of Venus* in the Uffizi in Florence. I was with friends and we were all very taken by the image. My friends, a young wife and her husband, their arms entwined, looked long and lovingly and quietly exchanged observations. Then the husband, sighing with feelings and overflowing with appreciation, nearly melted with tenderness for the beautiful Venus, stepping lightly in her shell, her thick hair blowing in ropes and tendrils around her, and caught up in all the right places. The wife disentangled herself and stepped away a little. She remarked that she didn't find it Botticelli's most *important* work. There were others, she felt, that were certainly more significant. She leafed through her guide and with an authoritative voice began to read what was said of another of Botticelli's great works—something to our right, she believed—a faint hint of scorn or irritation in her voice. But her misty-eyed husband was not hearing. He had succumbed to an "anima infatuation." That curious displacement of a man's inside woman, on an outer object. That mood that sends any sensible woman stepping smartly to the next painting. Disgusted. Jealous?

The unevolved King, whether smitten or rageful, allows his inner feminine side to be too either/or ("Are you from heaven or from earth? Are you a spirit or a human?")—a goddess or a witch?—and often projects this unrealistic duality on the women (or the gadgets he wants to buy) in his outer life. The limited number of pears may be a prognosis for the marriage relationship he offers the maiden.

The Handless Maiden as lover or new wife is vaguely aware of his limits. She works hard at trying to keep their romantic love alive. Even though she has, as yet, little sense of herself, she does have an uncanny sense of what her man's inner woman looks like. She knows just what to be to match what he's looking for in a goddess. She knows how to act, how to dress, what to read, what to cook, how to be coquettish, how to respond to him. She even knows how to feel. She is thrilled and surprised at how they both "seem to love exactly the same things!" She will be so weak, so fluid, so ignorant of her needs, that he can shape her any way he wants. She stalls her own development and certainly never expresses her own needs directly because of her total dedication to this man. She puts all her effort into being what she senses he wants her to be—because she is so dependent on this man for his admiration and attachment. What a cycle of operations she has to keep up! And what a perfect target she becomes for her man's "anima attacks," as my Jungian friends call his seizures.

The Thief as Member of the Relationship

Even as she searches constantly for his attention, the Handless Maiden begins to yearn for a deeper relationship—for something more. Romantic love at times feels frayed around the edges. Deep down and still out of sight something nibbles at her. Her intuitive sense indicates that this relationship lacks something. But until she knows who she is and what true intimacy is, her neediness, her clinging, may grow and eventually work against her. She wants to force her man into a change. After all, she married him because he was a King and a King is all-powerful. He ought to act his part. "He has so much potential and I can just see it." That's a lot of pressure to put on the bewildered fellow. He withdraws behind the *Wall Street Journal*.

Being handless has a way of further contaminating the issues of a relationship. Wanting what you want and not knowing how to get it—needing and not knowing what you really need—is muddy stuff. The moodiness of the man is a manifestation of his handless, nameless feelings as much as is the irritation of the woman with her vague needs. For the woman, who has placed everything into the relationship for the definition of her own identity, knows that depression drains her vitality, deadens her experience and gnaws at the partnership. The loss of the ability to make a picture-book image out of a marriage, or a marriage partner into an archetype, makes life frustrating and plunges one into depression.

As the female thief, she becomes sullen and difficult and then one day she wakes up to the fact that this man is no prince! When the woman cannot effect the evolution necessary, she often sinks into a funk and gets crabby and sulky. She makes sure to spoil the atmosphere by sinking deeper into her passivity. Her days look flat and uninteresting. She feels that life is passing her by.

She complains: "There's nothing on the calendar to look forward to." Neither will she be mollified by a suggestion: "I don't want to go to the movies tonight." Or if the calendar does serve something up: "I can't go to that party. I won't know anybody there and besides I've got nothing to wear . . . nothing fits. I feel fat."

She may be irritated with the man for having a world of his own. She wants the man to make her happy, and she sets up a whole series of hoops for him to jump through. She challenges him, making major demands on the relational side of the marriage because feeling and relationship were meager to non-existent in her own growing up.

On the negative side, her thieving can be infantile, needy and demanding. She is not clear about what she wants; actually she doesn't even know what she wants, being handless. She would prefer it if her husband would just guess—would just arrive at the front door with roses and chocolates at the right moment. He feels so bewildered or so trapped by all this neediness that he simply works longer hours at the office, flowers the last thing on his mind.

On the positive side, when her needs are quite reasonable, her thieving can be helpful to the relationship. Sometimes men can be clumsy or negligent in matters of intimacy and matters of the heart. They would rather leave "all that stuff" to the woman. A woman—and a marriage—do need caring and loving attention. And it is wonderful when a woman can draw out a man and help him to recognize and define his feelings clearly—and share them honestly and fearlessly with her. And when she can put forth her own needs and feelings clearly and risk asking for the attention and care that she needs, she can help the relationship.

When the maiden had eaten the pear . . . she went to hide herself among the bushes.

To bring about that growth in relationship, she will have to stop her infernal nibbling around the bushes and reach out her stumps and name what she needs, asking in such a way that she will be listened to and understood. Early in the relationship this seems almost impossible for a Handless Maiden to do because she either wants to make demands or she retreats into an angry silence. Perhaps she merely hints around, fearing that a negative response from her man will be a rejection of her whole being or the death of the relationship. And early in the relationship the Handless Maiden will tend to fear her man's feelings—she doesn't really want to hear them because she fears, just as much, her own.

Just now, the Handless Maiden in our story does seem to know two things quite clearly: what she craves and the truth of her predicament.

> "Oh, if only I could get inside this garden to eat some fruit before I die of hunger! . . .
>
> "I am no spirit, but an unhappy mortal deserted by all but the grace of God."

The Apple Tree and the Pear Tree: Two Trees for the Hungry

There is a curious parallel between the two trees in this story: the Devil has control of the apple tree in the mill yard and the angel has control of the pear tree in the moonlit garden. While some may think the Devil and angel motif must be a later addition to the tale, designed to make it a story with a Christian moral, other variations, even out of Africa, also have a spiritual being, some other-worldly or unearthly creature, like a mystical bird or a magical snake, who keeps appearing to help the young woman. (Please see the stories at the end of the book.)

THE APPLE TREE

In the Genesis story the tree of forbidden fruit is bedeviled with the problem of consciousness. The apple tree is the daylight tree of consciousness; it stands in our own backyard. It holds the masculine fruit of knowledge and differentiation or "knowledge of good and evil." To have the faculty of discernment, the Devil promises, will make us "like to God." Eating the fruit of this tree, and perhaps *because* it is forbidden and stolen, means to wake up, to become conscious and aware, to make judgments and choices, to know. And to know guilt.

Eve (like Pandora or Psyche) is the inner, feminine aspect of the psyche that wants to know, to uncover, to solve riddles, unlock secrets, open boxes, and shed light on a subject. Intellectual curiosity is a human quality and belongs to us all. We all come to crave the fruit of knowing and, having once eaten it, we discover that the Devil had a point: however could knowledge be a sin? Knowledge and the freedom to choose make humans of us. And sometimes knowledge even makes us feel like God. With our powerful tool called knowledge, we proceed to differentiate and judge and sort and divide—everything. We make and we choose, we invent and create. Sometimes we begin to believe that we are, indeed, gods and we think we can create ourselves.

We are also confused and ambivalent about our craving for this fruit, because it turns out that to be conscious and knowledgable also makes us responsible. We are not sure we want to be responsible for what we know and for the choices we make. We've divided everything up into little bits with our knowledge and have forgotten how to put it together again. We long for the time before consciousness, when all was One and Simple. With that we cultivate a contradictory attitude that says, Ignorance is bliss . . . let sleeping dogs lie . . . what you don't know won't hurt you. For didn't the Eden story warn that it was dangerous —in fact, flat out a sin—to become conscious? It is much the safest thing to remain ignorant, unconscious and innocent— otherwise we will bring suffering and death into the world.

Hence, we are distressed when technology enters the "primitive" world and the old ways begin to crumble and are certain to be lost. The old father's ways are replaced as the son is seduced by new methods. The native women no longer make earthen pots but fetch water at the tap in gaudy plastic containers. The old gods are scoffed at and their altars and ceremonies neglected. The new gods are the shiny implements of progress. The price of consciousness is the loss of innocence and a direct connection with God. No wonder knowledge has a forbidden ring to it. Lost innocence makes us homesick for the "good old days," for paradise, for whatever style it was that we once lived and no longer have access to. Lost innocence means the end of the old, simple ways and the beginning of new, complicated ones with responsibilities and serious moral overtones.

Out of one side of our mouths we say that it is a sin to become conscious, and out of the other we say that it is a sin to remain unconscious. In a family, when one members dares to become conscious—to become enlightened about the ways in which the family has functioned or, indeed, about how they have been dysfunctional for so long—his or her deviation from old family patterns is a heroic act that takes enormous energy. The collective family taboo that forbids awareness or true autonomy has a great gravitational pull to keep that roving family member in place. Any efforts on that person's part may be defined by the rest of the family as ungrateful or disloyal, crazy or dangerous. When someone shifts into consciousness and out of an assigned familial role it threatens to unbalance the whole family. Everyone will have to shift around to reestablish a new balance. Some members may even begin to make their own changes and risk new growth. But the person who risks change will be on a road to freedom and who knows who will follow?

The feminine quality of curiosity that resides in all of humankind, the quality of wanting to know what is still unknown, is not an evil quality in itself. Certainly Eve or "the woman" is not evil—as one perspective on the issue of feminine curiosity has viewed it. Knowledge brings about wonders, but it can have terrible consequences. If we use knowledge for personal gain at the cost of others, or to further our blooming hubris in order to play at being gods, our unexamined motives are the cause of evil. That is the tragic flaw that is coupled with knowledge. That is the tree the miller has eaten from.

If we use that knowledge to become acutely responsible for the way we conduct our lives and the way we relate to one another, knowledge is used rightly. That is the awareness that sends the Handless Maiden in search of herself.

We all want to know ourselves. Some have made psychoanalysis the new religion. Some take psychological tests to find themselves in a greater schema. Others religiously study their horoscopes. Expelled from the garden of our childhood innocence, we wander outside its walls. We work by the sweat of our brows, but we wonder what our lives are about. As sinners, we can't quite figure out who we are. We long for meaning in the midst of this pervasive feeling of homesickness. We sniff around the garden walls, wishing we could find the entry and a way back in to the bliss of our original innocence.

During the darkest moment of the Easter vigil service, there is chanted a powerfully beautiful hymn, the "*Exultet*," in praise of our salvation through Christ's death and rising again. It praises the mysterious paradoxes that make us whole and healed again. One line praises the sin of consciousness, and the next indicates that this sin is responsible for our reconciliation with God:

> O happy fault, O necessary sin of Adam,
> which gained for us so great a Redeemer!
>
> Night truly blessed when heaven is wedded to earth
> and humankind is reconciled with God!

Had we not committed the sin of consciousness, we would also never have brought heaven and earth together in the incarnation of God's own Son. Through God's flesh-taking, all of matter becomes a suitable, even a worthy container for the divine. All matter—this earth under our feet, nature, our bodies, generativity, women, feminine values, all that we have judged as lesser—has actually been blessed and made equal partner in a marriage to the divine. God, in the person of Jesus, is now one of us, and his suffering and death on the tree of the cross and his rising and victory over death have transformed the nature of that apple tree and made it a holy tree of paradox: the tree of suffering and the tree of life. The tree of the cross returns meaning to our lives and sets us free.

THE PEAR TREE

The pear tree in the royal, moonlit garden offers a feminine fruit from an orchard which grows in the mysterious world of the unconscious. This time an angel and not a devil suggests we steal the fruit it offers. The angel is the saving grace here and is no doubt the same angel who appears in the center of the forest later in the story. Surely the angel must be that grace which comes as a winged messenger, that being who lives in two worlds, bridging the gap between the unconscious world and the conscious world—between heaven and earth. In this story the angel brings us first to the riches of the world of the unconscious: to dreams, the inner life, to poetic, mystical realities. It is the dark, feminine fruits that nourish us in that inner world. The sunlight of consciousness does not enter this place. Here, the garden is surrounded by a circle of shimmering water and grows by the light of the moon.

Moonlight

In the night and by the light of the moon we see things in a different light. Thomas Mann coined the phrase "moon grammar" to describe that sense of an inner reality. "Daylight," he said, "is one thing, moonlight another. Things take on a different look beneath the moon than beneath the sun. And it well might be that to the Spirit the light of the moon would appear to yield the truer illumination."

The moon is also reflective. It has no light of its own but takes sunlight, which is too bright to see into directly, and returns it to us in a way which we can tolerate and even comprehend. Moonlight and feminine wisdom have their own ways of shedding light on a subject. Feminine wisdom is less concerned about "original thinking" or what is "new under the sun" but takes the creative world as it is and reflects on it—reflects the great light or the bright ideas back to us in endless variations, constantly making old knowledge new and ever applicable.

When I want to look in the night sky for the constellation called the Seven Sisters of the Pleiades, I find I see it more clearly by looking just next to it rather than directly at it. We can just as well say that a Handless Maiden must still her hunger by not being direct and clear. As yet she cannot wander up to the roadside stand in broad daylight and pay for a pound of pears. Just now in her development, she can only steal what she needs; she gets the pears underhandedly, rather than directly. And when she stills her hunger with that fruit, it brings a positive result.

The King said, "And if you are forsaken by all the world, yet will I not forsake you." He took the maiden with him into his royal palace and because she was so beautiful and good he loved her with his whole heart and made her his wife. And he saw to it that she was fashioned a pair of silver hands.

Chapter 9

SILVER HANDS

*The King loved her with his whole heart and made her his wife.
And he saw to it that she was fashioned a pair of silver hands.*

Being able to *do* something by way of either householding
or gainful employment is the necessary requirement if we
are to enter into the larger society and hold our own. So
the silver hands which the King (and that kingdom of cultural standards) has created for our Handless Maiden seem
exactly the gift necessary for this entry into her adulthood.
And marriage is generally accepted in most societies as the
arrival into adulthood. Certainly the spiritual, sacramental
standard of a marriage is both form and formation and may
be exactly the structure for our Handless Maiden to develop
within.

The King, in some ways, is indeed her salvation: he is a
new, loving and helpful male figure. He can take her into
his life, love her, fit her with silver hands, and he is not
quite her father.

Tedium vs. the Art of Doing

Adulthood, that state we have spent a childhood and youth looking up to as the apex of human freedom, is scarcely attained before we begin to bemoan our lost youth and the freedom of childhood. For when we enter this stage of development we discover that *doing* is in fact the definition of our state of being. And this doing may very quickly come to represent a depressingly tedious nine-to-five sort of existence: our work merely a means of earning money for survival, our duties all routine, responsibilities, social demands.

We might even consider that this limited understanding of doing as economic burden—as supporting ourselves and our families and leaving everyone else to muddle through in the same way or as best they can—is the malaise of an industrial culture that has come to grinding out an existence with the old miller's attitude. It is the attitude that has been the conditioning experience of the miller's daughter. It is the attitude that has infected the whole kingdom. It is represented in our story with uncanny accuracy in the gift of metal hands, the caring but only solution the King can offer his new bride.

Because the King outfits her with a pair of silver hands, what the maiden has to offer the world now are his hands. The silver-handed phase in a woman's life (or in the psychic life of a man) can last for a very long time. She may mistake her silver hands for a full cure or she may believe that the functioning of silver hands is of greater value than ordinary flesh-and-blood functioning. Or her silver-handedness may be only a mechanical doing of actions necessary for mere survival and may be removed from living a life.

We all function out of our silver-handedness when we are ambivalent about being adults and fail to grasp that our doing is not just a private act of survival but might be raised to the level of *art*, both sacred and social. The *art of doing* is our essential contribution to building and preserving a social order. To be adult means that we are able to transform our actions—work or play—into satisfying, even enjoyable participation in creating this world. The art of doing presumes a conscious acceptance of our responsible role in the making and healing of the social order and is satisfied with performing even the smallest gestures to this end—artfully.

Unfortunately, our Western society does not have the rituals to help us make the transition into responsible adulthood and leaves to chance, to fate or grace, to randomness or individual determination the discovery of how to become real and human down to the tips of our fingers. Hence the achievement of true adulthood may be the longest and messiest and most often failed developmental cycle that our Western society ever grapples with.

Borrowed Hands

With silver hands, the new bride in our story is really only a little better off than she was when she was handless, and until our fairy tale finally takes us into her evolution to authenticity she may spend untold years in dullness and tedium. She may settle into a period during which she remains acceptable, even pretty in her new, precious hands, but essentially still passive and helplessly "feminine." Without hands of her own—with these borrowed hands—she cannot be fully authentic. Her opinions are borrowed, even though she is not aware of it. Passive and opinionated, what she has to offer the relationship or the outside world are not her own feelings but the borrowed convictions or the shrilly delivered authoritative opinions of her King or the culture. It is common in women, especially early in their development, to live by the quotations or principles of others, especially the quotations of men or social systems they know and admire. They may also exchange their freedom for a constrictive "religious" system or cult. So, too, the feminine part of a man may be so constricted and shut down that he functions automatically by the unquestioned rules and opinions of a political party or a metallic, hard-edged fundamentalist system.

Detached from Feeling

It is possible that the intellectualized and "masculine" opinions on which the Handless Maiden has come to rely and which are somehow artificially attached to her begin to work alone. Like some eerily robotic function, they dictate to the rest of her personality. Silver-handed functioning is lifeless. It has no warmth. It has no soul. Only later will these hands be redeemed by spirited direction and perhaps by some authentic, artistic expression. But for now she continues to function indirectly; a direct mode of expression is lost to her. She is detached from her own feeling.

Sterling Accomplishments

Until she learns to listen, to touch, to taste, to feel, and even more importantly, until she is able to order and translate those feelings into conscious value and meaning, the Handless Maiden will use those silver hands in her relationships, both at home and in the community, to *manipulate* what she wants.

Having impaired natural responses, she will read all the *manuals*—the handbooks—that tell her "how to" function and what to think. *The New Yorker* carried a cartoon of a woman surrounded, floor to ceiling, by shelves of books. She was seated in an armchair amid all these books reading one entitled: *Women Who Read Too Much*. The Handless Maiden may devour information. She wants facts, results, sterling accomplishments, perfection. So she reads baby books, diet books, books on finding the right colors to wear, books on how to make friends, how to relate to men. . . . She rarely misses the advice columns in the newspaper.

After reading dozens of books and magazines on the subject of home decorating, collecting swatches and catalogues and agonizing over endless details, a Handless Maiden may throw it all over and choose to hire a decorator to do the living room and the family room in all the right colors. We do that because we can't afford to make mistakes and won't trust that we have any taste of our own. Also, it seems too risky to wait for the atmosphere to grow organically. The decorator, then, proceeds to do the perfectly trendy thing, and it probably looks just like ten other houses in the subdivision. Or maybe no one can live in the place because it is perfect—perfectly impractical.

As a child, I remember a woman who spent a great deal of time and thought redecorating her living room. I imagined that somehow it must have been utterly, splendidly perfect—but I couldn't say for sure, because the place was draped—always—in protective sheets and milky plastic slipcovers. Sometimes I liked to imagine who the honored guests might be for whom the covers would be removed and for whom the room would finally be revealed in all its splendor—because it never seemed to happen.

Slipcover days were also the days of hair curlers when some women, it appeared to me, lived in that uncomfortable hardware. It seemed they suffered the night in them, but next morning they might also arrive at church in them, lumpy and swathed in scarves. I would wonder when the great occasion might arrive when the woman could unveil herself and feel free to let down her hair.

I've been known to squirrel away bars of good scented soaps, all given as gifts—for how could I buy myself something so fine? I savor the moment when the perfect occasion arrives to actually use one of them. The silver-handed attitude seems to live on the brink of perfection—everything in perfect readiness until the perfect moment arrives. But does it? For the Handless Maiden, no moment may ever be perfect enough.

Charitable Acts

Being a "good girl," a Handless Maiden's good works continue to be a part of her routine. While she may be less the goody-two-shoes of earlier years, when she did what was expected out of fear, and though she does indeed have a deep capacity for doing good, for knowing the value of "works of mercy," until she comes to feel that capacity within her, her good deeds may be fueled more by a vague guilt or driven by a tedious sense of duty. She is now, after all, a new queen in the kingdom and her duties may resemble those of any first lady. Since her identity is connected to her husband's high position, her sterling goodness may be vast and public, generalized and abstract.

The volunteer work of women has a long history and has contributed much to keep the world afloat, but a silver-handed goodness runs the serious risk of being artificial and cold; pretty, to be sure, but done out of a Handless Maiden's bottomless need for public approval and recognition. She will be a fund raiser and philanthropist when it gets her picture in the paper or she is praised in her alumnae news. She may assign a greater value to service which is public and grand. And she may shun, in keeping with society's patriarchal thinking, the small, interior way.

William Blake said, "He who would do good to another must do it in Minute Particulars. General Good is the plea of the scoundrel, hypocrite, and flatterer." Christ called the doers of pretty deeds "whited sepulchres." The hypocrites were do-gooders, and Christ hauled out the miller's millstone and said: "It were better that a millstone were hanged about his neck and he be cast into the sea."

There is also the insidious Handless Maiden attitude that says, unless it can make grand changes, an action is not worth doing at all: what's the use? You throw up your hands (the ultimate handless gesture) and say: "My not drinking from this Styrofoam cup isn't going to stop pollution." It is that masculine—from the top down—view of the whole universe that leaves one feeling hopeless and helpless about the mess. It is the favored viewpoint of men, and one that we women easily adopt, perhaps because it provides us all with an excuse not to take responsibility for our part in the world community at all. Wendell Berry, poet and farmer, reminds us that the world has been spoiled by individual actions and only individual actions will clean it up again.

Some volunteer work in the past seemed vaguely off the mark. And many women today refuse to do anything without pay or power. In a search for liberation, some have rushed to the other end of the scales. They do not want to be part of the tribe of "vestal virgins" who hovered around the pastor, baking him brownies and scraping up candle wax on sanctuary floors. They would rather just be the pastor. In any case, many institutions, from the Church to the Red Cross, have had to change the way they function for lack of women volunteers. And many women, doing some sort of mindless work, day in, day out, wonder why being paid for this is called "liberation."

The truly "subversive" and revolutionary action that can bring a society around to a new consciousness has, in fact, often been the domain of women who have vision and who have volunteered their time and energy to that vision. In the earlier stages of the more recent women's movement, the issues of peace awareness, of ecological action, the cause of children, the poor, minorities and the third world, the preservation of animals and the natural world were made known through the quiet, steady work of women who had not yet been swallowed into the energies of a work force. It has become a serious loss to these movements that the energy and single-minded dedication to these issues have been watered down because women have since been liberated into a world of the paying eight-hour day. Or perhaps *all of us* have degraded the feminine value of voluntary work—works of mercy or stamp-licking—because there is no power in it. At least not masculine power.

Mother Teresa, as a model of a woman at home in her own skin—brave, wise, ordinary, direct—functions most simply: charity begins at home. And she makes her home where she is most needed and does not have to wander far. The child dying in the street, lying in her very path, is Jesus and the person sent to her care for today. She has it together—heaven and earth, together in the same place. When asked how she does it, she says, "With love—with love you can't make a mistake."

Competition

The Handless Maiden in us too often cannot even fathom that kind of power—the power of love. She prefers being "in love," if not with a man, then with masculine power. When a Handless Maiden is so overly, helplessly "feminine," she feels powerless and only receives a sense of power from her connection to men. Being disconnected from life, she has no share in masculine power, so she craves the recognition of her man and her world. While a part of her may have a natural gift with her children and family, she still rather mistrusts those feminine values either in herself or as one of the good qualities necessary to her family or her culture. "With love you can't make a mistake." But she harbors a view she inherited from her father—the patriarchal system—that power has greater value than love. That men are more important than women—well, she may not *say* that to-day, but she inflates with energy both the ratification and the criticisms or insults she receives from men and ascribes to them a very great power over her.

And while it is true that no one is justly disqualified from sharing in masculine power, because of her silver-handed attitude, a Handless Maiden may mistrust anything that has no "real value," anything impractical or that doesn't lead to something tangible. So she may urge her children to be "number one" in "math and science," even when these subjects do not particularly suit their personalities. Or she brings a formidable pressure to bear on them to become competitive and successful in all the ways her father—or her inner masculine critic—would approve. She wants from her children the same sterling performances she requires of herself. And with all the grades and trophies and plaques to prove their worth, she may never have noticed that competition can be hard on love.

Perhaps the Handless Maiden adopted this competitive attitude hoping that her children would not repeat her overly feminine early experience of passivity or helplessness. Or she so mistrusts or undervalues the practice of cooperation that competition, though she fears it deeply, is the position she functions from personally much of the time—or lives out through her children.

How quickly she's forgotten her own oppressive experience—forgotten that someone, somewhere, pays a price for the one who wins that "number one" place—because competition means there is a "top of the heap," and hence an underdog for the bottom of the heap. Now it has become feminine value itself that "knows her place" and is relegated to the bottom of the heap. Collectively, the oppressed feminine value is manifested, for instance, in systems of power that contribute more to the making of "smart bombs" than to the making of "smart children," or education. Her vigilance and mistrust may be the Handless Maiden's way of repeating the crime committed against her by her father/culture by keeping the feeling and sensitive relational value smothered and unrecognized—even maimed.

Envy

Where there is competition, where there are unaddressed feelings of uselessness and emptiness, where there is "unlived life" and unused intellect, or where ambition and the need for recognition lie just beneath the surface, envy thrives and its poison seeps into everything. The problem of jealousy occurs with great intensity in our next story and will receive greater attention there. But our Handless Maiden with her unlived life is a close relative to Cinderella and her envious sisters. It is easy for a Handless Maiden to see herself as left behind in the dust, while her sisters in the community live the glamorous life. It is also easy for her to see herself as the sweet, good one, envied by greedy sisters bent on persecuting her. As long as a Cinderella or a Handless Maiden fails to see how she envies or how she causes others to envy her, her transformation is stunted. But when her goodness becomes pure and joyful, it makes her whole.

A Fear of Machines

It may be the heritage of a "miller's daughter," the result of her conditioning experience with mechanics and technology, that renders her befuddled with her household and office machines.

My own handlessness manifests itself in seizures of terror over technical things. I would have no microwave oven and no food processor if they were not delivered as gifts to my household by others. I don't have a dishwasher and there is no way I would have a trash compactor. Recently I was caught in the act of singing incantations and making obeisance to my computer before risking a tricky maneuver. I have never quite mastered the stereo, certainly not a VCR, and never will I submit myself to the automatic bank teller because it combines two of my complexes: money and machines. Neither, in my estimation, can ever be "user friendly."

And with regard to driving, my children, peering with horror through spread fingers, have often implied that I have no talent for traffic; they have even suggested that it would be in the community's best interest to supply me with a driver.

Should any new bit of equipment intrude on my life, I will study the user's manual carefully. I will pore over that manual until I am ready to confront the machine in question. With my husband in tow for courage and assistance, I hope to conduct its maiden firing up. But promptly my husband starts to punch the buttons and dial the knobs with great interest. Since I know he never studied the manual, I can only flee the room. Surely he is about to blow us all up.

A Mistrust of Process

In the business world a Handless Maiden is both impressed and frightened by her boss's "bottom line" mentality. "So what's the bottom line?" "What's it doing for the Gross National Product?" Product and production are what pressure—and impress—her. The feminine side of work—process—is suspect for its impracticality and is seen as less valuable. She has learned to feel guilty and useless about her process and unproductive when she has nothing to show for herself. One time, when my husband asked me what I had accomplished that day in my drawing, I pulled the loaded wastebasket up from under my desk and presented it with a flourish. I was trying to make light of my guilty feelings. While "the primrose does not hate the mud it grows in," the value and necessity of process are often lost to the Handless Maiden. Anxious for the product, she can wring her silver hands with the best of them.

I still have a nameless fear that lies at the pit of my own handlessness. I am perfectly aware that the Handless Maiden can be so overly feminine that she can circle and circle around an idea and never quite get off the ground—rev up and rev up and never take off. It is an old fear that I've had to look at. One day it occurred to me that my process simply was not a masculine process. I didn't think in a linear fashion and I could never write an outline for a paper until I wrote the paper and knew what it was about. All these years I had nursed a useful sense of inferiority which excused me from certain work. I was excused because of my "handicap." No, I was excused because I didn't trust a process that was unconventional or "impractical" or feminine.

When I write something now, I first write on hundreds of bits of paper. I get scraps of paper from the printer down the street. They come in many colors and they sit in tidy little piles and baskets by every telephone for messages. They lie in the glove compartment of the car. They poke out of books as markers and, as a result of their handiness, they carry reminders and messages and quotations and ideas and inspirations and insights into the subject matter currently brewing in my head. Finally, when I am ready to begin the paper, I start to gather up all these bits—it's almost like raking leaves—and I get down on the floor and begin to arrange them and add to them and make a pattern of what I see growing there. It takes the form of a circle. Every day I switch and shuffle and poke in new bits like spokes in a wheel—here and here and here. Over the days no one can walk in that room. The wheel grows, each circle surrounded with another circle. Soon the pattern takes up the whole floor and looks curiously like the makings of a star quilt.

Then I find a place to cut into the star pattern in order to create a beginning and an end. I straighten the papers out and tape them into a long river. Where the river stops brings me back to where it began. Perhaps the process will turn into a paper, but I can never be sure.

Then came the word processor. Now would I have to think in a straight line? And I can't see where I've been or where I am going, I can only see eighteen lines on the screen at a time. So I print out a mile of paper. I lay it down the hallway and into the bedroom and with my shears in hand I crawl up and down the hall, cutting out this, pasting it there, taping that bit up there to this down here. I am back at the business of tailoring.

Craft

For all that mistrust of process and anxiety about product, the Handless Maiden is curiously handy. It is possible that she is attracted to and learns skills that will tease her dormant intellect just a little but not threaten to develop it too much. I think, during waves of cultural pressure to remain slow-witted and helpless, relegation to "mechanical skills" may have contributed to the creation of Handless Maidens. A woman was safe as long as she wasn't doing "anything really important." But, for all that, a Handless Maiden does, ironically, know how to get certain things done.

The Handless Maiden or the maiden outfitted with false hands comes upon some important choices here: She can opt to continue to do the silver-handed thing which contains no blood or passion and is only "perfect." She can call her work unimportant or unappreciated and so take no real interest in it or responsibility for it. Or she can come to value what is feminine about her process, imbue her work with her deepest reality—wounds and all—and turn even the simplest tasks into sacrament. A sacramental, artful way of living will bring feeling into her hands.

A Handless Maiden may be a wiz as a secretary or a receptionist. Even great with the mechanics of phones and the computer. She may do her job with magnificent, silver-handed precision, but she may avoid making simple decisions that are not initiated and approved by her boss. She fails to be creative or to take risks. She has no faith in her creative ability or belief in her purpose.

Or she may be the kind of secretary who has a devotion to her job. Many companies, church offices, libraries, universities are kept running smoothly by wise women who have embraced their value and feel fulfilled and rewarded for the patient, tender, creative ways they make things tick. They have not only a great talent for details but a great talent for relating to a host of different personalities, building bridges of understanding between them and helping each of them to function well with the others.

Perhaps a silver-handed maiden paints. But cautiously. In the old days, it was certainly painting by number because it afforded no risks and guaranteed sterling perfection. She does needlepoint, but sometimes the major part of the design is already finished and all she need apply is the background. She can put together a stained glass window to hang in the landing—of a skier or a sea gull—from a kit with patterns.

I came from the era of silver-handed ones who learned to smock little dresses. We knit, we crocheted, we embroidered, quilted, sewed. We are the ones who know how to paint the kitchen, refinish old furniture, plant a garden and put up the produce. We know how to make baskets from garden clippings, cut the children's hair or cut the dog's hair. We still know how to darn socks, take up hems and let them down, turn collars and let out seams.

This handiness of the Handless Maiden may be born in compensation for her imposed incompetence. It may be necessity

that allows her to be the mother of invention. But it may also become an initiation into her healing. For handwork, skills and crafts have the capability of serving the high art of living, or even high art. Often, and over time, these skills do develop and mature and make significant contributions to her very soul, her family, work, or the larger community.

Thrift

A desperate miller's wife, trying to run her household in poverty, will naturally teach her daughters all the ways to be thrifty. So did the experience of the Great Depression make of our parents string savers and teachers of thrift. As a youngster I drew and I painted and pasted and built all the time. It was my father who, with admonitions not to waste it, doled out what I needed in paper from the pile of blank blue-book pages, old cardboards and carefully sliced-open backs of used envelopes that he kept (and still keeps) neatly in a folder behind his desk. And some of our parents still save used twisties and meat trays, yogurt containers and old pickle jars because "you never know when you'll need them."

Necessity made better "ecologists" of them than affluence has of this generation. It certainly made wonderful folk artists if you consider old quilts that were fashioned from scraps or rugs made from rags. As daughters of a miller's household, we develop useful skills, learn thrift as a virtue, and some will come to turn thrift itself into art. I have a sister, I swear, who knows how to make a gourmet dinner from an old hiking boot.

Beyond thrift, there is another great advantage to those homey skills. They take time. So we take time. They are a legitimate form for quiet, interior musings, for letting some outer pressures go, for setting things in order. Certainly the ordinary tasks of an ordinary household might offer the same nourishment. Patching, ironing, making the hearty soup. Digging in the garden, making compost, pulling weeds. Making the baby a pair of warm crawlers out of an old sweater feels like making "something from nothing." I make stitched, thick, squared dustcloths from my soft old flannel nightshirts.

Women, it seems, have known forever how to make what is useful and the useful into a thing of beauty. From sewing good buttonholes to baking bread, these tasks can offer an experience of creativity, of grace, of sacrament. All this has been good, healthy "pear nourishment." It belongs to us.

I was giving a family workshop not long ago and in the very front rows four people were knitting. One was a young father—a great, gray sweater growing out from his needles. I can't say that I see this too often. Perhaps this was only a patch of the sixties preserved through some oversight. Or these people, with an intuition about the wounding that a technological existence might do them, found comfort and antidote in knitting. They seemed an endangered species.

This "taking of time" and "the time it takes" to be handy in this way are also endangered as values. When we *took* time—had "time on our hands"—I think we had a greater chance of restoring those hands to flesh. What is too much and too fast in our lives today interferes with processing the simple happenings of everyday living. It robs us of challenge and takes away purpose in simple acts. And our notion that the value of silver supersedes the value of simple, common flesh lets us forget that we do still need healing. One day we may learn, once again, to return to the ground of our being and give up our complicity with a system that exploits our energies and robs us of religious experience.

The object of life is to live it with feeling and passion and art—minutely—because without the paper scraps, the sticks and rags and soups, without sunrises, or compost piles, without babies, and loves, without spinning an atmosphere for family, neighbors, and friends, there is no taste of God.

"Woman's Work"

One of the major differences that separate older cultures from our culture is our modern incapacity to live our organic lives as a sacrament. At one time the fundamental issues of love and food were surrounded with ceremonies which put a people in touch with life itself. The ordinary, fundamental acts transformed into ceremonies brought about a religious experience. They freed a people from performing in a merely automatic, physiological, silver-handed manner. They freed a people from losing a sense of meaning—from nothingness. In parts of India the mother of the household rises early and before the doorstep of the house makes a fresh design of colored rice flour. It lasts until the first persons come and go. It has nothing to do with the practical but everything to do with setting things right. Some of the ritual foods which tradition has seen as a mother's task to prepare may also be experienced as her invitation to collect herself and return to what is uncomplicated, direct, organic—soul nourishment for herself and food for her family. In the Orthodox Jewish family the father has 213 prescribed ritual tasks to perform each day, but the Jewish mother has three—one of which is to bake the bread, the challah. Perhaps she has only three because the other two are to keep a kosher household and raise the children. But it is the bread—its making and its sharing—that holds the family together. Inner feminine values are quietly being nourished and strengthened as the Ukrainian women stay up all night to decorate beautiful Easter eggs. These were once painted in silence, as prayer.

"Woman's work," and all those fundamental details that we have relegated to inferiority, may actually be the place of religious meaning and insight. "Women's work" may, in fact, be priestly work and not just the privilege of women alone.

And though "domestic skills" may have been taught by a horrified mother knowing no other way to save her daughter during those fateful three years before the Devil arrived, the Handless Maiden, I feel certain, learned every domestic skill that was once defined as "woman's work." She learned those practical and ordinary skills, later honed in the marriage circle, which, best of all, provide the very simple stuff for a sacramental attitude that the marriage most needs.

I remember, only weeks before my own wedding, being stricken with a panic so overwhelming that I couldn't eat or sleep. Surely I was about to enter the most foolhardy agreement an ordinary mortal could undertake. That I should throw in my lot with another ordinary mortal—this was nuts! Marriage was madness! How might I get the word out quickly for all to ignore the invitations which were already in the mail? My bones felt cold, my skin tingled painfully all over. I stood in my mother's kitchen, white as paste, my tongue a piece of thick leather in my mouth. What was I to do?

I think my mother was horrified just to look at me. So she did what I imagine the mother of the Handless Maiden did even as the Devil came up the driveway to get her. She pulled me over to one of her pots on the stove and thrust the wire whisk in my hand. "I don't know what you should do. Hush. And learn to make white sauce."

I stirred up the roux according to her instructions and added stock to it and stirred some more. She fussed a bit over my shoulder when she thought I might let it get brown or too dry. Slowly I added more stock and then milk. I whisked steadily to make sure no lumps formed. A little more milk. A spot of stock. A squeeze of lemon. Bubbles formed and died with small velvet explosions. I turned the heat lower and reached for the salt . . .

I became absorbed in the action. It brought me down to earth, centered me, calmed me. Of course love and marriage are madness. Neither is ever quite "perfect." There is only perfect madness. This whisking of white sauce was a small sacramental act that nourished my understanding of the sacrament of marriage as *human* love. Human love as everyday love. Everyday love as down to earth. Caring. Ordinary. Committed. Holy. How could I ever stir anything and not be brought back to that moment?

I know, now, that over the years our human relatedness is often nourished and expressed in "woman's work," the actions—those lovely, holy, *ordinary* actions—we perform in the service of one another and as humble thickening in this sacrament we share.

Out of Touch in Relationship

Until a Handless Maiden comes around to the sacramentality of the ordinary and feeling functions of her life she may struggle in a prolonged period of silver-handed functioning which interferes with the development of mature relationships. A mature love is not yet possible for the Handless Maiden until she has learned to give. And she cannot give until she has learned to ask. She won't know what to ask for until she has "gotten in touch with" her feelings or names what she longs for.

Her actions may be sterling, but often they are still chilly and lifeless as stainless steel. With silver hands, she can neither feel nor be touched by feeling. *Silver hands do not conduct feeling.* Because she does not know her feelings, she cannot feel the feelings of others, which is empathy and is the deepest requirement, essential to love and the creation of a better society.

Without hands of her own, she succumbs to "wishing for" rather than asking for things or helping them to happen. She makes wishes—but silently. These are almost always intense wishes for the relationship. Ask any teen-aged girl what her wish is as she blows out the candles on her birthday cake. She wants a boyfriend. Or she wants her boyfriend to commit himself to her deeply and with feeling. "He loves me, he loves me not . . ." She is always looking for some information about this relationship. She reads his horoscope as well as her own. She is almost addicted to sentimental expressions of romance.

Sometimes this longing for a male relationship becomes a compulsive search for a father figure to approve and notice and validate her femininity. She feels incomplete and thinks she is nothing without a boyfriend, a lover, a husband, a mentor. To the outside world she may seem very popular and glamorous with the men, but there is often little genuine mutual understanding or intimacy in her relationships. There is only tragic despair.

In her marriage, she continues wishing for relationship and for signs of intimacy. These are wishes which the husband is supposed to divine. In her silent world of wishing, she can almost be greedy because her need is so great. Since she tends to look at her married life as the joining of two halves which only together make a whole, the man continues to be necessary to her completion. She tries every way she knows to make him be her hands. But what she's afraid to develop, being handless and outfitted with silver hands, are the "we" feelings of empathy. She can't imagine that her husband has feelings quite separate from hers. If he is particularly inept at knowing his own feelings and expressing them directly and simply, a common enough handicap in men with their own handless feelings, it certainly doesn't help her. Furthermore, if he, too, is a neophyte with his own feelings, he may resort to dramatic emoting. He may rage—or be oddly sentimental. Strong feelings terrify her. She wants none of them. She can't handle them.

As romantic love fades, they discover that the qualities in each other that caused them to fall in love in the first place are now the very qualities that they dislike most in each other. That discovery has a complicated twist in the following story. A woman sought counseling when she found herself in love with two very different men and couldn't decide which one to marry. One man was well established in his career and already a very successful attorney with an even more promising future. He was dedicated to his work and liked what he did. He made a good living, owned a comfortable little house and was utterly dependable and practical. There was little doubt in her mind that he wanted to look after her and any family they might have with care and kindly dependability. He was an honorable and decent person and he loved her very much.

The other man was a gifted, imaginative musician. He played and wrote music for his living but had no regular income and sometimes was so flat broke that their dates were picnics in the park, feeding the ducks at lunchtime or singing songs by the fire at night. He often arrived late or didn't show up for appointments "because he chased rainbows." He was funny, creative, loving, full of surprises, delightfully unpredictable, often preoccupied, and, "well, somewhat impractical." The musician was keen for them to get married and was certain that somehow, between them, they could make a marriage that was sure to be a creative, wonderful adventure.

Some years later the counselor ran into the woman in town. She was pregnant.

"Well, now I'm curious," said the counselor, "which man did you marry?"

"The attorney." She smiled.

"Congratulations! And how are you doing?"

She looked at her shoes and then she looked at him and said, "We never feed the ducks in the park."

The poignancy of her answer says it all. What she loved in her attorney is what breaks her heart now. But what she loved in the musician would, if she had married him, surely be her agony now.

When the romantic era fades, and the qualities we once loved now irritate us, we begin to stir up each other's smothered feelings. We reinjure each other, opening the old childhood wounds. And we project our own negative traits onto our partner. The Handless Maiden and the man's wounded feeling side find it difficult to express themselves or to help the other articulate feelings. Most of all, they find it impossible or threatening to feel each other's feelings. But empathy and compassion are necessary to the next evolutionary cycle—properties necessary to a mature relationship.

To be empathic, you must be able to reach out with feeling hands and include another's experience in your own. Perhaps that is the meaning of that turn of phrase: "to give your hand in marriage." With consciousness, you make the effort to understand exactly how other persons see things—how they think, what they feel, what makes them anxious and why this is so. It presupposes that each is willing to be open and trusting in exposing his or her deepest self to the other. Empathy is the ultimate goal of mature relationship and love. It takes courage and practice. And it takes time.

The King and his silver-handed bride give it a year's time.

After a year, the King had to go on a journey, so he gave his young Queen into the care of his mother.

Chapter 10

THE KING'S MOTHER COMPLEX AND THE QUEEN'S FATHER COMPLEX AS PARTNERS IN THE MARRIAGE

Included in every marriage is a complex assortment of invisible personalities who mysteriously slip into the scene and promptly take up their roles in the unfolding drama of the couple's relationship. No one sees them exactly. They are difficult to define. They shift and move around the stage and speak their lines and make their demands, often by possessing one or the other of the hapless couple.

It is an important factor in this marriage too, for the Handless Maiden has married a man with a live-in-mother complex. His complex is a rather fitting match to her own devilish father complex. The mother is kindly but ineffectual, and the Devil is tireless, intrusive and destructive. A messenger who continually falls asleep on the job is also a member of this partnership. He passes messages only after they have become twisted and convoluted. There are angelic messengers who do a better job of passing along meaning, but they appear only after things have reached their greatest point of disintegration. The old complexes—positive or negative—that define our still unknown selves smuggle their way into our relationships and our marriages to play out their roles.

> *The King had to go on a journey, so he gave his young Queen into the care of his mother. . . .*

The King's Complex

The King soon leaves on the proverbial business trip—or he is "out to lunch." He thinks that he can conduct a caring and loving relationship with his wife—from a very great distance. He removes himself completely, leaving behind his mother or his mother complex to mind the household—and the marriage—in his place. A man's mother complex shows up in the very emotional feelings, positive or negative, that his mother—or, more accurately, his mother's effect on him—can call forth. Her power over him has remained archetypal rather than just personal. Somehow, somewhere, she still has a say in his choices, or in the way he demands to be cared for or feels he must care for others. His emancipation from her, or, more exactly, from what the Great Mother has come to represent to him, is still incomplete and in process.

This King doesn't mean to make trouble. Not consciously. He loves his wife. Didn't he invite her into his kingdom, that virtual paradise where she will never have to be troubled by her mutilating father again? Here—because she is handless—he will provide everything for her happiness and well-being. One hears an ominous echo down the halls that sounds like something her father once promised: "Now I will keep you handsomely as long as you live." As the story continues to unfold, one is inclined to add: the road to hell is paved with good intentions.

The story seems to say that the King has withdrawn in his masculine form. Being "a good provider" who wants to please his helpless wife with every good thing, he may be off putting most of his energy into his masculine affairs—the building of his career or the ruling of his kingdom and the fighting of his wars. Perhaps he is given over fully to his work by day and replaces himself in the relationship with his complexes or his moods, his demands or his impossibly "good intentions," by night. Perhaps he regresses to the boy his mother either pampered or neglected. Unwittingly, he may set his young Queen up to repeat the mothering he knew as a child. Either he wants the same pampering or he will prove to her that she—like his mother before her—has failed him. Wiped out by the demands of his stressful day, he may regress to demanding and tantruming by evening. Or he pouts. He's in no mood to be receptive. Perhaps he becomes passive. The man pushes himself away from the table and retreats in front of the TV. And all along his every intention has been to make his wife happy—to keep her in blissful dependency.

The Handless Maiden's Complex

All this mysterious carrying on drives his Queen wild—her devilish father complex kicks in automatically. She finds her husband demanding and ungrateful. She finds him moody or infantile and silly. She feels used and, frankly, fed up. She would love to berate him for withdrawing, for being a bore, for being unhelpful, for not listening to her. She could go off on a devilish rampage and give him a tongue-lashing.

But her style as a Handless Maiden is more likely to make her become intensely defensive—because, deep down, she has allowed herself to feel guilty for the fact that they relate so badly. She believes she has failed this man somehow. She is, after all, helpless and mutilated. How could she ever serve a *King* as he deserves to be served? She has nothing to give him in return. She is impaired, flawed, inept. How could he possibly love her? Isn't she just his little charity case? She should feel grateful! Think where she'd be without him.

> "If my wife should happen to bring forth a child, take the very best care of her, nurse her well and tell me of the birth at once in a letter."

A great chasm has opened between them. It is too wide to talk across. In fact, are they talking at all? The story tells us that it is really the mother and the Devil who now carry on the correspondence.

How could the evening have turned out this way, when all she really wanted was some relationship and intimacy? When all he wanted was some quiet time or nurturance? Between them they've made certain that closeness and caring will not be possible—not this evening. Somehow neither one's needs have been expressed with honest directness. Neither has been served. And neither meant badly by the other.

> *And it so happened that the young Queen did indeed give birth to a fine boy. Promptly the old mother hurried to announce the joyful news in a letter to her son. . . . Now the Devil, who it happened was indeed still and always looking for an opportunity to bring harm to the young Queen, exchanged the joyful letter for another and said that the Queen had given birth to a terrible monster.*

We may have thought our Handless Maiden was safely tucked away in the kingdom called marriage. But even here the young Queen is not safe from her Devil. This Devil is always going around "seeking whom he may devour." He still lurks in the background, looking for ways to ensnare her. She avoided one devilish possession in her girlhood by doing everything rightly and properly. She feels that everything in this relationship should be just as right and proper and she may be doing everything she can to make it so—it's just that her definition of "right and proper" has been contaminated by her father/Devil complex which tells her all must be perfect—or it is nothing. Because she gave up her living hands to save herself and her father, flying off now on a great devilish toot is one possible reaction by her and is often the response of a Handless Maiden trying to break out of a vicious circle. But more likely she will begin by feeling somehow at fault, becoming defensive and losing all hope.

Then the devilish complex will usher her into dark depressions. "The Queen has given birth to a terrible monster." Everything she does seems like so much sawdust in her hands.

Nothing catches her interest. Her efforts are worthless. All of life is tedium and boredom. She is condemned to extended bouts of passivity, isolation, hopelessness and inactivity. Deep down, very deep down, she mourns and secretly longs to develop the unlived life that she set aside in that sacrifice she made to save her father, thereby rendering her own self handless.

The combination in this relationship of a negative mother complex and the demon/father complex can create in her a great lack of energy. As a "daughter-in-law" to the mother complex, a Handless Maiden can become negative, indecisive and listless. That's quite understandable, for she has no real hands and cannot grab for what she wants. In fact, how can she even afford to want? Like a black hole, her indecision and passivity simply suck in the negative mother. She has to deal with the Devil on the inside, which is a lot to defend against, so the "mother-in-law" or the mother complex of her husband takes over matters on the outside and makes all the decisions and dictates what a real relationship between them should look like.

In some variations of the Handless Maiden story, the Devil and the mother figure merge into one and proceed to work their devastation in concert. In our story, the mother seems well meaning, for though she doesn't avert the disasters, she helps to lessen the degree of devastation wrought on the young Queen.

The Archetype of Mother-in-law

In fairy tales, mothers, stepmothers, mothers-in-law often come off rather badly. (Just as men are often described as ogres, devils and stupid giants . . .) We might understand their bad press if we remember that fairy tales aren't speaking of literal women or men but rather of some quality or complex that is best described in this guise. Not every feminine value is nourishing and grace filled. Repress it, and we get the same archetype in reverse. Feminine archetypes aren't always nurturers: they can just as well eat you up. We also know that sometimes we ourselves become possessed by one of those complexes or archetypes and, being thus beside ourselves, can do quite a little damage to the people around us. We'll find ourselves carrying on with a passion that rather surprises us: we *become* that witch, that ogre, that devouring mother, that meddling mother-in-law.

Any one of us is capable of playing out the role of the mother-in-law archetype. We can bustle into the life of a Handless Maiden and find her inept. We will tell her how our boy likes his soup thickened or his birthday cake frosted. We will tell her how she should raise the baby, how long she can decently nurse him, certainly that his brother should be potty trained by now. This is also the kind of mother-in-law who provides all the major "gifts" to fill in the household gaps as she sees them. She generally runs the young woman's life and unravels the delicate fabric of the young people's relationship. At least, this is what the gifted but undervalued, underengaged mother-in-law may have done in the recent past.

On the other hand, it is also possible that the mother/mother-in-law is now on the way to a wise old age. On some level, the sensitive, mature woman is always needed to contribute her wisdom and talent to the kingdom:

> "If my wife should happen to bring forth a child, take the very best care of her, nurse her well and tell me of the birth at once in a letter."

Grandmother may no longer sit in the rocking chair and knit afghans as the old stereotype would have it, but she may translate that knitting of things—or that fruitless knitting of brows in anxious concern—into a knitting together of factions in her own family: in the young family and in the community around her. In her thoughtfulness and wisdom she may now have a vision of how the world might work. There is a true vocation awaiting these energetic and wise grandmothers of today which has nothing to do with meddling and unraveling but mends and makes whole. I imagine a kind of matchmaking that wise women can effect, bringing together people who might otherwise never come to know one another. Old factions may be reconciled or institutions or people of opposite talents may be convened to benefit from combining their gifts. I know a

woman who makes it a personal project to bring together re-
search teams on child care and education with political com-
mittees. I see both grandparents (if they have not withdrawn
too early into an attitude that says, "It's our turn now") developing an educated level of child care and parent training that
makes good use of their experience and wisdom. When the
young parents are struggling to grow up and juggle professions
and raise their children in a stressful situation, a grandmother
can represent a warm and uncomplicated, steady presence to
her grandchildren: to her grandchildren and to the children of
society—personally or professionally. She can bring to the
professional world a gift that turns meddling into explaining
people to one another. She can gently untwist the twisted messages between people. Above all, she can integrate what has
been scattered and imbue with meaning anything she under-
takes.

That is the rich possibility of a positive mother complex in
the young couple's marriage and the positive possibility of a
woman's rich old age.

A friend who is a mother of eight grown children is also a
professional in child development. Recently she saw the need
and an available space for a Head Start program to be set up at
a mission church in our Latino community. Slowly, steadily,
she checked around and gathered a massive amount of information and facts about everything from fencing to free lunches.
She offered this to the pastor of the mission and provided him
with contacts for an excellent opportunity to purchase portable
classrooms. She looked up young women in the community
who were looking for Head Start jobs and connected them with
the regional office. She was facilitating and introducing all over
the place in a gentle, helpful fashion. When she hit a snag (and
there were several) and was tempted to lose her patience, she
would catch herself up, refresh her motives, take a deep breath
and walk back into the fray—that confusion of messages that
always occurs whenever a number of people gather to build
something. She helped each person to do what he could do best
and in such a way that he could only succeed. She explained
each to the other. In three months' time she had an established,
bubbling, well-run and well-attended Head Start program ex-

actly where one was urgently needed. Quietly, she slipped out of sight and is rubbing her hands looking for another place to be helpful.

The redeemed Handless Maidens in the older generation are often powerful and quiet founts of wisdom and help to young parents and the children of society. They are adults in the best sense of the word, able to make sacred and communal that which is otherwise secular or self-centered.

Chapter 11

GETTING
THE MESSAGE

The Messenger Sleeps

That other ghostly member of our story's marriage takes
the form of the messenger. This drowsy messenger must
be an archetype: don't we stand outside the drama of *Romeo
and Juliet* and watch the selfsame fellow with his vital message rest and thus fail to get to Romeo in time to tell him
that his Juliet is just asleep and not dead? And we, the
desperate witnesses, know what Romeo does not know.
We know she only sleeps when he, in finding her, is sure
she's dead. There we sit and watch, with aching hearts, as
the drama swells into its famous, tragic end.

> *Promptly the old mother hurried to announce the joyful news in a
> letter to her son. She gave the letter to a messenger to hurry away
> and deliver. But the messenger, weary with the long distance, rested
> by a brook and was in fact so tired that he fell asleep.*

And there follows an increasingly garbled and twisted
exchange, passing in complex ways from the mother,
through the messenger who always falls asleep, through the

Devil's distortions to the King and back again through the same complicated psychological network.

Whom can we blame for this "problem in communication" that, from our vantage point, just causes dreadful pain and leads to a senseless tragedy? We cannot berate the messenger—he was hot and tired. He wasn't out to cause trouble. He didn't know what was going on.

This messenger, who becomes unconscious at all the crucial moments, seems just the opposite of our story's angelic messengers: they enter in the nick of time at all the other crucial moments. The angels know the story and the truth and come to help whenever they are called. But when the bearer of the truth gets foggy about it or goes to sleep on the job or checks out of his responsibilities for just a moment, he leaves a vacancy wide open for the Devil to slip in and translate everything to an evil lie. Maybe it's exactly this winking out on awareness that causes evil things to happen—that *is* evil. Something takes advantage of our blind spot and allows the hidden, unconscious message to be sent. What we thought we'd said and what we really end up saying are opposites. The unconscious world, tired of being ignored and repressed, springs into any vacancy it spies and makes a major, archetypal mess.

It happens all the time. It happens internationally, we do it in the community, we garble things between the very people we love. We do it within ourselves by sleeping to our own realities.

When we fail to hear our own deepest messages, we are asleep to our own meanings. We fail to know our true selves and share them honestly. When we fail to hear and understand the messages sent us by others and are more caught up in delivering something back, we are asleep to the meanings of others. We are no longer speaking heart to heart.

Heart to Heart

That the young Queen and her King sincerely desire to speak heart to heart and directly is central to their relationship but too often falls apart in an obscured, confused effort that is just a painful exercise in missing, first, their own, personal meaning and, secondly, the meaning they wish to share between them.

The young Queen remembers the experience of their mutual in-loveness. It is a feeling that she wants to preserve intact, one that she wants to communicate, in turn, to her King. Certainly, with these silver hands she will know how to make some very pretty gestures of communication. She will remember to make the heart-shaped cake for Valentine's Day. Hearts and flowers are the very signs of affection that she herself most longs for. In fact, she is still so in love with romantic love that she may care more for explicit signs of affection than for the real relationship before her.

Small wonder that she is nostalgic for that feeling of "in-loveness." It was a *feeling*. It had mythic depths and classic proportions. It carried moments when she thought she knew herself as never before. She never felt more alive. She could see the good in everything. She could taste God. If she does not wander the world in search of catching that fever again and again—falling in love with all sorts of men, or trying to get all sorts of men to fall in love with her, or falling in love with the romances of her daughters—she may settle into a perpetual longing and search only for the signs of romantic love. The romantic ideal will haunt her, and its every expression will have devilish twists.

Lovemaking, which can both build up and reflect our relatedness, is far more often referred to these days by men and women removed from their feelings as "having sex." For the Handless Maiden the love relationship may be performed artificially and without spontaneity. It may take an act of will. Her lack of instinctive response results in silver-handed mechanical actions, in dead gestures or "pretty" signs.

Perhaps she has decorated the bedroom with so many frills and flounces—porcelain hearts, little wicker rockers with the teddy bears and rag dolls of innocent girlishness—that a man will feel like a clumsy bull in a china shop. He will feel the intruder rather than an equal partner.

It is coincidental that St. Valentine's Day and Ash Wednesday often meet or merge in February, but Scripture readings from the Ash Wednesday liturgy and from the early Lenten season offer some instruction and promise which are oddly useful to our traditional Valentine celebrations. We hear the words: "A clean heart create for me, O God, and a steadfast spirit renew within me." The "clean heart" will be a heart with honest, direct feelings, cleansed of sentimental motives and distorted concerns. Steady my resolve to see our relationship for what it is and where we have yet to take it. Wake me up to what I am alive to. Help me to perceive a divine numinosity in what is simple and nearby. Transform what has stopped beating and pulsating with life—what has become paralyzed between us in our fear and woundedness. Intoxicate us with hope and the joy of living . . . for which we are given that wonderful promise (which also occurs in the early Lenten readings): "I shall take away their hearts of stone and give them hearts of flesh."

Twisted Messages

Until that kind of transformation begins to glow in the embers of the relationship, the man with his mother complex and the woman with her father complex get to passing messages back and forth between them and some devilish twist will miscommunicate or obscure the meaning. Even here in our story, where it is good news, like the birth of a child—the symbol of a new possibility for them both—the message is twisted and its truth delayed or obscured.

"Well, you know . . ."

"How should I know? You never tell me!"

"Why should I have to tell you? After all these years of living together—if you *really* don't know, I'm not going to tell you."

The Handless Maiden part of ourselves continues to be afraid to state, even to know her own mind or what she wants, because deep down she fears that to have any needs will jeopardize the relationship. Ironically, that's exactly what does jeopardize the relationship. So inclined to be passive, she is not yet able to be assertive. Assertion sounds too harsh for her—to her, it still sounds aggressive. So her solution is to be passive-aggressive: in chilly silence she goes about her business, punctuating the tension with huffs and little sniffs of hurt.

A man, smoldering with resentment because he gets stuck clearing the dishes three days a week sends the same passive-aggressive message. He is sloppy and inefficient. He scrapes off the plates but drops a fork down the garbage disposal. The fork gets mangled. "Well, I *did* the dishes! What more do you want?"

On Sunday there will be a family outing. One person wants to go to the beach, another wants to go to the mountains, another wants to stay home. The husband figures his wife probably wants them all to go to the museum, so he announces that it will be the museum and of course that's where they are headed a half hour later. They're all driving down the freeway and it soon becomes clear that nobody wanted to go to the museum. Now that they're headed in the wrong direction, his wife finds it safe to say, "We never go to the zoo." She doesn't dare think, "Next Sunday, I'm going to state my request clearly." Instead, she adds to the general bad mood by muttering, "We *always* do what *you* want to do." And she believes it. He doesn't dare admit, "I really should have asked the troops what they wanted to do." He mutters, "I can *never* do anything right by you, can I?" And he believes it.

In the restaurant, faced with a menu, a Handless Maiden is overcome with panic. Choices are often paralyzing for her. She doesn't have a clue what she wants. She can't afford to want. She may discover she hates what she ends up choosing. What she'd like will most likely be too expensive. So she doesn't read the items listed, she reads down the price list, quickly checks to see what's least costly and says: "Well—I guess I'll have that baked chicken. Again." She hasn't heard what is true in herself.

She hasn't answered to what is true in herself. And she won't admit to that failure but rather sighs like one making a major concession.

She may develop a judgmentalism which is not an indication of what she wants or likes but an expression of her anger and frustration. Her judgments size up everything and allow nothing to be simply what it is according to its own aims. She dismisses a painting at the museum and declares she "doesn't like it." And her reason? "Because it wouldn't look good in our house." Really? No, not really. She scorns the country western station her husband listens to in the car and quickly slips in a Vivaldi tape, because she thinks it's the more sophisticated thing to like. By passing judgment, she puts everything in its place and never needs to look at it again.

Perhaps the messenger has delivered a certain truth after all: the love they had between them has only given birth to a monster.

Understanding the Child

The silver-handed young mother in her fearful rigidity can maintain a stiffness that allows her few spontaneous reactions, especially to her children. She can't really read them—doesn't understand the messages they give her. She simply does what is right "according to the book." Sometimes, though she would be the last to admit it, and because of her insufficient or mistrusted maternal sensibilities or sense of self, her children are a great annoyance to her. In place of functioning in an honest, natural, maternal way, she responds, not in a consistent way, but in a clinical or routine manner.

And wasn't it routine that ground down her father? She becomes mechanical as her father was before her. Grounded, uncomplicated motherhood has a natural or "instinctual" sense for children. A woman at home in her motherhood is more able to perform the routine tasks that have to do with raising children without being overwhelmed by them, as part of a day's work. She takes them in stride. She can bark sharply at the children in warning one moment, and in the next can gather them up with a hug. Feelings of anger and love are promptly expressed, aren't long and drawn out and in no way cancel each other out. "But the woman," says von Franz, "with the negative father or mother complex has an unredeemed negative side to her which would let her go too far," if she ever gave in to her anger.

Communicating Anger Directly

Her growing frustration and depression are really results of her unfelt and unexpressed anger. In depression she sends just the "twisted message" of anger. In depression she fears feelings, fears admitting these feelings and has no appropriate channel for their honest, nondestructive expression.

The more frozen she is in her anger the more she may be the "good mama" to her children, trying never to explode. She reasons with the children. She follows closely the collective models and standards. She reads her manuals on child care— never being authentic with the child and always in fear of "breaking his spirit." Actually she's angry with the child's power over her and afraid to take charge for fear of the power struggle that might result between them. She's afraid she might really blow up.

> The Devil, who it happened was indeed still and always looking
> for an opportunity to bring harm to the young Queen . . . said that
> the Queen had given birth to a terrible monster.

The child wants another cookie and pesters her while she tries to avoid saying anything at all, especially saying no. She fears "no." She fears that it will sound forth like some crack drill sergeant. If she trusted herself to decide what was right, she could actually refuse the child in a firm and at the same time friendly way.

Having to refuse someone is not evil or cruel or wrong, so the refusal doesn't need to be shouted in order to defend its validity: "I said, no! I mean no! And I don't want to have to tell you ONE MORE TIME!"

You can say no *and* be friendly. You can refuse a request *and* allow/encourage the other to have feelings of disappointment. You can say no and, because you don't feel guilty about it, mean it:

"I'm sorry, but no. Makes you so mad, huh? You really want to watch that show, and now you feel sad and angry. Isn't that *just* so aggravating? Show me your face—let me see how *mad* you are. Brother! That's pretty mad!"

"No" is the minus on the yes-no polarity. It is negative, it is, in fact, feminine, and her basic mistrust of the feminine makes a Handless Maiden feel guilty about negative answers. She thinks them bad and not equal in value to the masculine, active affirmative. The Handless Maiden finds it difficult to say no.

You can observe that phenomenon in particularly exaggerated form in what I've come to call the "university syndrome"—the parents who have so lost their feeling instincts that they operate totally out of their intellectualized opinions and theories and out of fear of their hidden feelings. Authoritarian responses to children (which they are trying to avoid) are unfeeling ones. Reasonable and loving responses, however, can be spoken with the sureness of authority. But these parents think they owe the child a reasoned response to anything asked or observed. Delivered in an overcontrolled and well-modulated tone, they offer long, complicated reasons and logical explanations to the child, even every time he whines: "How come I gotta go to bed?" A parent could just laugh and say: "Because I said so and I'm the boss." And mean it.

Woe to the parents if the child should stump them on a good reason why he should have to clean up his room. If parents cannot believe that creating clear boundaries for the child is to everyone's advantage and comfort—if they cannot commit themselves to being the adults for their child, if they don't believe that they can be directive *and* loving at the same time, if they finally burn out on endless reasoned excuses and changes of mind—the Handless Maiden that permeates their parenting style may simply give up and turn the other way, refusing to engage or even notice the child's behaviors. The parents have given the child an unspoken message: "You're the boss." This twisted message leaves the child trapped and frantic about how far he must go now with his misbehaviors to get someone to stop him.

In a relationship with a partner, the Handless Maiden faces the same dilemma. Sometimes a woman in her anger thinks: "I can't live with this man . . . but then again, I can't live without him!" So she cannot afford to be spontaneous. Certainly her spontaneity could well be filled with untold and inappropriately expressed rage! That might blow him off the map forever. Far better, she thinks, to continue to do her sterling-mother, sterling-wife routine. She is careful—very careful—with her man. She sends out a twisted message. She is so afraid to ask for anything and risk refusal that she would rather do everything herself—and, in fact, do it perfectly. And as a martyr. "Never mind"—and she gives it another twist—"I'll just do it myself."

"Handlessness" in being a parent, in a marriage, or in wider relationships contributes to the distortion of those messages we must first know, then feel, and then express with simple honesty. It comes of a great fear that to express any wish, desire or feeling is to risk the relationships—and it is on relationships that a Handless Maiden remains utterly dependent.

At the bottom of the Handless Maiden's plight, then, are those devastatingly undeveloped or inferior feelings. And these unfelt feelings are heavy with anger and rage, ambition and aggression. They are also heavy with greediness, with desire and with a massive need for recognition and acclaim.

A Strong Man Is Hard to Find

Hearts of flesh, hands of flesh—a real prince of a man can be very helpful when he finds his woman in a state of handless confusion, bogged down in her own convoluted messages. He may be tempted, because of his own mother complex, to allow her judgmentalisms—allow her to judge their friends or settle for her dismissal of people or her pinched choices. It takes real strength not to join in her anxiety or become disgusted with her indecisiveness. In the restaurant, for instance, he could recognize her anxiety, name it and help her imagine the items on the menu and how they might taste. Perhaps he'll cover up the prices to remove one of the elements that rattle her. He can make a game of it with her and give her generous encouragement in making up her own mind. And his encouragement will need to be genuinely empathic and not patronizing.

Often, when she is afraid to state clearly her needs, she will resort to subtle manipulation. Then a man must be strong enough not to be manipulated even as he remains loving.

"Hey, the garbage is overflowing in here." She is afraid, once again, to ask directly and makes it sound as though there's no desire on her part, it's just the garbage's fault that it should need a husband to come in and attend to it.

"Did you need to be rescued? Could you just say, 'Please take out the garbage?' and I'll be happy to rescue you!"

Humor helps, sarcasm is a big mistake.

A man can be strong—that is, quite clear about his own reality at this moment—and do what needs doing most.

"I'm going to finish adding up these columns, then I'll take the garbage out—for sure."

And he can help her feel quite capable by defining her as strong enough to handle his clearly stated reality:

"I can't meet you for lunch tomorrow. I have a meeting over the noon hour. Could we try for next Wednesday?"

He can take part in her healing: "*You* tell me which film you'd rather see. First of all, what sort of mood are you in? You want to see something lighthearted and silly or something serious?"

But being strong means that he needs to know what he is feeling in turn. That means he can't give in to his moods or rages or blamings or withdrawals or searing criticisms or putdowns if he wants to be present and honest and guided (not dominated) by his own inner feminine.

"I'm feeling tired and needy tonight—like I need rocking and holding. I've been acting like a baby, I guess. Can you be patient with me?"

He doesn't blame her for how he feels but takes responsibility for his own feelings: "I have this real thing about finding my laundry in piles all over the bed. Like when I found the socks outside the drawer, I feel like you're leaving this last little bit of work for me to do just so that I can feel guilty about all the work you did. And like you just can't bring yourself to do that last little loving act for me . . . like you don't really care about me."

He has to be more masculine (that is, strong, not bullying) than she is when she gets caught in one of her sharp, cutting seizures. That means he must be kind, certain, direct, present, active, and vulnerable . . . even if she's being judgmental, aggressive, opinionated, bossy and definitely "right!" She may make some pointed observations about his TV viewing—what a waste of time, what poor taste he shows, how deadly dull and unavailable he becomes.

"Well, I guess I can see it from your point of view. You feel like I check out when I watch the game. I guess I do! Maybe I need time to vege out as much as you want time to relate. I suppose we can figure a way so that both of us get some of what we need."

What muddles a man is that the woman's observation is offered in a certain reasonable fashion—full of proofs that she is right—that she was right all along and that she is always right. The problem that confuses both of them is that she really is right! What makes him want to groan that she's being "unreasonable" or "illogical" is mostly that she is right but at the wrong moment or in the wrong manner. She may be speaking for justice but there is no mercy. "I told you so!" is perhaps the major point she really wants to make, and it is salt in the wound. But he can respond with manly courage and not with a simpering defensiveness:

"Yep, you were probably right, honey—absolutely right. I should have taken a left at that last stop sign, like you told me. Will you forgive me for being obstinate?"

"Will you forgive me for being demanding?"

"Will you forgive me for blaming you for my bad mood?"

Poof! . . . But a strong man is hard to find!

And a Strong Woman Is Hard to Find

A woman needs to be strong for a man, too—be more feminine than his "anima attacks" during which he gives in to those bad-quality feminine moods of blaming, accusing, of licking his wounds or withdrawing and being passive. Being "more feminine" has little to do with hearts and flowers and a black negligee, however much these have their place in the grand scheme of things. "Being more feminine" is strength, because it is undefensive—it is the courage to take a vulnerable stance. That's the paradox of it all: it takes great courage and strength to be "weak," or vulnerable.

If she actually allows and draws out his hurt and disappointed feelings, acknowledges them, mirrors them back to him to be sure she understands and hears him rightly, she does not need to take all his accusations and criticisms personally. Sometimes his accusations have truth to them. A wife is always "committing sins of omission" as far as her husband is concerned. She just never does things as promptly or as well as his mother did is the unconscious implication. Or she is always letting him down at the wrong moment—just as his mother did. She may have cooked a fine supper, typed his report, done the laundry, but she didn't put his socks into the drawer? Really! That's the reason for his moping around? She'd love to scream! She'd just love to list all the things she does day in, day out without his considerate notice! But when she's defensive, it means she really feels guilty—she acts out of weakness and she really rather believes that she *is* a failure to this man and should have put the socks in his drawer. She bought into his wounded feelings and has taken the blame on some level.

Rather, a strong woman will separate her reality from his outburst: "It looks like your feelings are hurt. Can you tell me again what I did and how that made you feel? That made you feel ignored? Uncared for? You mean like I'm not really focused on you like you deserve? I'm sorry, really I'm sorry you feel like that."

That's it! She is a real hero. If her statement is not followed by, "*But* I think you ought to remember . . ."

She doesn't need to be defensive. Because she doesn't really accept the blame. She refuses to get hurt. She gives and she forgives. Gives before it goes another step. Gives up having to be right, or righteous or "fairly treated," or "appreciated," at least, not just now, because that's not the issue at hand. She can separate his confusion of feelings from hers and is strong enough to hear his perceptions because she is not hurt no matter how silly the accusations. Because after all—and though he *can* be difficult sometimes—she loves him. But a strong woman is hard to find.

Most of the time, in our encounters with our spouses, we are actually safer when we step in front of our defenses than when we hide behind them. That's what "being strong" means.★ Without defenses, a partner becomes an ally and not an enemy. But many couples don't seem to know how to make those jumps over their own complexes at first, to help each other grow and develop. We don't always share our own reality with one another soon enough. We aren't clear. Our messages are twisted and garbled because the messenger has gotten weary trying to span the long distance that we keep between us. The messenger sleeps by the brook. Sometimes it takes a long time to shed ancient fears and childhood hurts. We would always rather blame someone beside ourselves for the feelings we are having. We want someone else to be responsible for healing our ancient wounds. It takes grace and leaps into graciousness and generosity before we can wake up and hear the deepest messages of our own meaning and translate into meaning the messages that someone is trying to deliver to us.

★ There is a very clear distinction to be made here between hearing out another's feelings or being nondefensive toward their perceived reality—and staying around for abuse. Verbal roaring around needs something like, "Say, it seems to me you're pretty mad and you'd like me to be your verbal whipping post. I think I'll just go take a walk (or why don't you go take a walk) and when I get home you might be ready to talk about it." Just as you don't accept responsibility for unfair blame—though you'll encourage the expression of the bad feelings— you don't accept abuse. And you *don't* stay around for abusive expressions. We have been speaking here about nonviolent interaction between people who are struggling to express their feelings and trying to do so with honesty and maturity.

Chapter 12

INTO THE WOODS

Banishment or Separation

It seems to be the fate of many a marriage to come to a moment of truth at midlife. Even though she longs for a relationship more than anything else in the world, the Handless Maiden has not been able to effect a real relationship. She has to admit, now, that she is lonely and that even a "charmed" or "well-meaning" relationship is still not a real relationship. And her King may be confused and bewildered, angry and needy for his own reasons.

They have not been able to express themselves clearly or to understand each other—unable to communicate over so great a chasm. Because of their distance, they have allowed the mother complex and the father/Devil complex to do all their talking for them. These, in turn, routed their communications through the weary messenger. This causes the young love and the new life the couple had created between them to be seen now as a monster and an aberration. "The Queen has given birth to a terrible monster," says one letter. And another message says that "the Queen and her little child are to be put to death."

What is meant to be loving care on the part of the King—and the conventional world—now becomes the directive to murder the feminine—not by the King's own hand, but indirectly by the hand of his own mother. If the young Queen's devilish father complex took away her feeling hands, her marriage and its devilish interventions threaten to take away her seeing eyes and cut out her tongue as well. Blind and mute, she would be unable to see her reality or speak it—positive or negative—paradise or hell. That would make her as good as dead.

Now the old mother wept to think such innocent blood was to be shed, and she caused a hind [or young doe] to be brought her by night and had her tongue and eyes cut out. And these she kept.

Then she told the young Queen: "I cannot bring myself to have you killed as the King commands, but here you may no longer stay."

There is little cultural support for us at this moment of challenge and virtually no fitting ritual for crisis in marriage or the midlife transition. In marriage we had hoped to be offered a general absolution of the fate that made us who we were: the history, the family, the country, the cultural bias from which we drew our first breath and which formed us, willy-nilly. We were blinded to that fate even as we carried it into our young adult lives and into our relationships. For just as the wounded maiden carried both her handlessness and her virtues into her marriage, we carry the wounds and the joys of our early experiences into marriage and into the relationships we form.

Our story has shown us that the giddy bliss of the Handless Maiden's good fortune—to be swept up into the love of her King—is clearly not the whole of the story. We were tempted to believe that this very love experience would be, at least for her, her salvation. It would give her purpose, identity and meaning. So powerful is our longing to maintain the highs of romantic love that our culture knows how to use it to sell us everything under the sun. We are surrounded with messages that imply that "happily ever after" is a state easily bought and maintained, and that romantic love is the goal and the end of the journey. But the love of the King and the young Queen was a blessing which could bring either of them only so far in their search for wholeness. Before very long a new reality took shape and the high promise of romantic love began to fade. The wounds and complexes they carried into their relationship had yet to be healed or these would rend them asunder. "Put the Queen and her little child to death." *Something* will have to die, so that a deeper love can begin.

The midlife challenge—within a marriage or not—is also our invitation to the next evolution in spiritual and psychological growth. Sometimes it may take some dreadful misunderstanding or some horrible jolt to set this next evolution in motion. Jung says, "Seldom or never does a marriage develop into an individual relationship smoothly without crisis. There is no birth of consciousness without pain."

On *some* level, then, the marriage may simply have to fall apart. And there are marriages that are beyond all repair. But if a marriage breaks apart literally and dissolves, sometimes it is an unfortunate abortion of what might have been possible, if only the couple could have held out for each other and worked through their next developmental challenge. Because we do, unwittingly, often choose the very partner we need to shatter our illusions *and* team up with in the holy work of making a real partnership.

The Call to Separate Work

What the fairy tale seems to say is that a separation *is* necessary:
The Queen must be banished and the King must return from
his business trip and find her gone—so that he will launch his
own painful search for wholeness. The story says that this necessary separation will be painful and difficult. But, because the
story tells mostly what is "true on the inside," this separation
does not have to be literal: the unconscious inclination to act
out that archetypal drive to separate may lead some couples to
make a decision on the wrong level.

More important, this separation means that *each one* is required to do the *separate* work necessary to become whole. This
is the kind of separation that is our call to develop individual
authenticity and wholeness, which is ultimately requisite to
deeper human relationships and responsible commitment to
community.

Choosing a Path

> "Go forth into the wide world. Take your child and never come
> back to this kingdom again!"
> The poor woman tied her child to her back and went away weep-
> ing. Day and night, she walked and walked . . .

What a powerful image—and a tender one. Just as she left
the chalk circle of her childhood, wounded and bearing her
wounded arms on her back, now the young Queen must leave
the circle of the kingdom that sustained her and gave her, for
a time, a better home, a love and a marriage. This time she
bears the child of that marriage on her back.

The young wife and mother is cast out of every convention,
denied all that the world calls acceptable. Here she shows us
how her new fate is endured—and even redeemed. And we
will know ourselves in her struggle and in those waves of
resistance-attraction-resistance which well up in her. We will
recognize her dread, her bouts of despair, her cynicism, her
rage, her hurt at the injustice of it all—and we will know her

prayers, her angel's grace, her embrace of the challenge offered her. Seven years of solitude in the middle of the woods—seven years and seventy times seven—it takes a long loneliness and divine intervention, in fact a religious experience, to discover who really lives at the center of our being.

The Handless Maiden begins another major transition in her life. Her banishment is, in fact, a kind of death. Like her father before her, who fell from being a successful miller to being a woodcutter, she repeats a certain pattern and falls, as Queen of the kingdom, to being a handicapped and homeless mother. With a child as her "baggage" now, she bravely shoulders her burden of responsibilities. The child, however, is also an image of new life, a promise of growth and the hint of something in the future. Though the young Queen's life, to this point, has been filled with amazing experiences, on some level life has passed her by. What lies before her is the next task: the Queen has *not yet drawn meaning from her life*. T. S. Eliot said, "We had the experience but lost the meaning." The search for meaning, for a Handless Maiden, seems most particularly to be the task of the second half of life.

The Prescription

Day and night, she walked and walked until she arrived in the middle of a deep and wild wood.

Wisely, she seems not to get caught up in the "wide world" that she is sent into but rather passes the wide world by and heads directly into the woods. In the woods she can sort out her experiences and learn to draw meaning from her life. To have entered the forest is, perhaps, the most important choice that she ever makes. "Entering the woods" turns out to be the story's clear prescription for healing the wounded feminine. She has made an important decision between falling into a fruitless or neurotic depression and entering a chosen form of deep suffering that allows true healing.

To go into the woods is to go into the "unconventional inner life," as von Franz called it, to the most primitive condition of all, the vegetative. This has nothing to do with "vegging out," which is destructive passivity and inertia. But the Handless Maiden can no longer run her life in the light of the sun or turn to reason, to activity or to attempts to control everything. Her silver-handed activity no longer works for her—those chilly attempts to control and be perfect. A way in the "wide world" won't work for her. She has been separated too long from the patient, nurturing qualities of the earth, from the reflected light of the moon, from darkness and the deep heart of the forest. It is there she must enter.

Of course, she can protest. She can bang her head against the trees. Scream. Lacerate herself and the baby in a frantic effort to find a way out of the woods. Fight it. Fight everything. But neurotic suffering and frantic attempts to control the situation will only seem futile. It is just a doing of something, of anything. Fighting and frenzy would hurt both herself and the child. And resolve little.

Sometimes a divorce court becomes the arena of prolonged, expensive wounding and fighting. It becomes a devil's cauldron of wounding in the name of "justice" and "rights" where, more often than not, the victim is every feminine value, and too often the woman herself and the children.

When the pain that divorce brings is engaged on the deepest possible level (how did this happen?), then the danger of repeating the original wound over and over in subsequent relationships is averted. There, where we were *first* rendered handless and powerless, is where we alone must change and can heal.

Crisis in life is often to be understood as the invitation and initiation to maturity—to another level of true adulthood. And a "spiritual emergency" or even a "madness" that has the look of a possession can be an initiation into spiritual meaning—a process which our modern culture is slow to understand as a creative illness. Jung compared this "dark night of the soul" with the powerful, painful and often uninvited inner experience that initiates and defines the making of a shaman. It is always critical whether this experience will become a blunder into an eternal hell—a hellish possession—or the cleansing passage *through* hell to the other side where the creative *daimon* awaits one. Having first been dis-membered, the person is then re-membered, and emerges again healed and in possession of wisdom and the gifts of healing.

I have known women, long the Handless Maidens of a shattered relationship, finally "enter the woods" to suffer terrible sadness and loss, and then come out of it again, each like a phoenix from the ashes. One such woman, stripped, most unfairly, of everything, descended through the divorce, became further stripped of every defense and there, in the pits, found the courage to feel the wounds of her abandonment as a little girl and there conquered an addiction. Even as she was racked with pain and afraid, she took gentle, unselfish care of her children and, after three years of healing them, returned to life herself, glowing with wisdom and new-found abilities. Her "death and resurrection" are an example and encouragement to others. More than that, she has grown far beyond being merely an "independent individual" but has become a participant in the creation of a better community around her. Divorce, or being single, can just as well be the "hothouse" of death and resurrection which people in a marriage or a locked-in relationship may drag out, delay or avoid.

To withdraw into solitude is a conscious entry into our wounded reality and also into introspection and inner work where dreams, stories, Scripture, prayer, poetry and the messages of the inner world are taken in slowly and lovingly. It is a place for writing, for painting, perhaps for therapy or analysis, but nothing for the outside world to see. Nothing to be taken into the world's sunlight.

The Vernal Wood

Nature seems always to have offered a place of healing, when one developmental cycle comes into crisis with the next stage of development. There are planned experiences designed to immerse adolescents in an intense experience of nature—programs which have something of ancient initiation rites to them. The young people are taken into the wilderness where they learn to know and respect the environment, to suffer the fear and dangerous uncertainty of desert dryness, mountain cliffs, wild beasts and insects and—often as solo experiences—to survive. They get a good look at themselves—at their own character, stripped of all their usual comforts and defenses of loud music, fast cars and hamburgers—and, returning to their peers, they know themselves in a new way and discover better ways to interact and cooperate with their fellow initiates.

> One impulse from a vernal wood
> May teach you more of man,
> Of moral evil and of good,
> Than all the sages can. (Wordsworth, *The Tables Turned*.)

Often the young people emerge from their wilderness experience healed and confident. For the adolescent transition, but also for the Handless Maiden's in midlife, this stripping down to nature is the stuff of healing. This is the "vision quest" appropriate to transitional periods in a lifetime and bears a resemblance to powerful Native American rituals of initiation.

It is the rite that Jesus undertook when he withdrew into the wilderness to fast and pray and empty himself of any temptation that might stand in the way of his true vocation. Jesus overcame the temptations proposed to him by the Devil, for easy wealth and power—the same kind of temptation which the miller at the beginning of our story was unable to resist. Even he, the God/man, emptied himself of the temptation to play at being God, so that he could be God's own beloved Son and live his life and die his death stripped of hidden motives and refreshed with a clear vision of his true identity and purpose.

Such rites of initiation celebrate and recognize the dangers we face when we need to grow from one developmental level of consciousness into a new awareness. For it seems that, as we leave one circle of our development and enter the next, we are strongly tempted to grab hold of this uncertain life we've entered and we feel a need to take control of it—create it as we think we can create ourselves. We want to drag our defenses and habits from the old circle into this new and frightening, unknown place. Youngsters want to take their boom boxes along on camp-outs. We want to continue our attempts at silver-handed manipulation. This is where we want to loathe our fallibility, or refuse to make or see our own mistakes and deny our human weaknesses. We may still want to be "right" at all costs, even if we have to step all over people to be right. This is the moment when we are tempted to worship power —when we might hope to gain the whole world by bowing down in homage to the evil one who offers it all to us—for a hidden price. We are tempted to opt for a public form of power and give up love in exchange. In essence, we might lose our humanness and vulnerability to frantically play out our poor imitations of God.

If we fail, here in the wilderness experience of midlife, to strip ourselves, empty ourselves of ego dreams, then we give

away what is human in us. We have committed the sin of
hubris—we have fallen up! And it is in coming *down* to earth
that we find a way for healing.

Down to Earth

Very often we experience for ourselves those smaller healing
ventures into nature that we take—or that take us—just at a
moment when we need them most, when we feel we need
"grounding." Gardening, camping, mountain hikes, beach
walks, an experience of silence in the woods while cross-
country skiing, even these small experiences are often curiously
refreshing—in fact, the miller's wood-gathering place is not a
bad place to revisit.

Not long ago I returned home after a period of flying to
several cities across the country for work. It was good to be
home again, but I didn't yet "feel at home." I felt rather as
though my soul still hovered over the Rio Grande somewhere
and I couldn't quite settle down. It was midday. The family
were all away at school and work, so I pottered around the
house. Then I went into the garden to see how it was doing.
There had obviously been a big wind while I was gone, and
the trees had been well shaken out. Twigs, leaves, pine needles,
pine cones were strewn everywhere. Here and there I thought
I even spotted some pine nuts on the ground. Torrey pine nuts
are unusually large—handsome rusty brown pods, smooth and
satisfying to rub between a thumb and finger. I picked up a
few to feel and to roll around in the palm of my hand—to rattle
in a loose fist. Then I found more to put in my pockets. Then
I got a small bowl. On hands and knees now, I fingered through
the grass and leaves, combing out a seed here and another one

there. I could crack these and make a pesto. I filled the bowl.
I could find enough of these to share with my friends. I filled
another bowl. My hands and knees were black now. My vision
sharpened down to the smallest details. I picked out the nuts
from between the pebbles. I felt them out from under needles
and leaves. What a contrast, these details of the ground, from
my airplane view of the earth of just an hour ago. I was down
to earth all right—and blissful. All these seeds felt holy, filled
with possibility. They could be ground into a pesto, or I could
just scoop and drop them in the bowl over and over. Or perhaps
I could fling them into the wind again and they could grow to
giant trees . . . but I think they became smooth little conduits
of grace and meaning, little brown pods of energy bringing sky
and earth, spirit and flesh, a little closer together.

I think of the people who tend and turn the compost, sifting
the new soil between fingers with a pleasure and satisfaction
akin to some alchemist's joy as he tries to turn base metal to
gold. I think of the men I know—like my own husband—who
love to potter among their roses or in their greenhouses of a
Saturday morning. In the greenhouse, you poke little seeds into
frames. You sprinkle seedlings tenderly with a watering can
and fish emulsion. You whistle aimless little tunes through your
teeth as you transplant and make cuttings. Your mind switches
into a kind of detached dreaming and imagining. You think
of everything and you think of nothing.

In Unhurt Virgin Ground

In nature, we can learn to love the world in gratitude, receiving
it as a gift. Which is not the same attitude as assuming the world
belongs to us to use—in fact to abuse—rather than to "keep
and tend." Culturally, I think that the environmental movement is our instinctual concern for the holiness of that "in the
woods" experience. We have a basic sense that the health of
our very souls depends on the ground we stand on. And some
have become acutely aware of how our greedy consumption
of nature's resources is a reflection of our inability to overcome
the temptations of ready gratification. The environmental

movement may be our collective response to a global "midlife crisis."

My daughter Sara tracks and studies the rare spotted owl someplace in a woods at 9,000 feet. She keeps owl-hours. All night, on snowshoes and with a radio tracker, she searches in the moonlight. Each owl has a name—usually for the canyon that is its territory. She tells me, after two or three hours of trying to track one down who's been evasive for days, you get mad. "You don't call him 'Murray' anymore. You swear at him through clenched teeth. And then—you hear a faint signal! You crash through more bushes, and as the signal gets stronger you take off your snowshoes and tiptoe in, parting branches quietly, whispering to it in gentle irritation. 'Okay, you little bugger, where are you?' Oh! And then you see him—lovely Murray. 'Sweet Murray. There you are. I've been so worried about you. Oh, thank God for little Murray.' " Then she stands there and talks to him in the dark. Tells him things.

These owls need thousands of acres of virgin timber to survive. She works for the Forest Service, which wants to know just how *many* thousands of acres—among other things. Last week she found three of her eight owls dead. Three in one week! She cries. Sobs on the phone. "I get so attached to those lovely, foolish things. How can I help it! All night, every night, I look for them and worry like a mother!"

It isn't just the owl that needs saving. It's virgin timber. It's our natural history and last link of respect for the ancient past of our earth. The logging companies don't see it that way. All around the edges, the forest is being slashed and hacked away and mowed down. The logging trucks bear bumper stickers: "Spotted owl tastes like fried chicken." "To them, an owl's home means millions and millions of dollars in timber. Big business can't see the forest for the bucks."

The miller couldn't "see the forest for the bucks" either, I remind myself.

Thoreau said: "In wilderness is the preservation of the world." Wendell Berry says: "In human culture is the preservation of wilderness."

But even more than that, to return to nature—to what von Franz calls "the unhurt virgin ground of the soul"—is what preserves and heals the Handless Maiden. When you feel so low, when—given the chance to be relieved of all your shoulds and oughts—you can't imagine that there is anything left to do but weep, when you can only do nothing—you have arrived at the virgin ground of the soul where healing begins.

Ashes, Ashes, We All Fall Down

The earth is a living mother because she is fertile. Everything that is born of the earth is given her life and everything that returns into her is given new life. If we don't go into nature to seek a reconnection to the earth, there are rituals that bring the earth to us. In the Christian tradition and with the same invitation to engage the "virgin ground of the soul," on Ash Wednesday the faithful receive the blessing of blackened ashes on their heads. We wonder, in fact, why people flock to churches for these ashes—people who otherwise may not even go to church. What is it that's "being given away free"? I think that, deep down where they do not even know the word, people know that they want to be made human again. We are not merely humans made of earth because we die, but we are humans who can live because we are born of this earth and we will be reborn when we are willing to return to it.

Ashes are not so much to remind us of the "mere nothingness of our beginnings" or to "warn us" of our final death. Rather, they remind us that every day we die a hundred little deaths—

in losses, in failures, in longing and rejections. We die a little with every separation and letting go, because we cannot love each other and give life unless we also give each other the freedom to be separate. The earth from which we were all fashioned and the earth to which we return is, literally, our common ground. "Ashes, ashes, we all fall down."

Some deep realization calls people for that blessing. With a smudge of dirt we are brought down from our fancy plans and lofty opinions, brought back to the original, virgin dust out of which we were made. We look for that black blessing because we have some hunch about our origin, which speaks well for us. Lewis Thomas says that it is from the oldest language we know, that we took the word for earth and turned it into "humus" and "human" and "humble." It is a sacred sign, a grace which invites us into our own mystery.

It's a gift, then, to be simple, as the Shaker song tells it. And being human is really all that is asked of us. We always want to forget that. We always think that we have to be superhuman and then berate ourselves for failing that expectation. So that's why we have symbols and rituals, like ashes and graces and sacraments. They are there to remind us and help us and ground us. What a comfort to remember at the testy stages in a marriage that it, too, is sacramental and sacrament. The graces necessary are contained within the institution and conferred on each by the other. And in our woundedness, it takes all the grace we can get. As always the Word must be made flesh—our sterling gestures turned to human, loving acts—the divine made incarnate in our love and dogged faithfulness to each other. In grace and sacrament we transform experience to meaning. And meaning will give form to our actions. There is no other container for the spirit than the life we live out daily.

In patient waiting—in subtle, slow, hidden ways, in everydayness—the spirit heals. When you can only do—nothing—you have arrived where healing begins. For us to grow, it takes waiting. In our culture this is the hardest part—patience and waiting. For when we allow a process to unfold in its own rhythm and to grow at its own mysterious pace it often feels as though everything has come to a halt. We mistake it for a total stagnation.

Stagnation

It is terrifying for any of us to enter willingly what looks like a period of stagnation. For some, it takes the form of a kind of "writer's block" or "spiritual dryness." For some, it is those sleepless nights—long sleepless nights where 4 A.M. is the grayest hour and every anxiety and failure looms bigger than life. And the handless maiden in us tosses with niggling doubts and fears.

What has gone wrong? How did I get into this place and however will I find the way out? Once, the world told us that if we just brushed our teeth with the right toothpaste we would always be loved and valued and cared for. A likely story. If we were "good," then people would approve. Good! That's all I've been. I live my life doing what's expected of me. I depend on being told what to do. I'm just some dependent drudge swilling out the toilet bowl. That martyr, cleaning under the mop board with a hairpin. The maker of a zillion sandwiches and the stuffer of as many envelopes. This is my life? This is significant? Really, it's not funny. I am nothing. Stuck in nothingness. And alone.

Suddenly no action works for her anymore. Anything the desperate woman has ever produced seems "rich in sorrow." Many try to turn back. They reject the angel's invitation into a spiritual, solitary retreat. Some will insist there simply are no angels in their lives.

It is possible to suffer out such a stagnation in the jungle of a city and the business world—in "the wide world." But there it seems to take even more grace and genius to grasp religious meaning in a place so bursting with action and the pressures to perform. It *is* a jungle out there—in the world that roars at us with what we should do to be successful and gain power.

But "in the woods" is to let go and let be and thus, being in a right attitude, we are always in the right place, in society or in solitude. "In the woods" is what we ultimately create in our own hearts; there only the trees whisper, and there we finally learn to ask: "Who am I? And what is my purpose?"

Regression and Repetition

We might also say that this retreat away from life and into the woods of a chosen depression looks suspiciously like "going back to square one." Like regression. In fact it looks like a return to the beginning of this very story. Is the young Queen going back to the same woods where her father once failed? Has she come to the end of her *father's* rope—to redeem her father—to pass or fail the same test for the family name? There, where the Devil tempted her father away from engaging his failures with the promise of wealth and power, a woman returns, to redeem an old failure and restore her own soul. Has she returned to recover what she once lost—what was real and made of flesh and blood?

It seems that we each have the opportunity to repeat the "father's sin"—to push the culture further off its course. Or, at the crucial moments of transition, we can transcend the father's level of consciousness—or the patriarchal system—that has gotten us off the track. We can redeem his sin; we can do our small part in easing the culture back on course. For "the sins of the fathers" are the wounds and the blind spots we inherit. Whatever the parents or the preceding generations have not worked out is left to the children to work through—or tragically repeat.

Culturally or personally, a crisis points out the importance of retelling and rehearing what went before us. For history is destined to repeat itself if we don't go back and remember its stories.

Here, what looks like a regression is to enter the darkness of memory and painful recall in the inner world of the psyche. We call to memory what has been forgotten. We tell our stories. We share our burdens. We re-member what has become dis-membered. And we seek to understand.

How odd, to retreat into the darkness for illumination. To the outer world, this going to the "feminine place" to heal the "feminine wound," this retreat to beginnings and the chosen task of *feeling* again what went wrong, seems hopelessly foolish. The handless maiden who has the courage to choose this way will also have well-meaning friends who are uncomfortable with her inward turning. Puzzled or afraid to engage with her the loneliness of her task, or unwilling to stay with her and encourage her to tell her story, they will see it only as useless or foolish. They want to apply temporary solutions from with-out. There is always the friend who will say: "Pull yourself up by the bootstraps. Shape up, sister! Stop crying and feeling sorry for yourself! Get out there and date, take a class, volunteer for the Friends of the Library, get a job. Heavens, you're not nuts. You don't need to waste your time digging up your past."

Whatever method the Handless Maiden takes to reenter that "forest" and learn to feel again, she must not be diverted from falling to its darkest center. She must not be prevented from feeling her painful woundedness and terror.

Her prayer is like a plaintive chorus, a haunting plea, that runs through her days and nights.

> When in trouble I sought the Lord,
> all night long I stretched out my hands,
> my soul refusing to be consoled,
> I thought of God and sighed,
> I pondered and my spirit failed me.

You stopped me closing my eyes,
I was too distraught to speak;
I thought of the olden days,
years long past came back to me,
I spent all night meditating in my heart,
I pondered and my spirit asked this question:

"If the Lord has rejected you, is this final?
If the Lord withholds his favour, is this for ever?
Is his love over for good
and the promise void for all time?
Has God forgotten to show mercy,
or has his anger overcome his tenderness?" (Psalm 77:2–9.)

Prayer vs. Wishing

She fell on her knees and begged God for help, and with that an angel of the Lord appeared before her.

In her crisis, the young Queen prays again. She prayed when she left the chalk circle and she prays when she leaves the moated kingdom. It seems to say something that all the while she struggled to build her marriage she didn't pray—the Devil and her mother-in-law, through the befuddled messenger, were her agents. During that whole tedious period of silver-handedness, she forgot to call on God. But each of the other times she has prayed, an angel has come to her aid. In prayer she is not just *wishing* that things would be different. She is not passive, as wishing implies—wishing, with its aggressive counterpart—but she is assertive and authentic in her prayer.

Father, if it is possible, let this cup pass me by.

Assertive prayer is ready to take a responsible role in the process and willing also to include its own counterpart: receptivity and yielding.

If this cup cannot pass by, but I must drink it, your will be done.

She may long for her old days in the kingdom but learns to pray for a new kingdom.

Thy kingdom come. Thy will be done.

Stripped of earthly wealth, she carries only her baby on her back, the fruit of her life as she has lived it and the possibility of the new life ahead of her.

Blessed are the poor in spirit, for theirs is the kingdom of heaven.

At the center of her pain, she does need a friend, some angel to come along and encourage her to hurt and feel it with her.

Engage it. Go deeper. Oh, little one, I know how much it hurts. Cry for a while. It's all right to cry. Tell me more. What else happened? What did that feel like? Really? If it was me I'd feel terrible, betrayed even. Sure it was horrible. It was so horrible, wasn't it? What's to happen with you now? What's the worst thing that could happen? And then what? And then? Oh, you feel so sad, so angry, so betrayed and abandoned. No, I can't take it away. It does feel hopeless. . . .

What takes place is an implosion of feelings. Every day, waiting in that dark place, there is more to be recalled.

For a long time the prognosis is: doing better—by feeling worse and doing nothing. Feeling perfectly dreadful is the only way out. It is the feminine route and the only route that heals what is feminine. The only way out is into and through. Such a paradoxical prescription is difficult to pass along to a friend. It is not always easy to feel that much pain *with* someone. But a real friend will ironically encourage the Handless Maiden (and the King who seeks to find his wounded feminine feeling place) to hurt, to feel to its depth the wound and the loss that is hers. This is not an easy message to deliver. It is not an easy message to accept.

For, right now, it is not her task to go about trying to "find her positive masculine side." She must first honor and believe in the feminine. She never really valued herself as a woman or the qualities we call "feminine." Rather, she has always looked outside herself and looked up to masculine principles, to ideas and ideologies, to convention, to action, to lovers, husbands, mentors, men, all as extensions of her stunted arms. The principle here is: *the feminine wound must be wedded not to its opposite—not to the masculine—but to itself.*

Stagnation Transformed to Receptivity

A too-feminine passivity or a stagnation is not healed with a masculine solution, like action or aggressiveness. Such a solution does not heal the situation but only borrows a masculine tool and uses it clumsily or even cruelly. Then the woman just goes from passive to passive/aggressive. She may be driven by borrowed principles of rightness, duty and judgmentalism. It is a temporary "solution" which only prolongs her problem.

More often, the healing can only come about through waiting and remembering, feeling and allowing the healing to take place in nature and in God's good time. Without doing anything that seems practical to the outside world, a natural growing and maturation can transform the soul. Passivity is healed by the more evolved feminine quality of receptivity. The positive evolution of passivity, or an apparent stagnation, moves into a vulnerable receptivity. It awaits and receives the seeds of new life. And the seeds, now planted, need a period of incubation, a place to die and produce new life.

Receptivity Transformed to Incubation

That quiet incubation and waiting make me think of the Christian season of Advent which precedes Christmas. It is a time in harmony with the natural cycle of early winter—a quiet time when growing takes place under cover and out of our sight. Advent is that pregnant time of becoming when waiting is of the essence. The trees are bare and stark, the landscape is covered and muffled in snow. It is gray and cold. Unless you knew better, you would say that everything was dead.

Here in California we're not likely to have had rain for a year. The grass hills have turned brown. The scrub has dried into brittle sticks. The earth has become packed and hard. If we are lucky, the first rains come during Advent.

> Drop down dew, O heavens from above. Let the clouds rain forth the Just One. Let the earth be opened and bud forth a Savior.

That is the prayer of Advent and it means something in this hard, dry land where I live. But the graces of heaven cannot enter what is hard and dry and unreceptive. The earth needs scratching up, opening, turning over. It needs to become vulnerable and open for seed and rain, dew and snow to be healing and not to erode it. As an entire culture, we dislike that business of holding still and opening out and becoming receptive. The Advent season, as a celebration of preparation and waiting, sends most people into a panic. They hurry away to join the other fugitives in the shopping malls.

In one of his plays T. S. Eliot has a character say: "In a world of fugitives, he who would take the opposite course appears to be running away." The one who retreats and turns inward appears to be running away.

Embracing the Cross

What is wanting to be born and what has yet to die become almost indistinguishable. The young Queen in her dark woods weeping. Persephone in the depths of hell. Psyche, abandoned by her love. Mary, the salvation of all humankind lying dead in her arms. And Christ, suffering his agony in the olive garden, "was a man of sorrows and acquainted with grief." We all have grief in common. We all fall into the darkest pit.

> Yahweh my God, I call for help all day,
> I weep to you all night;
> may my prayer reach you
> hear my cries for help;
>
> for my soul is all troubled,
> my life is on the brink of Sheol;
> I am numbered among those who go down to the Pit,
> one bereft of strength:
>
> one alone, down among the dead,
> among the slaughtered in their graves,
> among those you have forgotten,
> those deprived of your protecting hand.
>
> You have plunged me to the bottom of the Pit,
> to its darkest, deepest place,
> weighted down by your anger,
> drowned beneath your waves.
>
> You have turned my friends against me
> and made me repulsive to them;
> in prison and unable to escape,
> my eyes are worn out with suffering. (Psalm 88:1–9.)

To reach out, even inept hands, and begin to accept may be the young Queen's most heroic task—to embrace and accept her cross, her heroic deed.

> The cross is heavy when we drag it and nothing when we embrace it. (Teresa of Avila.)

In some variations of this fairy tale, it is when the woman embraces a tree that she is healed. Here among the trees, all creation groans and travails together with her. Here in this place of trees, the tree is also a symbol of wholeness. It can be a maternal symbol for the place where fruit ripens until it is ready to fall. It is the place where children climb and build their own houses to have a place away from the "real world," a nest in a healing world of fantasy. To go up and down the tree is a process of rebirth. In some cultures it is the shaman who must live, isolated and incubating in a tree, waiting for a vision to bring back to the people as their new wisdom. And the cross of Christ is that place too, where death and redemptive rebirth are example and healing for believers. It is a bitter/sweet paradox. First, there is hell to pay: "Through the tree of knowledge, evil came into the world"—but then—"through the tree of the cross, we won life everlasting."

Asking

> Ask, and it will be given to you;
> search, and you shall find;
> knock, and the door will be opened to you. (Luke 11:9.)

I met a woman who had broken both arms at once when she tripped over a dog. "I've always been so proud of my self-sufficiency, proud of my independence. This accident has been a terrible shock to me and to everything I took for granted and everything I was proud of in myself. Imagine, first of all, the humiliation of having to explain *how* this happened to me. Can you imagine what it feels like to need my husband and my daughters to spoon cereal into me in the mornings? Can you imagine needing my husband to put on all my clothes for me —my underwear—tie my shoes, drive my car. Can you imagine teaching my classes without hands to speak with me or arms to hug? Can you imagine having to ask someone—to wipe my bottom! This is total reduction. And yet I've learned something about me—I've learned a lot about me. For one thing, how controlling I was in my great independence. But the most important thing I learned was how to be still. And how to ask, ask vulnerably. I know I'll never be the same."

> Have no fear! Stand firm, and you will see what Yahweh will do to save you today. Yahweh will do the fighting for you: you have only to keep still.

We ask, but it must be for nothing—nothing that belongs to the world of power or ego. We seek passionately, we knock madly. We weep. We pray. We call out. When everything is given up and opened out, we empty ourselves. And God fills in.

> When half-gods go, The gods arrive. (Emerson.)

The angels of the maiden in the woods don't just spill out of the sky, they seem to whorl up out of still depths.

> Come gently. Travel light. Consider the lilies in the field, how they grow! They neither toil nor spin. Poverty is closeness to nature—and to the nature of things. Look there, how they grow. "Nature has an equal mind," it does not judge. Your only possession in this place is Sorrowful, he, and the treasure of the moment. And this moment we shall live and feel fully with no worry for tomorrow: consider the lilies.

> Our Father, who art in heaven . . .

Even with an angel's encouragement, a Handless Maiden is tempted to regress: "Please, can't we go back? I think I'd like to go home—to the way things were." Or she is tempted to heal the feminine wound with the masculine plaster: "I could sell real estate! I promise, I can learn to be self-sufficient. I could go back to school!"

But to return to old ways or attitudes which mask the new challenge is to give up the hero's journey and is tragedy. I remember a friend who was in analysis and suffering terribly through a painful period saying, "Maybe I should just quit! Close up the whole thing and back out. What do you think?" "Well," I said, "my dear friend—back out the way you came in and it's sure to cause severe tire damage."

So you press on. Lost. Lonely and hurting. You pray. "Give us this day our daily bread—just *this* day. Just *bread*." And you hear: "My grace is sufficient."

An angel urges:

'[I] will prepare a way for banished ones to return.
Come now with me into the villages, walk through all the cities.
Though thou art taken to prison & judgement, starved in the streets,
I will command the cloud to give thee food & the hard rock
To flow with milk & wine; though thou seest me not a season,
Even a long season & a hard journey & a howling wilderness.
Though . . . cloud hide thee, & . . . fires follow thee,
Only believe and trust in me. Lo, I am always with thee.
(Blake, *Jerusalem, the Emanation of the Giant Albion*.)

Thy kingdom come; thy will be done.

As a Religious Practice

This "retreat into forest solitude" affirms a spiritual process that
has to do not with perfection but with the continued realization
of our human limitations, our desire to be transformed, our
sense of the great and mysterious Holy Other. We learn and
practice the sacrament of reconciliation—forgiving, telling the
truth, making reparation and accepting forgiveness. Daily tasks
of service and sharing become sacramental. We give up our
attempts to be poor imitations of God—to control—and place
our trust in the transcendent.

This "forest solitude" is also reminiscent of ancient religious
disciplines. In our culture such a retreat was the spiritual exercise
and the chosen practice of the medieval mystic. The mystic
sinks down to earth, down to the ground of our being, so that
there results a letting go, a giving up of all control. The mind
stops grinding out thoughts and becomes simple. The most
primitive feelings emerge. The practice and the behavior are
meant to bring one into the deepest introversion and to release
all attachments to and projections on external objects or persons. With that the inner world becomes enriched and enli-
vened. There comes a reunion of what is human with the divine.

Meister Eckhart, himself a medieval mystic, said something
like this: that in our complete letting go we come to stand in
the right attitude that allows God to be with us. And we can
learn to carry this attitude anywhere we are—as much in the

midst of many people as in the middle of the woods. In other words, it isn't where you are, it's who you are.

> Behold the handmaid of the Lord. Be it done to me according to thy word.

He also said that all paths lead to God and God can be found anywhere when we "know with transformed knowledge." Best, he said, to take God in any manner, in any thing, and not to have to hunt around for your own special way.

For the "into the woods" experience is sure to be your own special way. It is the way that "comes to you"—the unique path that only you can take. Nor does our "transformed knowledge" mean to imply that the material world entraps us and only the spirit world is free. No. The whole reality of spirit/matter is both and neither. Earth cannot escape heaven, says Eckhart; "flee it by going up, or flee it by going down, heaven still invades the earth, energizes it, makes it sacred." And the experience of such contradiction is also our initiation. It is, for most of us, only a life lived and felt passionately, even as we let go and sink into the dark mystery of God.

Chapter 13

HERE ALL
DWELL FREE

Initiation

The Handless Maiden's initiation is also an invitation to relinquish control, to let go, to give up her silver-handed way. "Into thy hands, O Lord, I commend my spirit." In reaching out her stumps and in a conscious embrace of loneliness—when there is nothing else to do—there is a death. The difference between neurotic depression and a healing suffering is consciousness—a conscious acceptance of painful regression. Of ambiguity. Of the mystery of life. It means *feeling* and not numbing out. To leave behind the world you have known and to venture inward is to find out whether you are really alive and is by definition painful and lonely. But here loneliness turns to aloneness. The natural healing begins and the fruitless depression is on its way to being dispelled. For God is at home. It is only we who have gone out for a walk.

The angel, in answer to the Handless Maiden's prayer, leads her to a little house in the center of the forest over whose door is written: HERE ALL DWELL FREE. From out of the little house comes yet another numinous angel who welcomes her and brings her inside:

> *"Welcome, Lady Queen."* . . . *[The angel] unbound the little boy from her back and held him to her breast that he might drink and laid him to sleep in a beautiful little bed.*

The angel—in this story—is a feminine, nurturing, caring aspect of divinity and is to be found here where darkness is deepest. Up in the other world, and in broad daylight, the Devil twisted all the messages that went back and forth and gave every meaning a devilish distortion. But an angel is a messenger who carries our messages between unconscious realms to the conscious one and connects our earthly words to heaven. An angel gives meaning to what has been obscure and returns the heavenly messages to ordinary mortals in such a way that these can be taken in.

This angel has heard the poor woman in all her pain, perhaps also because her asking has been clear and direct. Her heart has been purified by prayer, for there is nothing manipulative or garbled in her calls for help. But it can also be said that her prayer has been purified by the pureness of her heart. And so she is delivered from her pain and brought to a place of true freedom.

While it seemed fate that led her to such woundedness and fate that led her to the King and fate that interfered with her letters, now fate has less to say. Her passivity and her feelings of hopeless "giving up" she transforms, not first into action, but into a profound, conscious "letting go." She lets go her dependencies and her projections on men or masculine values. She lets go of any overblown ego plot to become great in the eyes of the world. Or to be perfect. This little house of freedom may be the "room of her own" where she is freed of all shoulds and oughts, and comes to the center of her own true being.

Freedom, however, is not being rid of responsibilities; it is being free of random shoulds and oughts. Freedom doesn't dwell in randomness but in conscious choice. The young Queen does her ordinary chores, caring for her child, in quiet little rooms. She knows, now, the truth about her own story—"and

you shall know the truth and the truth shall make you free."
And freedom shall make you true—tried, tested, honest. She
is no longer controlled by her past experiences or compelled to
reenact them with unwitting compulsiveness on her child or
on the society which is her own. "Freedom is not winning over
losing or living over dying." It is the discovery, says Zen scholar
R. H. Blyth, of *how* to win *or* lose, live *or* die. It is to give up
wrenching nature to suit your ego purposes. It is to accept the
nature of circumstances. It is to give up wanting.

> He who binds to himself a joy
> Doth the wingèd life destroy;
> But he who kisses the joy as it flies
> Lives in eternity's sunrise. (William Blake, *Eternity*.)

Freedom is an activity of mind and soul and body all at once
which flows with the nature of circumstances as naturally as a
bird flies with the wind currents and does not question what it
does.

Feelings and the Feeling Function

In freedom one gains true feeling. Silver-handed feeling was
inferior feeling. It was loss of contact with what was felt or it
put wrong values on things. It could not conduct feelings that
came from the heart and dispose of them and order them. Being
out of touch with the surroundings, the silver-handed feeling
often had no sense of timing or of tact.

True feeling (as C. G. Jung defined it as a function) is not
just having feelings, not touch, not intuition, not emotion,
affect, passion; rather, it is a function that disposes of the feelings
we have, expresses their contents and sets them in order. The
feeling function, then, will know the difference between the
feelings of authentic personal fault or blame and the archetypal feelings of angst, misery and profound despair which
belong to the human condition—belong to us all.

Many people who take psychological tests and register as

"feeling types" tend to congratulate themselves for having such a noble function. That's what we feeling types do—promptly classify a bit of information with a feeling value. But to be a "feeling type" may only mean that it is the function out of which we operate most readily, not necessarily most consciously. We may evaluate, appreciate, make distinctions, impart values, but we may do so automatically and merely with facility. The feeling function is second nature to us but not necessarily a conscious contribution. It provides a primary guide to what is valuable and important in life. And in general ways, our feelings about the value of a situation may rightly cause us to declare with alarm: "Children today have entirely too much stress in their lives."

Loss of Feeling

But in a society like our own the feeling function is all too often wounded and operating with silver-handed ineptitude or relational distance. It is "the famine over there" that alarms us or the impersonal "the children today" that brings forth an accurate enough judgment, but much closer to home the feelings that are the fire to such value judgments are themselves extinguished. Much more serious is the fact that our culture has lost touch with the very feelings that the feeling function is meant to express and order.

We have been traumatized too long—bombarded—with stresses and anxieties, with loud sounds and loud colors, with threats of loss and real losses, with a fast pace and too many choices. Children have been left for long periods in highly aroused states with no one around to gather them up and calm them down. They suffer separation from their parents at early ages and learn to spend hours in silent terror that they will never find their parents again. Or they are left to watch violent programs and films without anyone nearby who cares enough about them to relieve them in their terror. Being left in states of fear and stress for long periods causes the human organism to shut down feelings. We cannot cope in that state for long.

We grow numb. Better to feel nothing than to feel that way. In numbness we know neither joys nor sorrows. In numbness we no longer know our own feelings so that we can even relay them to ourselves, much less to others. Certainly, wounded in this way, we don't grasp the feelings of those around us. Without the ability to feel the feelings of others there develops neither a conscience nor empathy. In short, without conscience, we are breeding a growing crop of sociopaths without enough jails to warehouse them. And without empathy we are unable to form feeling, mature relationships with others. So marriages shatter at an alarming rate, to the advantage only of the divorce lawyers. Speaking out of my strong feeling function, I add: "What a bleak world!"

Of what use is the feeling function—to evaluate, appreciate, impart value, make connections between subjects and objects —if there are no feeling people to benefit? Of what use the making of judgments—balancing values, comparing tones? Why qualify, weigh the importance of things or make decisions on value if this reasoning does not go out from one feeling heart to another?

Writer Conrad Moricand, in a letter to his friend the novelist and diarist Anaïs Nin, writes of this discovery in himself:

> The poet in me . . . was precisely the instrument I used to keep life at a distance which I now believe was far more than an abdication, a sort of cheating, of evading life, because one must respond, one must feel. One must know tenderness, but with my temperament, a man incapable of love, as I have been, as I am, my somersaults towards heaven were only a derivative, an ultimate cheating. I took refuge in a cosmic existence. It was a very cold region. . . . [I have] a nostalgia for an earthy life, earthy and consuming, which I missed in my chimerical quest for wisdom and serenity. . . . (Gunther Stuhlmann, ed., *The Diary of Anaïs Nin*, Vol. 3: 1939–44, p. 6. New York: Harcourt Brace Jovanovich, Inc., 1969.

The story of the young Queen with the silver hands in search of freedom seems to teach us that the freedom we need and seek begins in the immediate environment and in the ground of our being. The search for freedom begins by deeply feeling what is a clear, direct, personal experience, and then, with the help of the feeling function, the meaning of that experience may be transformed into a religious experience—may evolve to an experience of inevitable transcendence.

> *Then, by God's grace and because of her faith, her hands, which had been cut off, grew once more.*

Growing Back Feeling Hands

In some stories we can see that the child himself becomes the redeemer of what has been spoiled—as in the Christian myth. Other times it may be the experience with a child or children that leads a person through a trauma and out the other side to healing and freedom. Perhaps the woman has, in this experience, given birth to her own true self. That the woman in our story has carried her child with her into this experience of healing and redemption is hardly insignificant—a phenomenon offered in interesting variations both in human experience and in other fairy tales.

It often happens that a woman's child may become gravely ill or psychologically troubled. Where, before, the mother was frozen in indecision and unable to ask for help for herself, she now, for the sake of the child, suddenly springs into action and in saving the child also saves herself. Her hands grow back.

In an African tale (and in the Russian version of this story, both included here at the back of the book), this becomes particularly graphic. A woman who has had one hand cut off by her brother is healed when her child falls into a stream and her guardian snake tells her to reach in and find the child. The woman uses her good hand but cannot feel the baby among the rocks. The snake urges her to use her other hand—reach in with her stump. How could this work? The snake won't do it for her—maybe even cannot do it for her, magical as it may be. This is something she must do alone and against all odds. She must do exactly what she is defined as incapable of doing: she must reach in and grab with the hand she doesn't have!

"Then, by God's grace and because of her faith . . ." —through some kind of miracle or a divine mediation—

through the mystical snake, by the angel, by God—the impossible becomes possible.

Suddenly her hand grows back. By finally doing for her own child what she needed done for her in her own growing up, a woman often heals herself. (Of course, this is just as true for a man.) She breaks an ancient spell. She changes fate itself. No longer is she condemned to endless repetitions of woundedness; she now makes sense of her life and discovers that she can choose. Above all, she can now heal others exactly out of the place where she was wounded.

Often a woman (or a man) will train for a career not fully aware that the chosen field of interest has its roots in an early and important experience. She goes into the field unwittingly to repeat the early experience over and over with the unconscious hope of conquering or curing what she had no control over as a child. As long as she remains unconscious of her own early wound, she may only be driven to repeat some aspect of the scene and to return to the early, unresolved feelings. But one day, when she comes to engage her early experience— when she grabs hold of it and gets to the root of it—she has the opportunity to become genuinely creative and gifted in her work.

A woman (or a man) in medicine, for instance, may have chosen the field because she had a parent who was chronically ill or may even have died when this person was still young or especially vulnerable. Now she vaguely hopes to gain the information and skills she needs to prevent illness and death— she wants some control over the powerful experiences that overwhelmed her when she was helpless. She wants to cure what the doctors and nurses failed to cure long ago. She may conduct her business through her intellectual skills alone. She repeats the situation until the experience finally brings her to the deepest feeling she suppressed and lost touch with long ago. And with that she finds meaning again. Now she is able to heal out of the very wound she suffered herself. The early fate is transformed by feeling to insight and wisdom—a "job" can now become art.

When a Handless Maiden's fate has been replaced by choice, she brings new meaning into her life. She weaves together, if you will, a new whole fabric out of the bits and scraps of her haphazard and often disastrous past. Her feeling hands restored, she makes order and value of all the feelings that now flow freely from her heart.

Sometimes it is a ritual or the simple doing of something with your hands that realigns feelings with meaning. I am reminded of a workshop I was invited to lead one weekend. On the first evening, after I'd given the opening presentation and the participants were milling around again, a handsome, middle-aged woman drew me aside and quietly talked of this and that which had touched her as she listened to the talk. She didn't know, however, whether she would be able to participate in the rest of the weekend. She hadn't been sleeping well, she told me, since her husband had died only five weeks before. She was in the midst of mourning and, with tears welling up in her eyes, she said she never knew just when she would need to disappear—to go off by herself or to grab some sleep when it came. Of course I understood, my clumsy, muttered concern small comfort in the face of her great sadness. I walked with her to the door and on the way out we looked at a loom which had been set up by one of the women for a communal project. Participants had been invited to bring scraps of fabric and yarns to be woven into a stole for the parish and we looked at the first beginnings taking shape on the loom. Then I wished the woman a good night and a good rest.

The next morning people arrived early to get their turn at the loom. Men, women, children, babies, youths, parents, singles, old folks—it was a great, grand mixture of people, all bearing scraps of cloth. Often these were remnants or swatches from clothing that had been worn at special times in their lives. We crowded around the loom and watched and took turns weaving. "There's my Easter dress from two years ago and Jenny's prom dress." "Isn't that the same fabric you used when you made that smocked dress for our daughter?" "I brought this to remember Carla. Don't you think she'd like to be part of this?"

The morning lectures completed, everyone returned to the loom. The project had a growing fascination. It was wonderful to see how the green warping united the many colors and calmed them down—made any combination quite legitimate. That the women would find the project fascinating seemed natural, but rarely have I seen a cluster of men or teenagers have so much fun together. They had moved on now to whole bags of fabric scraps. People were busily cutting more fabric into long strips or laying together the combinations of colors that they wanted to make as their next contribution. And there were skeins of remnant yarns being twisted together into colorful combinations by a small team of enthusiastic boys. And there, over at a quiet table by herself, was the woman who had talked to me the evening before. I walked over, touched her shoulder lightly and watched as she snipped open the stitches up the back of a tie. "It's his tie," she said. "It's the one he wore for our wedding." Carefully she opened out the tie, pulled away the facing and patted the fabric flat. "Now it goes back to the altar as part of a stole. That makes sense—right now it all makes much more sense." And with her shears she began to cut the tie carefully into long, narrow strips.

Religious Meaning

Now the Queen stayed in the little house for seven years and was well cared for there.

With the attentions of an angel—with a religious intervention—she is given the grace to care for herself in a reparative way. By engaging what she lost, she comes to appreciate her existence. This is where some people in midlife will come to grab hold of life with enthusiasm. They may become fit and healthy and at peace with their bodies. They may confront their addictions or embrace their relationships. Having richly earned a sense of strength and spirit which allows her to participate in life again, the young Queen is quite able to take worldly matters "into her own hands." With feeling hands, the ability to act returns.

But there is a far more valuable aspect to her healing than merely the ability to act or look after herself. For we have seen how this poor woman spent the first half of her life, removed from it and fated to exist in passivity and dependence: she saw life pass her by. That deep realization alone is enough to sink almost anyone in midlife who has discovered this to be his or her reality too. That is the Queen's wound—and her revelation. Having engaged what she lost, this woman who has been wounded wanders the whole world to find life and finds, in fact, the *religious meaning* of life.

Many women come to a true and deep religious life at middle age. They learn to pray, they learn to love liturgy, they learn to meditate, they become better poets and writers, painters and artists than they were before, and because they raised children called "rich in sorrow," they earn the serenity and the wisdom to help others, often becoming priests or rabbis, spiritual directors or healers or hospice workers, giving back meaning to those who are struggling with their own wounds. The woman who lives life as a wounded healer has a Zen experience— loneliness is transformed to aloneness. Atonement has been transformed to at-one-ment. She will have full consciousness of what she is doing and is rewarded for her suffering with a simple but deep contentment. Says the Chinese poet Toenmei (quoted by R. H. Blyth) of this poetic simplicity:

> The lanes are too narrow for fine carriages,
> And even my old friends are often turned back.
> Contentedly I pour out my wine,
> And partake of the lettuce grown in my own garden.

As Jung put it, a part of life was lost but the meaning has been saved. You can muddle through the first half of life as in a dream and finally wake up in the second half. While many may experience life and never find its meaning, the wounded person may have lost out on experience but, in healing, finds the meaning of life.

Knowing the meaning of life—the religious meaning of life—the Queen is ready to return to the kingdom she left: the very same castle, the very same people, and live out the very same marriage, but this time not limited to her personal concerns but with an awareness of herself as participant and co-creator of a new society. This time with enlightenment.

Enlightenment is not to be mistaken for a state of permanent bliss. It is not a matter of having "arrived." Enlightenment does not prevent one from suffering. The sufferings during an initiation are steps in a continuing inner process and we will have to pay a price in suffering again and again. But to suffer wisely and constructively is to grow mature. The compulsion to repeat the *same* suffering is always a danger. Often, after a woman has "grown back her hands" and has learned to reach out and do something with new grace, she will become vulnerable to a new "father figure"—an ideology or a system, a mentor, a spiritual director (usually male) or a guru—who was perhaps helpful to her healing but, at the very moment that her hands grow back, is quite willing to cut them off for her again. Women writers and artists have often been exploited by the men who have been important in their lives—as in the famous story of the sculptress Camille Claudel and her teacher, Rodin. A new way of being and interacting and wedding our gifts to the gifts of others has to be created at this stage in life. We give and we take as in a cross-fertilization. The masculine strivings for recognition must give way even as the healed feminine must reach out and reclaim. Over and over again.

Chapter 14

THE KING'S
JOURNEY

The King Learns the Truth

*At last the King returned home from his journey and his first wish
was to see his wife and the child.*

Only now after the young Queen's seven-year sojourn
in the little house in the woods—after she has earned back
her living hands—does the story switch scenes to the return
home of the King from his long absence. He "comes home
to the fact," actually, that his beloved wife and his little son
are long gone.

Jung used to say that in looking at our dreams, when two
very different events are juxtaposed, we might link them
up with the word "because" and catch new meaning—
"because this happened, that happened." So, *because* her
hands grew once more, the King returned home from his
journey. Or we can say, "Her hands grew once more *because*
the King returned home from his journey."

After such a major crisis in married life, when she was
cut off from a normal life for a time, a natural relatedness
finally returns for the woman. And *because* she has suffered

her part honestly and bravely and done the work necessary, _the King comes back._ _Because_ she has not spent herself in fruitless wishing that her King would change his ways, and has, instead, changed herself, there is a shift of balance in their relationship. _Because_ the Queen has changed, the King now has to change. For her, life in the collective works again and she can be alive and spontaneous. And her own healing paves the way for the King to undertake his _real_ journey this time—not just the "business trip" or the "journey of running away," but the journey into his own healing. For on his return to the castle the King sees the situation and his part in it.

> Then his old mother began to weep and said: "You wicked man! Why did you write to me ordering that I take those two dear innocent lives?" And she showed him the letters which the Devil had forged. "I did as you commanded," she told him. Then she brought forth the tokens: the eyes and the tongue.

His mother complex also tells him the truth because he is now in a right relationship to his mother/mother complex. He becomes freed of his own dependency on the mother complex that has been running him and in his emancipation can finally hear from her what is true. From the nurturing, caring, vulnerable part of himself he can hear the truth about his wife, too. He becomes vulnerable. He weeps. _Because_ he stands in a right relationship to his mother complex—_because_ he knows the truth about his wounded, inner feminine place—_because_ he knows the truth about the young Queen, her hands grow once more. Like a pebble dropped in a pond, the effects of one person's change ripple out in wider and wider rings, touching every thing—every one—around.

> With that the King began to weep so bitterly for his poor wife and his little son that the old mother had compassion on him.

Seven Years and Seven Years

The King has missed all his wife's important religious experiences. He has missed forming a deepening relationship and intimacy with her. He has missed the birth of their child, he has, in fact, missed the child altogether. And now he has missed their tragic death—or certainly their suffering and banishment. He has missed, on its deepest level, that part of his own soul and psyche that she and the baby represented where feeling and caring and nurture and all the feminine values grow and are honored. The King, too, has come to realize that a part of life has passed him by.

> Then the King spoke: "I will search as far as the sky is blue, and neither will I eat nor drink until I have found my dear wife again and my child. . . .
>
> With that the King traveled everywhere for seven long years and looked for her in every cleft in the rocks, in every cave, in every valley, on every mountaintop, but he could not find her and he thought surely she had died of want. During all this time he neither ate nor drank but God's grace was his support.

Isn't it the truth, in the spiritual and psychological development of relationship between men and women, that a young woman will long and yearn for intimacy and relatedness to her man and try everything she can to make a deep connection with him but not really know how to bring it about? And isn't it true that more often than not he is wary of commitment, afraid of intimacy and preoccupied with forming an identity in his career? A husband will want to go off on a business trip psychologically and abandon or avoid the relationship on some level. He may do what is necessary for his family but from across some great emotional gulch. The wife, then, muddles through. Perhaps she does the lion's share of raising the children and keeping the household in order and when the children are grown or gone she is ready for something else or ready to put to work the talents that have been merely simmering on the back burner. With a renewed strength in her hands she can handle the issues of the world and becomes much more at ease and interested in the development of her gifts and her new vision. Hardly is she out the door and involved in career, or education, or significant volunteer work when the man returns home—to find her gone. He's been missing the kids. His "empty nest" crisis is probably more severe than hers ever was, because he didn't have the close, daily experiences of the children's step-by-step emancipations. He's lonely and ready for warmth, intimacy—even a little romance. He'd like them to book a cruise. But since he is wobbly in his unpracticed feelings and their expression and still afraid to really reveal himself with intimacy, his wife thinks a cruise would be hell at sea. In fact, her committee is sending her to meetings that same month of the cruise.

X At midlife, men and women are given the opportunity to exchange places—if not on the outside, then surely on the inside. Knowing that the Queen in our story has suffered and earned a genuine and competent independence and sense of self, a deep and feeling ability in relationship, and above all a religious sensibility, we sense that the two "will not pass each other in the doorway," heading in opposite directions. Having suffered and grown in her archetypal seven years, she enables the King to thrash through his seven years of searching.

Seven years and seven years, and the King arrives at the middle of the forest not looking like an archetype or a king anymore at all, or even like the conventional man, the competent career man, the smooth salesman, the polished politician. He looks more like a wild man—a man who has been through something. Human. Vulnerable. His clothes are tattered. He hasn't shaved in years. He may be hungry from his fast and he probably smells, but it is the grace of God, the story says, and his fierce determination that make it possible for him to have come this far. "Winning the princess" this time around will be the result of having looked for her with purpose and determination, and it means that this time he also knows what to do with her. His compassion is larger than that of just "being nice to his mother." His vulnerability and compassion are those of a grown man, a conscious man. Despite his looks, he is a real king who is also a real man.

"Thy kingdom come, thy will be done . . ." and the archetype of the King with his earthly kingdom has been transformed into the ordinary man with extraordinary vision: "thy will be done on earth"—right here in the middle of the woods—"as it is in heaven."

Having done everything in his power to find his wife and

child, the King's will is now no longer in his hands but in God's hands. His response is not the stoic's response—cold, lifeless, heavy, helpless resignation. Not a sinking into a living death of a bored and bleak retirement. No, it is rather, "Now you must make use of me as you will. I am of your mind. I am one with you. I refuse nothing which is good in your eyes. Lead me where you will."

Grace is what it takes to even arrive at this place. Prayer and divine intervention—all those small graces and large ones—are what save a man and woman from passing each other by at their own front door, each heading in an opposite direction. An angel, that being who connects us with each other and untwists the meanings in our messages, who connects us to our own deepest selves, is also what connects us to transcendence and deepest Mystery.

Lead me where you will.

Only when the King, too, entered the forest does he come upon the little house whose sign says:

HERE ALL DWELL FREE.

From out of the house, the angel came forth, took him gently by the hand and led him inside, saying: "Welcome, Lord King. From where did you come?" He answered: "I will soon have wandered about for the space of seven long years. It is my wife and her child I seek, but I cannot find them anywhere." The angel then offered him meat and drink, but he did not take anything and only wished to rest a little.

God's grace has sustained him along the way and, just as the angel watched over the Queen and her child as she struggled on her journey, the angel has waited for him and has brought him to the end of his search.

Come, all you who are weary and heavy laden, and I will give you rest.

He lies down on a bench to sleep and places a napkin over his face.

The Napkin

What a curious symbol, this napkin, and the game with it which ensues. As soon as the King is asleep, the angel goes into the inner chamber where the Queen sits with her son, Sorrowful, and instructs them to go out and see, "Your husband is here." So they go out to where the King is sleeping and the napkin slips from his face. The Queen tells Sorrowful: "Pick up your father's napkin and cover his face again." This the child does, but the King in his sleep hears what is being said and finds pleasure in letting the napkin fall once more.

It seems like some small ritual in mutual revelation—husband and wife "at play" with offering each other their hard-won truths. It happens sometimes that some odd humor interrupts the harsh dramas of our misunderstandings and lack of connection with each other and the harshness which looked as though it could never end is suddenly softened: A woman, enraged and fed up with her husband—unable to take a second more—flings on her coat, grabs her purse, sweeps dramatically out the front door and, wanting to give it a satisfying, loud thwack of finality behind her, catches her fingers painfully in the door. Stinging with pain and mortification, she pushes the door again to release her hand and discovers her husband has rushed to her aid. "Oh, honey. Oh, you poor thing! Let me see your fingers—here, let's get some ice." And they sink into an embrace and laugh and cry and the impasse is over. They can talk now. Gently, they reveal themselves to one another. Slowly. As in a game. With humor. Not "letting it all hang out." Not in full light. Not in the courtrooms of the outside world where all is measured by standards of law and cultural opinion or conventional morality and "religious" rules. "Religious convention" or religious morality more often deals in rules and laws than with *religare*—the ties that bind this world to the spirit world, where meaning in life and relationship and love makes connections to the numinous.

Only when the King "blinds his eyes" to the opinions of the outside world can he connect with the sufferings of his feminine side. By closing his eyes and shutting out the old world view he harbored, he can look inside and begin to see the truth—

begin to recognize his own wounded, inner feminine. Blinded, like St. Paul in the moment of his conversion, his old views based in self-centeredness—in absolute self-importance—are transformed to a true vision of the other. And the exposure of himself as human—wonderfully human.

A man, though it is his lifelong task to become "wonderfully human," most especially is pressed to this reality in the second half of life. For him as well as for his queen, true feeling, differentiated feeling, is the art of the small, the subtle difference, the gentle touch. It is patient with the unfolding of relationship, helping it grow gently, feeding it lovingly. Loving without fear. True feeling knows the difference between needing and demanding, between what one likes and what one wants. Even from behind the napkin, the King can look without taking and have without wanting—because he has come to know who he is.

Sorrowful

By now Sorrowful, their child, must be about fourteen years old. How curious that parents must face the challenges of midlife just as their children are in the throes of their own adolescent crises. It seems not quite practical—or fair—to have the whole family in turmoil and shifting all at the same time. Or is it *because* the parents are shifting that the children will shift? Or *because* the children are changing, the parents must change? There is nothing like the nose of an adolescent to sniff out the "fake" teacher or snort at a parent who is role-playing with him. Adolescents in a house demand that parents finally grow up themselves and be authentic, or else the young persons feel hampered in getting on with their own developmental process.

The adolescent Jesus, lost in the temple and then found there by his anxious parents, tells them: "Did you not know that I had to be about my Father's business?" He brushes aside the role of the human father at this point in his adolescent development and indicates that the heavenly Father has more important designs on him. Here, in our story, the child, playing his own role in discovering his father as a real human, says to his mother:

> *"I have no father in this world. I have learned to say the prayer, 'Our Father who art in heaven.' You have taught me that my father was in heaven's kingdom, and was the good God, so how can I know this wild man to be my father? He is not my father."*

Hardly has the adolescent looked through the King and had a clear view of the humanity and vulnerability of his father—the authentic father—than he is called by a higher order into his own development. He is called to the business of his Father in heaven. Sorrowful speaks the truth. He begins to see that the new life ahead of him is a sort of awakening of self-consciousness, while his parents' development has entered the process of un-selfing. The un-self in that progression points to the Self in God and heaven and the kingdom as growing within each one of them.

Along with Sorrowful, we want God as a Father—in fact as our father/mother!—because we cannot be satisfied with some intangible, flowing concept. We want whole things. And Sorrowful wants a whole family.

In a Russian version of this fairy tale included here (at the back of the book), Sorrowful is a mysteriously beautiful baby, "golden up to the elbows, his sides studded with stars, a bright moon on his forehead and a radiant sun near his heart." Such a miracle child was able to "illumine the whole room." Indeed, sorrow has its reverse side: beauty, value, salvation, joy, light.

I have posted in my kitchen a blessing from one Isaac of Stella, 1169. I wish I knew something about him. But this blessing of his is also clearly a play on his own happy name, which means "Laughter":

> May the Son of God,
> who is already formed in you,
> grow in you
> so that for you
> he will become immeasurable,
> and that in you he will become laughter,

> exultation, the fullness of joy
> which no one will take from you.

To be fully human and fully adult is to know well one's own inner child. This is the child with a direct "entry to the kingdom of heaven." It is to know joy just as well as we know sorrow. It is to find God, immanent and transcendent. Perhaps it is the great insight of Sorrowful to show us at this holy moment of reunion that what is immanent contains the transcendent.

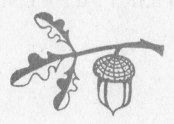

Chapter 15

AND THEY LIVED CONTENTEDLY TO THEIR HAPPY END

Transformation Through Disenchantment

True to the form of fairy tale wisdom (and contrary to what we like to think of as "enchanting"), our story points out that we are transformed and made whole through our experience of disenchantment. We finally see clearly through our illusions by disillusionment.

> *"Here I cannot stay. I must go forth into the world."*
> *"Here you may no longer stay. Go forth into the wide world. Take your child and never come back to this kingdom again!"*
> *"How can I know this wild man to be my father? He is not my father."*
> *The King noticed her living hands and said: "My wife had silver hands."*

Disenchantment breaks an old spell or possession. The angel reintroduces the family and each comes to know the other quite clearly with divine help or religious intervention.

> *By God's grace have my natural hands grown back again.*

There is no magic, but there *is* the grace of God. No longer are you "beside yourself," but you see yourself as you truly are and share yourself as vulnerable and fully human—real—all the way down to your flesh-and-blood fingertips. Heart to heart.

When he saw the old silver hands brought forth,

> the King knew most certainly that she was indeed his dear wife and this his own dear child, and he kissed them, and was glad and said: "A heavy stone has fallen from my heart."

We could say that what had been stony in his heart has become a heart of flesh—just as his wife's hands are no longer metal but living hands of flesh. Each, through an individual and painful journey—for their very natures are different—has become what he was always meant to be. Each has become fully whole and each is fully equal to the other. Not just personally but as collective genders, we must come to know clearly—and be empathic with—what makes us different from one another. Then we can appreciate our common ground and our equality in value. That transformation is not effected by magic but by perfect love of one person for another.

Perfect Love

After the children have left home and the man has achieved his kingly position in the world, he is ready to relate more deeply and with vulnerability to the woman. And the woman, grown authentic and autonomous, carrying a wisdom about the meaning of life, is ready to relate vulnerably to the man. It is a great chance for the marriage to become what, deep down, they always hoped it would be. If they don't pass each other like ships in the night, they will indeed "marry each other again." They can discover a new love, a perfect love.

The Danish philosopher and theologian Kierkegaard said that perfect love means to love the one through whom one became unhappy.

That means that after we have removed our projections from the other we can stop being unhappy with him. We can now see him and love him for who he is. Our unhappiness with one another almost always comes about when we cannot force the other into the mold we want him to fit. For that mold is ours. It is part of us and of who we are.

When we come to being who we must be, we allow the other to be who she must be. We bring—each of us to the other—a whole self, because we have brought about that *necessary inner marriage of the masculine and the feminine*. We have done the necessary separate work. The marriage of the King and the Queen—any marriage in a fairy tale—is *first* the right balance of yin and yang, if you will, within the individual. That right mix and tumble of masculine and feminine values within is the necessary prerequisite for our right relationships to one another in the outside world. That inner marriage in wholeness within each of us is what makes our communion with our sisters and brothers, wherever/whoever they are, a communion of true and perfect love.

"Perfect love," Scripture tells us, "casts out fear." We cast out the fear of allowing each to become whole in her and his own right and we make way for perfect love.

Empathy

We cast out, for one thing, the fear that we cannot have from the other all the things we think we want. We concede that the fantasy marriage we yearned for is not the marriage we are meant to build between us with patience and love and hard work. We give up wishing and, in freedom, begin to choose and to ask. Above all, we develop the art of empathy for one another. In empathy or compassion, we become keenly attuned to the feelings of the other. We try to share and accurately understand his or her perceptions, thinking and the causes of pain. With feeling hands we reach out and include the other's experience in our own. With a heart of flesh we acknowledge the experience of the other. This is the ultimate goal of mature relationship and love. We come to share ourselves truthfully and trustingly with our mates and our friends. We come to know them, warts and all, and love them.

Bread of Angels

Because each one of them now sees and knows and loves the other, just as he is, the angel offers them a feast and eats with them. What a nurturing angel this has been, and a house of hospitality. But this time the food is not pears from a royal garden— stolen food, not shared, eaten like a baby, without hands. This is "communion in the hand." Food taken. Food shared. This is communion in the best sense of the word, heaven and earth joined at table—feasting the real wedding about to take place.

The Return Home

After that they returned home to the King's old mother.

To come home again! What a ring of relief there is in it. We have been wrenched enough from one home to the next in this story—or was the hero always more homeless than "at home"? We identified with her and felt with her the eerily poignant feeling of homesickness and loss as she struggled from place to place, even as we hoped that her loss of home would always turn out to be a progression and her return to home not a regression.

Eva Hoffman, in her personal retelling of leaving Poland in 1959 as a young girl, speaks of leaving "paradise." She wonders, when she compares her paradise to those of others, that she could see it as a paradise at all. She grew up in "a lumpen apartment in Kraków, squeezed into three rudimentary rooms with four other people, surrounded by squabbles, dark political rumblings, marks of wartime suffering, and a daily struggle for existence." And yet, when it came time for her to leave, she felt pushed out of Eden.

> When the brass band on the shore strikes up the jaunty ma-
> zurka rhythms of the Polish anthem, I am pierced by a sorrow
> so powerful that I suddenly stop crying and try to hold still
> against the pain. I desperately want time to stop, to hold the
> ship still with the force of my will. I am suffering my first,
> severe attack of tesknota—a word that adds to "nostalgia" a
> Polish tonality of intense melancholy yearning. It is a feeling
> whose shades and degrees I'm destined to know intimately,
> but at this hovering moment it comes upon me like a visitation
> from a whole new geography of emotions, an annunciation
> of how much an absence can hurt. Or a premonition of ab-
> sence, because at this divide I'm filled to the brim with what
> I'm about to lose. . . . (*The New Yorker*, December 5, 1988.)

Uncanny how she can describe the feeling. Words like "pierce," "nostalgia," "melancholy," "yearning," seem to tell it well—describe that same sense of loss and homesickness that permeates our story. But is it relief we feel, I suddenly wonder, knowing that soon everyone will be together again at home? True to everything we know about being kicked out of our Edens, however much we had to leave them, we know, and this story says it too, you don't return by the same route you left it. You are different now, and that changes everything.

For our original paradise where we were first named evolves into the kingdom we think we can create in sweat and guilt—evolves, with grace and agony, to the place where ALL DWELL FREE whose enlightenment carries us home, to the world where everything is the same, and nothing is the same.

Now "home," because of the journey that got us here, is charged with the mystery that created us and the mystery we have become and the Mystery that is our ultimate Kingdom.

This archetypal yearning to return home is a frequent theme in myths and tales. Freud (and Jack Zipes, a professor of German who discovers social history in fairy tales) casts some light on the reason for such poignancy by looking at two words, *heimlich* and *unheimlich*, literally: homey (or familiar and "at home") and unhomey (or unfamiliar). In German, however, the word for unfamiliar has an even deeper nuance; it also means uncanny, weird, eerie, spooky. Freud argues that what is uncanny brings us in closer touch with the familiar or *das heimliche*. What we find eerie or uncanny is familiar or at home to our unconscious world. But what is "at home" in our inner world has become unfamiliar to us in the outside world, that is, alienated by denial and repression. So *heimlich* has also come to mean the opposite: secret or mysterious. This is, according to Freud, because the uncanny touches on emotional disturbances and returns us to stuck phases in our evolution. What strikes us as eerie and weird is what touches chords in that secret place in our inner world that we've forgotten about. That place where we got stuck and haven't yet sprung forward. So the recurrent theme in fairy tales of the quest for home (*heimat*, also related etymologically to *heimlich*, mysterious, and *unheimlich*, uncanny) is as powerful a progressive attraction for the heroes of fairy tales, Zipes says, as it is for us who read the tales and allow ourselves to be opened up to still possible futures.

With the Handless Maiden of our story, we found ourselves looking forward to her reunion with her King—to a reconciliation and the sort of "future wholeness" that we often cling to in fantasy. And those unfulfilled yet possible fantasies have their place. Through imagination we cultivate what might become possible; we cultivate such fantasies because they represent a primal urge to a restructuring of our whole society and to redemption, so that we can finally achieve Home. Not merely to "wish for" or to yearn but actually to "hunger and thirst for justice" is to know that such a Home, such wholeness, is something that we can indeed strive for here and now.

Through imagination we fuel with sanction, inspiration, orientation, and dynamism what moves us to join with other people to make the world a better home for all. Through our efforts and surely with the grace of God, we participate in making that "kingdom come on earth"—little by little.

The Handless Maiden, by comprehending herself, creates, rebuilds, transforms the hidden aspects of her unconscious world and establishes a domain of true freedom in the woods. This allows her to return to a kingdom of liberation and real democracy—a kingdom without alienation and numbness, without foreignness—but to something *familiar*, that is of family and imbued with "at-home-ness." She has, in fact, become familiar with the secrets of her inner world which have always been part of her but, until now, were forgotten or unrecognized. She did not give up or give in to her "fate"—her stuck places—nor did she adjust to life's unfairnesses, but rather came to transcend her fate and reweave it into a revolutionary personal and/or community change.

The very revolution of the sexes today would be clarified in its purpose, be encouraged and instructed and cheered on, by the process and outcome of this story. For now the Queen can live together with her King. The Queen has become a real woman. Whole, not helpless. Feminine but not prissy. Keenly oriented to relationships but not dependent. In touch with her feeling nature. In right relation to her inner, masculine guide—guided and not driven by him. Passionate about life and love. Compassionate and not manipulative. An artist and a healer in her work. The King has become a real man. An adult, grounded in his relationships and work, but not dull and listless. Decisive but no bully. A caring man but no goody-goody—not sentimental. Feeling and empathic, but no wimp. Charming but not manipulative. Committed to relationship as much as to his work. Passionate about his life and love.

Now they are equals who have had similar but different experiences. They have healed their own wounds, done their separate work, shared in the same grace and hope the same hope. That same good news that the fairy tale announces is magnified in the Good News we call the Gospel.

The family returns home to the King's old mother—who rescued the maiden once and now appears again as Holy

Mother. In some versions of the story the old mother has been allied with the Devil and worked untold terror on the Handless Maiden. Only in that unfortunate archetypal form of mother-in-law as jealous mother and troublemaker is that solution a seemingly regressive one. In the Russian version, as a wicked sister-in-law, she is miserably dragged behind a horse in an open field until only her braid is left yet tied to the horse. But in an Italian version, where the mother-in-law was a wicked woman, she is not allowed to be punished because the wife says to her husband: "If you really love me, you must promise not to lay a hand on your mother. She will be sorry enough as it is. The poor old soul believed she was acting in the interest of the kingdom. Spare her life, since I forgive her all she has done to me." The hero, in this case, rightly takes her own dark shadow aspect home—that is, takes her to heart. She knows her to be an aspect of herself, allows that she is a member of the same household and family. By accepting her—by taking responsibility for her own darkness—there will no longer be the destruction that occurs when darkness is projected outward and denied.

The King too, after all, is transformed and his relationship to his mother complex is also capable of bringing enormous richness to the transformed household. While this is not necessarily a literal mother-in-law, even if it were, the King and Queen can now live in harmony with all persons and be loving and at peace because they are inclusive of all reality.

And if the new kingdom is also the vision of heaven's kingdom, we need to take the ambiguous feminine to the same place for the sake of wholeness. If you leave her out of the picture there is hell to pay, as we will learn in our next story. But include her and she will bless you beyond measure.

Just as with dreams, we are taught to look at the numbers of people who make up a construct—especially at the beginning of a story/dream and at the end of it. At the beginning of this story we have a loosely formed household of a miller and a devil, a mother and a daughter, and that quaternity is on the brink of dissolution. Then, as the story unfolds, we watch the quaternity constantly shift, split, scatter and restructure itself. Finally, when the story comes to its conclusion, we have a rich and possible quaternity again of young and old, masculine and feminine. Four is the vision of wholeness, and the balance of a wise old woman, a queen-mother, a king-father and a young son filled with possibility and potential is a quaternity of peace and promise.

And They Were Married Again

There was great rejoicing throughout the whole kingdom, and the King and Queen were married again.

The whole community, the entire culture, benefits and will bloom again when even two people become conscious. And the King and Queen are married again. Not in the ceremony of moral duty and obligation, but in a ceremony of free choice of new beginnings and happy, holy union. The whole kingdom rejoices because Eden will be known again as Paradise. Because the return home was the long route around and into and through what had become stuck, repressed, forgotten, handicapped, unfulfilled. Now all is redeemed and can be made new and possible and whole in any place we call home. Here everything is the same and everything is different.

And they lived contentedly to their happy end.

Part II

BRIAR
ROSE

Chapter 16

THE STORY OF
BRIAR ROSE

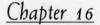nce upon a time
there were a King and Queen
who longed for a child.
Every day they sighed: "Oh, if only we had a child!"
Days passed and years passed
and still they wished and waited.

One day as the Queen was in her bath,
a frog jumped out of the water
and, sitting at her side, he announced:
"Your wish shall finally come to pass.
Before the year has come to an end,
you shall have a little daughter."

What the frog had promised came true,
and before the year was spent,
the Queen gave birth to a little girl
who was so astonishingly pretty
that the King could hardly contain
his delight and joy.

He ordered a great feast to be prepared
to celebrate his daughter's birth
and invited not only
his kindred, his friends and his acquaintances,

but he also invited the Wise Women.
He wanted the Wise Women
to be well disposed toward the child and kind.

There were thirteen Wise Women in his kingdom,
but the King had only twelve golden plates
for them to eat from.
Hence, one of them had to be left out
and she was not invited.

The feast was held in magnificent splendor,
with meats and cakes and music and dance.
And when the feasting came to an end
the Wise Women stepped forward
to bestow their blessings on the baby girl.

One gave virtue.
Another gave beauty.
Another gave fruitfulness.
Another gave truth.
Another gave wisdom.
Another gave curiosity.
Another gave charm.
Another gave intelligence.
Another gave joy,
and so on down the line so that the child was blessed
with every good thing one could ever wish for.

Just as eleven of the Wise Women
had bestowed their blessings,
the thirteenth burst in
filled with rage and vengeance.
She wished to avenge herself
for the humiliation
of not being invited to the feast.
Without greeting,
without looking at anyone,
she simply cried out
in a tremendous voice:
"The King's daughter
shall in her fifteenth year
prick herself with a spindle
and fall down dead!"

Without another word
she turned on her heel
and swept out of the castle hall.

The people were shocked!
But the twelfth Wise Woman,
whose blessing and wish
remained yet unspoken,
came forward.
As she could not undo
the evil sentence just pronounced
she chose to soften it.
"It shall not be death that overcomes her," she said,
"but the princess will fall into a deep sleep
for one hundred years."

The King, in his alarm and deep concern for
the well-being of his beloved daughter,
moved to keep her from any misfortune
and decreed that every spindle
in the kingdom
be burned.

Meanwhile, the gifts and blessings of
the Wise Women were generously
fulfilled on the young princess.
She was beautiful and virtuous.
She was good-natured and wise.
She was unpretentious and charming.
She was curious and intelligent.
She was such that all who saw her
were bound to love her.

Then it happened
that on the very day of her fifteenth birthday
the King and Queen were not at home.
The maiden was left in the large castle
quite alone.
So she went around
to discover all the corners of the castle.
She looked into rooms and halls,
into galleries and libraries,
into cupboards and bedchambers
just as she liked.

At last she came to an old tower.
She climbed the winding stone steps
until she reached a little door.

A rusty key was in the lock,
and when she turned the key
the door sprang open
onto a tiny little room.
In the room sat an old woman
with a spindle,
busily spinning her flax.

"Good day, old mother,"
said the King's daughter.
"What are you doing there?"
"I am spinning,"
said the old woman, nodding.
"What is that thing
that rattles around so merrily?" asked the girl,
and wanting to spin too,
she reached out to grasp hold of the spindle.

But hardly had she touched the spindle
when the magic sentence was fulfilled,
and she pricked her finger with it.

In that very moment when she felt the prick,
she fell down upon a couch that stood there
and slept a deep, deep sleep.

This sleep, like a cloud, spread over the whole court.
The King and Queen, just arrived home and
entering the great hall,
fell asleep on their thrones.
All the courtiers and cooks,

the servants and the knaves fell asleep.
And all around the castle grounds
everything dropped to sleep:
the dogs in the yard,
the horses in the stable,
the chickens in the coop,
the pigeons on the rooftop,
the fish in the pond,
the flies on the wall.
Even the fire in the hearth became quiet and slept,
and the roast meat left off sizzling.
The wind fell.
The flag on the roof ceased to flutter.
The trees before the castle moved not a leaf.

But slowly,
around and about the whole castle,
there began to grow a curious hedge of thorns.
It grew and it grew
and every year it grew thicker and higher.
It closed in on the castle,
it covered its doors and its windows.
It rose up, climbed over the tower, and covered it too
so that soon there was nothing of it left to be seen,
not even the flag on the roof.

But the story of a beautiful
sleeping princess called "Briar Rose"
went around the country.
From time to time and over the years
kings' sons came from far and wide
and tried to slash through the thorny hedge
to enter the castle.

But they found their efforts useless
and entrance impossible.
The thorns held fast together
as though they were hands and arms
twined around the castle.

The youths got caught in them
and could not get loose.
They thrashed and struggled and tore to get free,
but they could not
and so they died in the thorns
a miserable death.

After long, long years
a king's son came riding into that country again
and he heard a story from an old man
of a thick and mysterious briar hedge.
It was said that the thorny hedge had grown
to envelop a whole castle.
Inside the castle, it was said,
and so had the old man heard it told,
was a wonderfully beautiful princess
named Briar Rose.
The beautiful princess, it was said,
had been asleep for a hundred years,
and with her the King and Queen and all the court
were asleep as well.

Many a king's son, the story went,
had already come
to try to penetrate the thorny hedge,
but each became stuck fast and died there pitifully.
So had the story been passed from father to son.
So had the story been passed, said the old man,
from his own father to him.

Then the youth said,
"You can speak to me of dreadful thorns
and death by sticking,
and yet I will not be afraid.
I will go and see the beautiful Briar Rose."

The old man's efforts to dissuade the youth
were of no avail.
The young man would not listen to the old man's words.

But by this time
the fated hundred years had just come to an end.
The day had come when Briar Rose was to wake again.
When the King's son approached the thorny hedge,
it was covered in nothing but beautiful, fragrant roses.

These parted from each other as of their own accord
and so let the young man pass unhurt.
Then they closed again behind him
like a hedge.

In the castle yard he saw
the trees where not a leaf stirred.
The wind was still.
The fire was out.
The flies slept on the wall.
The fish hung motionless in the pond.
He saw the pigeons sleeping on the roof
with their heads tucked under their wings.
The chickens roosted in the coop.
He saw the horses in their stalls
and the dogs in the yard, asleep.
The knaves and the servants,
the cooks and the courtiers all slept.
And as he entered the great hall,

slumped on their thrones,
he saw that the King and Queen slept too.

He went on farther still
and all was so quiet that a breath could be heard.
At last he came upon the tower,
climbed the winding stairs
and opened the door
of the little room where Briar Rose was sleeping.

There she lay,
so astonishingly beautiful
that he could not take his eyes from her.
He stooped down and kissed her.
But as soon as he kissed her,
Briar Rose opened her eyes and woke
and looked at him without fear
and with clear eyes.

They went down together and entered the great hall.
The King and Queen awoke and the whole court with them.
They looked at each other in great astonishment.
Then the cooks began cooking,
the servants served,

the knaves got on with their knavery.
The dogs in the yard stretched and wagged their tails.
The horses stood up and shook themselves.
The chickens flew down from their roost.
The pigeons flew off into the open country.
The fish circled the pond.
The flies buzzed off the wall.
The fire flared up again
and the roast on the spit turned and sizzled.
The breezes blew once more
and the leaves on the trees shimmered and shook
and the flag on the roof fluttered and waved over it all.

With great splendor and with feasting and thanksgiving
the King's son and Briar Rose
celebrated their marriage.
And they lived in happiness ever after.

Chapter 17

THE AWAKENING
OF BRIAR ROSE

An Overview

In the story of Briar Rose (or Sleeping Beauty, as she is also known) we have a deceptively simple story about a universal theme: the holy child, the long-awaited one, who finally appears but then disappears and reappears rather like springtime in the cycle of seasons or like the phases of the moon. She is the apple of her father's eye. She is blessed by a whole series of mothers. But she is also cursed by a mother. While this daughter withdraws from life, as did the Handless Maiden, Briar Rose does not go into the woods to work out her salvation but disappears into a deathlike sleep and becomes completely passive at the center of a formidable tower. This tower is her prison. It is the only aspect of her that the world can see, while she lies dormant inside. But this tower is also her protection. This is the place to wait in quiet incubation until the time is ripe for her rebirth.

The Two Heroes, Back to Back

The Handless Maiden, as we learned, was caught in a too black-and-white dilemma: she could keep her hands and cause her father to become the Devil himself. Or she could try to save him from a devil-possession—maybe even keep him human—by giving up her autonomy. Bearing the burden of finding her father's very destiny in her hands, she must give them up and relinquish any grip on her own life for the sake of her father. She "chooses"—if this can even be called a choice—to be a good and responsible daughter and staves off the Devil's possession by becoming overly feminine, helpless and dependent on men.

If we could stray in our imaginations, for a moment, and merge our two stories, Briar Rose, faced with the dilemma of giving up her hands or being taken by the Devil, would have kept her hands, thank you, and hooked elbows with the Devil. Her personality and conditioning experiences are quite different from her sister the Handless Maiden's. She is much quicker to reach toward her autonomy. She's curious and fascinated with what's "forbidden." She can handle this. But once in the Devil's possession (like her Greek sister, Persephone), she would become his captive in the world of the dead. Certainly her feminine nature would fall into a deathlike sleep. All that would be left for the world to see—of her spunky, blooming, adventuring self—would be the gray walls of her tower.

Resisting the Story

There is an ironic element in our consideration of the Briar Rose story that we might want to address early on. For many of us, the Briar Rose inside us kicks in even as we read her story. Things go tolerably well until we find the princess finally languishing on some velvet couch, waiting for a handsome prince to kiss her awake. Then we balk! It's precisely our Briar Rose-like nature that is put off by this scene. We try never to "languish" through any aspect of our lives and we certainly dislike being defined as helpless or passive by our culture. Handlessness was a difficult enough problem to resolve, but in this story of Briar Rose we find it very difficult to identify with that passive bit of feminine fluff who, it appears, will need a man to rescue her.

The Briar Rose in us tends to be literal, historical, practical and just. Some women will argue that it was the patriarchal world that destroyed a once blissful and perfect world of the wise goddess. Some say it was the patriarchal world that ascribed jealousy, vanity, rage, conniving, plotting, evil ways to the woman excluded from the feast. It makes perfect sense that none of us will accept the implication that our biology determines our destiny, and none of us will accept a cultural/historical definition of women as "damaged goods," or even as passive or unconscious. Others say it is a patriarchal culture that renders the feminine inactive—because that's where men like us best. God knows there is truth in all of this. The patriarchal problem that we assign this story annoys and angers us and, in what is our healthy striving for autonomy, we find no solution here. We want to kiss Briar Rose goodbye!

It is difficult to maintain a mythic vision of the work and ferret out the truth in archetype and symbol. It seems, however, that this is the place we most often get hung up as Briar Roses. If we say that there is no real difference between men and women other than the culturally enforced one, then it follows that there is no masculine-feminine polarity central to the structure of the human psyche. And such lack of structure may prevent us from gaining any identity at all.

The masculine-feminine polarity, while subject to cultural influence or biology, is not the product of a culture. Jung would argue that polarities of opposites are a part of the psychic structure and are the source of tension or energy. This tension sparks the psyche to life—is the life energy of the psyche itself. It is intrinsic to our growth process—our journey to wholeness and healing—that we struggle constantly to balance and integrate these inner polarities. Earth and heaven, flesh and spirit, passive and active, internal and external, process and product, feminine and masculine . . . these are the polarities where we—woman or man—confront in ourselves what we deem "other."

The Briar Rose in us, ever tempted to function from an

• •

externalized point of view and seeking autonomy, is then tempted to favor the masculine values. "On the outside," and in reaction to any deadening passivity, we will attempt to be ever rational and active. Unwittingly, Briar Rose is herself inclined to lock up what is inner and feminine and allow it to become immobilized—locked up in a prison tower.

Cut off, then, from a symbolic approach to the feminine and its psychology, we are cut off from the language that speaks of certain aspects of psychic or spiritual realities within us. The psyche speaks in symbols as the best possible way to express what is inner and would be almost unknowable except for such language. The psyche uses symbolic masculinity and femininity to give us information about our deepest selves—information that will wake us to living more fully in the everyday world.

That entire cultures, and individuals too, will unwittingly act out the myth of whose truth they are unconscious is here the issue. If we don't know our archetypal propensities, then we will get caught in them, forever hanging ourselves up on the thorns of our complexes, stuck in the process of our own redemption.

Archaic Roots

Dreams, myths and fairy tales are our access to this darker world where the truth is told in mysterious and ambiguous ways and only slowly becomes accessible to us.

To enter and engage the feminine process—to see it as a *symbolic* journey—allows us to see that this process has always had its moments of fruitfulness and its dark times of quiet incubation. This pattern of ebb and flow seems to be the nature of feminine mysteries. Ancient peoples in many prehistoric civilizations found in nature, and in the cycles of the sun and the moon, a paradigm to chart the riddles of darkness and light, of woundedness and healing, of barrenness and fruitfulness, of death and rebirth. On to the very cycles of the sun and moon they projected the mysteries in their own lives, just as they experienced them. Their stories of lost innocence and love, or lost innocence and rape, lost loves and married loves, lost marriage partners and remarriage . . . all mirrored the cycles of the heavenly bodies.

There are noteworthy parallels to the story of the Handless Maiden in many of the archaic sun and moon stories. And the death/sleep/regeneration themes of the sun and moon stories reappear in the Greek myth of Demeter and Persephone as well as in this fairy tale of Briar Rose.

The fact that these themes are old and recurrent seems to indicate that cycles of feminine strength and weakness, introversion and extroversion, fat and lean, dying and rising, are not new patterns. These concepts seem to have been with us since our loss of original innocence or even since the invention of the sun and moon. For the theme in our story is old, and feminine value, it would seem, is always in danger of death. But the prescription for healing is actually filled with hope.

Above all—and most importantly—we are, again, not merely talking about women and men. Though both genders will find much that is personally applicable in this fairy tale, we shortchange ourselves and constrict the metaphors if we do not allow them to intersect the linear view which is personal/ sexual/historical—linear ways in which we have gotten caught in the journey.★

I think the story says more and, whether it ever meant to or not, warns us that here *the feminine value itself*, and not just women, *has been wounded and has gone to sleep*. This can happen within us as women or men, personally. The story states what we cannot deny has happened as well, both culturally and historically. On the broadest, deepest level, what concerns us here is how things went wrong, if they did go wrong, and our hope for the reemergence of a strong, whole, fruitful, feminine principle—one that the ages have longed for.

★ Such a linear view of the story has been extensively and well handled by Madonna Kolbenschlag and is worth examination. (See Bibliography.)

Problems with This Story

This story also has other problems. Most of us are of an age to have had the Disney imagery of this story well etched into our memories. That imagery, fine as it was at the time, is too personally Disney's and too sentimental for our use today. We need to reimage every character in this drama with a profoundly new, strong, archetypal conception. Reshaping those images may be a good exercise for us to employ, even as we enter this story to hear its wisdom.

The story of Briar Rose is also only half the story that the Handless Maiden was. It does not take us past what looks like a girlhood moving to adolescence. And that makes it a more anemic tale, it would seem. A Freudian, like Bruno Bettelheim, will handle this tale basically as that—a tale of a girl's growing into womanhood. But I would like to think that we could understand the story as that and more. I would like to think that we could "recycle" the same themes and patterns and glean more wisdom by seeing it as a story of girlhood growing to womanhood, indeed as the continued evolution of woman growing to wholeness in the second half of life, and as the collective feminine principle waking up to its own gifts and vital contribution to the culture and time.

Chapter 18

THE HOPEFUL KING AND QUEEN

The First Line as Diagnosis

The first line in the story of Briar Rose, just as in our story of the Handless Maiden, pronounces the general condition or "the state of the union." We are told the personal condition of the King and the Queen but, far more, we hear the diagnosis of the larger culture: the King and the Queen of the collective consciousness are barren. The whole kingdom is barren. The culture is barren. Without new life there can be no future.

Is there a cause for this sterility? Or is this just fate? Perhaps it means that the King and Queen have an undeveloped or immature relationship to one another. The relationship between the sexes throughout the kingdom/culture may be sterile and fruitlessly immature. The cross-fertilization between masculine and feminine principles may be unproductive or uncreative. For it is when women and men in relationship, and feminine and masculine in the individual psyche, can bless each other and affirm each other that they effect the cross-fertilization necessary for a vital creativity and a fruitful culture.

The King and Queen know that. They know that what the situation needs is new blood and new life. That would break the dreary impasse and redeem them from the bleakness of their fate. So they hope and they dream that one day they might have a child.

The Prescription: Waiting

There is a long period of waiting before the child is conceived. This long season of hope and expectation is a familiar theme. In Hebrew Scripture we know that Abraham and Sarah waited long for the birth of their only son, Isaak. In the Gospel of Luke, Elizabeth and Zechariah waited into their old age for the birth of John the Baptist. And so did the world await the coming of Christ. "Rejoice and be glad, O daughter of Jerusalem; behold your king shall come to you; fear not, Sion, for your salvation shall quickly come." It would seem that nothing of value comes to us without a period of anxious, hopeful waiting.

In our fairy tale the long period of waiting is also a clue that the child who will be born will be much needed—a treasure for the whole kingdom. She will be challenged to carry out the holy work of a hero with a distinctly feminine role in this kingdom. The story says that what the world needs now is not so much "a child" as specifically a daughter—the new, emerging feminine value.

Hidden Growth

The darkness, the depression, that dreadful feeling of emptiness and cautious hope that a period of waiting extracts from us may also be understood as a period when creative energy must quietly accumulate. Deep down where it is dark and moist, in the hidden place, the germ will sprout. Only in darkness will it take root. Darkness, so often seen as negative, is clearly necessary to fertility and hidden growth. A great energy is building and growing where we cannot see it. All of life seems silent and asleep before the creative breakthrough.

In myths, the fields must lie fallow and receptive before the corn goddess will allow the grain to grow again. In our own experience, any great work of art, any real relationship, certainly any healthy baby, needs a period of silent, undercover becoming. The creative process makes one, essentially, pregnant.

The value of this time of lying fallow is not very popular in Western culture. We don't like darkness. We don't like to wait patiently for what is unseen to gather the energy necessary to come to light. And if we want something, we want it now. Instant gratification is our constitutional right. Waiting is something to be done away with. Labor-saving/time-saving devices are invented to shorten every period of waiting.

But it turns out that the time we save is only reinvested in a faster pace. What has saved us some work has given us more time—to work more. The hurried, busy way in which we live out our lives has less to do with keeping a schedule or with efficiency—it has much more to do with our terrible aversion to waiting and to the feminine value that waiting represents.

When I have a paper to write and the deadline looms, it is easy for me to fill with panic. I think that, were I disciplined, I would just sit down—get going—and just produce the thing. But when I sit down nothing comes and my anxiety increases. What if I have nothing to say or to paint? What if I am barren? That is the fruitless, unconscious approach to what I don't quite understand or name or face. Then I've learned it's much the best thing for me to go out into the garden and weed, or pick plums, or do the ironing—something that doesn't require thinking—and I pass into a peaceful place of waiting and quiet mulling.

Better yet, I can put forth the *conscious* rituals of preparation that call down to the deepest part of me: I order and honor and bless my world. I name the four holy corners of its walls. I offer prayers to the Spirit over my head and bless the earth under my feet. I walk through the mazes of this walled and inner garden and come to the wellspring at its center. The water is black and deep, but cool and moving. I let myself down the well. Diving, but slowly. Slowly. Deeper and deeper. Deep down—way deep down—something is indeed stirring. Here is another world. Here I may find what has actually been conceived and incubating all along—here the Spirit fructifies what waits. Waiting is impractical time—good for nothing—but mysteriously necessary to all that is becoming.

The Christian Celebration of Waiting

We have mentioned already that the Christian tradition actually has a season that blesses the value of conception and waiting. A season is given to engage collectively that mystery of the marriage of heaven to earth, of Spirit to matter, and believers are invited to make conscious that marriage and resultant holy conception. Advent is the season that celebrates all the issues and developmental cycles in our lives that require a marriage of opposites. It celebrates all the periods of waiting that are the utterly human experiences in our lives, whether it is waiting for the paint to dry, or the muse to inspire, or for ourselves to change. Advent is a holy season of conception, pregnancy and waiting in all its forms. And this waiting points ultimately to every human hope for salvation and the completion of all time.

A Cultural Chauvinism

How the Western world actually engages the mystery of waiting before that archetypal season is symptomatic. We celebrate the arrival of the child-hero *before* he is born—perhaps even before he is conceived. A frenzy is stirred up by all the shops, and Christmas parties begin the moment we have wiped Thanksgiving turkey from our chins. The pace picks up and pushes us without a rest.

When Christmas Day arrives, we are not touched. We wonder what this pressure was all about. The day just doesn't work inside us. So, Christ is born. We're finished. Now let's get this mess cleaned up.

A child is born! The fruit of heaven and earth! Redemption is at hand! And we can't hold this baby—this new life—this hope—the very thing we longed for most. There is no time to nurse and nourish this small flame, not for its own life or even for the salvation of us all. And we don't celebrate. We thought the "Twelve Days of Christmas" came before the feast. We don't assimilate or incorporate what's given to us here. Time's up. We're sick of it. We're moving on to see what else is new.

I think this is some measure of how deep there runs in us the cultural chauvinism that despises darkness, the feminine task of incubation and waiting and is sick of the Child after it is one day old.

In our story of Briar Rose, waiting for the birth of this small daughter is a most important element of the story, and what is more, it is not the only waiting that we will have to endure. For there will be another period of waiting ahead which is just as necessary and even more painfully extended. Waiting, in this story, becomes the prescription twice over. Whether we are waiting for a birth or for a rebirth, we stand before a religious task. And it is the business of religion to adjust us to the inevitable.

The Frog

Finally, it is time to announce that the long-awaited conception has taken place. The annunciation is made by none other than a frog. He comes to adjust us to the inevitable. He jumps out of the Queen's bath and announces to her that she is going to have a daughter before a year goes by.

A Freudian interpretation would have the frog also be the father of this miracle child. If we think of the frog as the human father, however, then we would have to say that the masculine principle is not very developed here. The frog is one of the last in the creature chain to metamorphose before our eyes and to crawl out of the water as an amphibian—like a little man with two legs. The frog might also predict that the father lacks a certain maturity which will later prove to be true. He suffers a deficiency and does not have a mature sexual relationship with his wife.

Moreover, perhaps we should say that the relationship here between the masculine and feminine is still at an amphibian stage. It has not developed far enough and promises, to be sure, that there will have to be more evolutions to come. For in other fairy tales the metamorphosis of a frog seems to extend itself into further transformations when the frog actually becomes a human being.

But just as we define the frog as masculine, von Franz points out that in ancient folklore the frog also is a maternal animal, used to help women at childbirth and as an aid to fertility. It is associated, too, with "spring fever" and sexual desire.

A Miraculous Conception

And yet the frog seems almost like a holy intervention: the ordinary, human wish to conceive and be fruitful has suddenly slipped into the numinous sphere of miracle and mystery through the message of a frog.

The child to come will inherit the frog's ability to metamorphose: she will be required to continue the evolutionary process and is destined to bring about a vital transformation. But she will have to be wounded, and she will have her own time of darkness and waiting to endure. For after that long period of waiting for her conception, and the fifteen years of her happy childhood, we are introduced to her hundred-year dormancy. That long wait is a necessary ingredient in her healing and wholeness. It is necessary for the revitalization of all the kingdom, of nature and of the culture. This is a metamorphosis to be reckoned with.

Chapter 19

THE FORGOTTEN GODDESS

The child is born and is a wonderful, beautiful daughter just as the frog had predicted. The little creature is a delight, an answer to prayers, and the King throws a magnificent party to celebrate her christening. He invites, among other important guests, the Wise Women of his kingdom so that they might bestow their blessings on her.

There are thirteen of these women, this story says, but the King has only twelve golden plates, which causes one of these Wise Women to be uninvited—or left out. This seemingly trivial detail proves to be a terrible oversight with long-ranging consequence. This detail may signal the moment in mythic history when the goddess world has been offended and upset by an emerging or an ancient patriarchy.

Twelve Golden Plates

Someone, something, very important is going to be left out of the party because of the lack of plates. Perhaps the patriarchal culture that has developed to this point in our history has been able to dish up only so much consciousness, but now it has run out of "place settings." We had twelve plates to bring us to this stage of our development, but now comes the moment of truth. The balance has tipped. The "oversight" in the conscious world will only gather energy below and threatens to erupt soon into the light of day.

The King as symbol of our culture's system of law and order excludes an important aspect of the feminine from the justice system he has invented for himself. He has found a "blameless" reason for inviting some but excluding someone else. There results, then, in the culture no place for the "dark element"— or what is actually deemed dark by the dominant culture—the poor, the minorities, women and children, third-world countries—all are made homeless and have no place at the banquet feast. The disenfranchised are excluded from coming to the table, either to eat or to confer.

Back When the Wise Women Ruled

Perhaps the feminine, relational element in the King himself is itself so excluded that he functions only as a benevolent frog. He simply does what is necessary for the furtherance of the species and then checks out. Then the new mother and her little daughter and the whole community of Wise Women might just as well form an almost impenetrable bond.

We like to think that in pre-Hellenic times the goddess may have ruled. And we like to think that, when the feminine was ascendant, all was fruitfulness and peace and the whole world perfect. Many women imagine, now, forgotten Eden stories of a goddess paradise. Perhaps there was a time when only the Wise Women and their gifts and blessings reigned and baby daughters grew up bathed in women's mysteries.

And one can make the case that then the masculine descended on this Eden and with brutality, in rape and pillage, brought the goddess era to an end and that the patriarchal world ascribed to women, and all that had been good, cunning traits—evil and negative traits called jealousy, vanity, rage, conniving. I cannot say. I don't know enough about pre-Hellenic myths. And in trying to untangle myth from history, I find it's always wise to keep what is mythic truth quite separate from what is historical truth—and only then, when things are clear, strike out to find the place where both truths intersect.

Be that as it may, I suspect that any Eden, masculine or feminine, will have its day and that we can never have it back the way it was, in the "good old days," "when golden plates were plentiful" and there was bliss enough to go around for all. I only know that any archetypal world has its hidden, shadow side—where what hasn't yet been brought to consciousness is bound to create its necessary mess.

The Mother/Daughter Identification

When such a goddess—mother/daughter, or sister to sister—relationship is lived out in the real world, it has its own delightful, nourishing, affirming side to it. We know that joy in bits and snatches. But sometimes it is in danger of reaching mythic proportions. Such a relationship took place as archetype and was in process in a town where I once lived.

A mother, her grown daughter and the man of the house lived together in one of those simple houses in a suburban subdivision: a two-story box with a classical facade fronting the structure, pillars and cornice reaching grandly to the top floor. My children, still quite small, confused this house and its architecture with a very similar-looking structure in town which was the mortuary. When we rounded the corner and glimpsed this house, they always referred to it as "the dead house." It came to pass that we learned to know the folk who lived there.

The husband was a kindly, quiet, self-effacing man, somewhat withdrawn and rather nondescript. The mother and daughter were pallid, identical images of each other. Both wore the frilly dresses of children when they went out, and their age difference was blurred so as to make them look more like sisters. They told me that from time to time the daughter would try to attend the college in town. Her mother would accompany her to classes because when the young woman once tried to attend a college out of town she developed a heart ailment and had to return home after only a few weeks. Curiously, the mother developed the very same heart ailment at the very same time. And now they had discovered that they could never undertake anything apart from each other because both of them would fall into this heart problem if they separated. They wore each other's clothes, finished each other's sentences and spent the greater part of each day behind closed window blinds, wearing their robes and watching the soaps and game shows. They held each other, cuddling on the couch, with a dog on one lap and a cat on the other. And the affable, kindly man of the house brought home the groceries, repaired the screens and puttered in the garage.

Another variation of that feminine mystique was being played out in another corner of town. Our children took group music lessons every Friday. Another participant in their group was a pale, blond, lethargic little girl. Her hair was always caught up into a curly, waving little plume on the very top of her head and tied with lace and ribbons. She was flounced out in shades of lavender or purple—always. And arrived—always—as the third party of an inseparable trio: her pale, blond, lethargic little mama and her pale, blond, lethargic little granny. They, too, wore their hair in the same little topknots and mostly they, too, dressed in shades of lavender and purple. They were a self-contained little pod and found little need to interact with the other parents and children. Aside from a pair of glasses on the grandmother to break the progression just a little, you felt, to see them, that you were turning a little dial from face to face and could make the same image age before your very eyes. One day the father appeared for a recital. He looked a lost and fairly useless appendage trailing the procession.

These mother/daughter stories may be examples of how "the good old days" of the pre-Hellenic matriarchy look when they are continued into the twentieth century and are left unrestructured. The same can happen when sister is bonded to sister in such a way as to exclude everyone around. The male is there only in the service of the women. Things have grown regressive and are almost dead.

Daddy's Girl

Our story, however, says that Briar Rose is clearly "Daddy's girl." "The King could hardly contain his delight and joy." The arrival of this firstborn daughter has totally caught the King's attention and affection. So he is the one who throws the party for the little daughter's initiation into the kingdom. He is the one to send out the invitations and joyfully call the feast together. He is utterly taken with the new and long-awaited feminine being that has entered his life. He is, indeed, not at all afraid of incorporating this aspect of the feminine—a "baby" feminine value—into his consciousness. But notice that, from this moment on, we fail to hear significant mention of his Queen again.

We know, in families, the difficulties that occur when a new baby enters the household. There is a basic shift in the old, familiar order. Siblings will demonstrate their difficulties with the adjustment. But sometimes it becomes clear that it is the husband in the family who does not have "enough plates to go around," and he slights his wife on some emotional, libidinal level and favors his young daughter. The missing plate seems to be no one's fault in particular. It is just fate. And sometimes it is just fate that the firstborn daughter catches a shade too much of that father energy and unwittingly calls down a curse upon her feminine development.

Or sometimes a father so openly and clearly favors one daughter over her sister that it is not only the disfavored child who suffers rejection but the favored one who suffers great guilt and discomfort and receives only hate and jealousy from her sister. She comes to mistrust her own femininity for the way it alienates her from her sister and binds her too closely to her father.

In a more exaggerated case, the father's feelings are still froglike—that is, immature. He's short on golden consciousness and socialization so he turns his sexual energy toward the immature daughter with whom he feels safer. He is maturationally shortchanged and cannot relate to his wife and engage her in a sexually, psychologically mature way.

When the father transfers his feelings to his daughter and slights his wife on some important level, we can expect that there will be trouble: a conflicted bond between the mother and her daughter, too tight a bond between the daughter and her father, and trouble between the husband and his wife.

Trouble in the Kingdom

The old goddess world itself, or the realm of the Wise Women, has been tipped off balance with the birth of the new little goddess, and she may be as much the cause of trouble as any lack of golden plates. The new feminine is a threat to the old feminine. For we can guess that it is, in fact, his wife the Queen that the King has slighted, ignored or bypassed in his transference of feeling to the child. And it is some aspect of the forgotten wife who turns up now as the hurt and vengeful goddess.

Just as eleven of the Wise Women have bestowed their blessings, the thirteenth bursts in filled with rage and vengeance at having been excluded. She crashes the party at its holiest moment and pronounces a curse of death upon the child: *"The King's daughter shall in her fifteenth year prick herself with a spindle and fall down dead!"*

The whole party are stunned. They have been celebrating new life, their only hope for a future for the kingdom and the culture! And with this curse their hope is dashed. The princess-of-promise is doomed to an early, tragic death. Luckily, the twelfth Wise Woman has not yet delivered her blessing. The only blessing left to her is to soften the curse on the child and say: *"It shall not be death that overcomes her, but the princess will fall into a deep sleep for one hundred years."*

Hell's Fury

The goddess with hurt feelings is a terrible fury to be reckoned with, and this motif of the ignored goddess is a recurrent one.

Each of the Wise Women in this story, *even the fateful thirteenth one*, was quite willing and able to bless the new princess. And indeed, they did bless her with virtue, beauty, wisdom and every grace that one might want. Only the blessing of the thirteenth goddess was reversed into a curse and that was because she was ignored and left out.

> Heaven has no rage like love to hatred turned,
> Nor hell a fury like a woman scorned. (William Congreve.)

Aphrodite is such a goddess. Demeter is such a goddess. Snow White's stepmother is such a goddess. The modern woman, who returns to the goddess power within her, knows that this power can both richly bless *and* curse.

To be ignored is an injustice that women often take person-ally. Von Franz tells of the little girl at a party who first cried because the little boys pinched her and then cried because they ignored her. Of the two, she would much rather be pinched than ignored—an embarrassingly recognizable feminine reaction.

To ignore the goddess is a sin for which she will demand expiation. Hallmark makes its fortunes supplying the altars of goddesses who must not be ignored.

To be ignored collectively, however, is what gives purpose to the women's movement. For to ignore any segment of so-ciety is also to deny personhood and dignity to those who have been forgotten.

Modern men will very often ignore the goddess element in the very women they know best, but most especially when they have no conscious respect for their own inner feminine. A man will be enraged with women's demands for attention and equality when he denies the basic dignity due his personal feminine, feeling, interiority. A man will fall into the forgotten goddess's spell and allow her to be his voice when he rages and seeks revenge, or when he wants to "put to sleep" what is new and growing and a threat to his personal power or his personal future. He falls into her spell if he arrives home needy and tired and generally unaware of the source of his discomfort and pro-ceeds to poison the whole household with his angry, vengeful mood.

Leading the goddess into the light of day, recognizing and honoring her gifts and transforming and humanizing what she can give to us, is the task at hand. The primal power of the forgotten goddess bursts through in our human responses. And until we tame her somewhat through the process of conscious-ness, repentance, and a profound feminine evolution, we won't always get the best out of her, and certainly we get no blessing.

For the story offers us a profoundly important principle quite early: *any complex or archetype, even a good and benevolent one, if left forgotten in the unconscious, will become dangerous and explosive simply because of having been left out of our conscious awareness.*

We know this principle to be true whether it is some part of our body, some member of our family, an unfelt or unexpressed feeling, a repressed complex, or a segment of our society: if we ignore it, it will pay us back. The tooth will rot and pain us, the child will bear the burdens of a black sheep and trouble the family, the inner complex will poison our outer relationships, and the voiceless among us—racial minorities or women, children or Mother Nature—will rise up eventually and in revenge pay the world back.

The Revenge of the Forgotten Goddess

Revenge is the primal or archaic feminine response to neglect. The rejected and repressed side of the feminine is an image of the mother gone negative. She poisons the crops, brings misery and disease, fertility suffers, nature suffers. The action of Mother Nature herself has no time for fairness and justice. Revenge lays waste the just and the unjust.

While the "civilized," masculine world which bases itself on law and order attempts to deal in fairness and justice and to mete out punishment it thinks appropriate to the crime, revenge creeps in from underneath and contaminates the laws with systems of cruelty—because the patriarchal system has turned its collective back on feminine blessing. Our laws and righteousness, our power and "justice" systems are cursed when they provoke revenge.

Ignored or upstaged, the forgotten goddess—that repressed feminine value—(in women or in men) resents her position. She becomes driven by competition and jealousy and, being filled with the need for revenge, she wreaks destruction and lays waste the land. We see her handiwork in the destruction of a delicate ecology. We see her reach into governmental systems, into international relations, into any overly masculine or patriarchal system that, in its lack of true virility, tries to keep its own feminine values repressed.

Blake gave us a powerful and frightening view of undifferentiated feminine rage just in case any of us should never have had the honor of knowing it raw:

• •

And she put forth her hand upon the looms in dreadful howlings
Till she vegetated into a hungry stomach & a devouring tongue.
Her hand is a court of justice; her feet, two armies in battle;
Storms & pestilence in her locks; & in her loins earthquake
And fire, & the ruin of cities & nations & families & tongues.

She cries: "The human is but a worm, & thou, O male, thou art
Thyself female. A male, a breeder of seed, a son and husband."
(William Blake, *Jerusalem, the Emanation of the Giant Albion.*)

    She has a point—and she will make it.

When a Woman Is Not Served

When we as women ourselves are ignored and find it difficult
to be honest about our emotional needs and our feelings, we
may allow vanity or resentment to take over in relationships.
Sometimes we think that we should be able to overlook the
fact that no one brought flowers on our birthday, or be silent
about the fact that none of the children remembered us with a
card on Mother's Day. We may repress resentment over being
sidestepped for a deserved promotion or award. We may not
acknowledge that this hurt. Instead, on some other occasion,
one that seems somewhat removed from the issues that hurt
us, we are likely to be overtaken by a dogmatic or judgmental
mood. Everything and everyone around us is not quite up to
our standards. We become reproachful or opinionated. "The
milk of human kindness" turns sour in a woman's life when
we have overlooked our emotional needs and failed to ask for
what we need. When we are afraid to recognize, admit, name
and get over hurt feelings, we are in danger of becoming the
personification of an undifferentiated, irate goddess, out to exact
her due.

    Let's say that a woman prepares Thanksgiving dinner for her
family—laboring over all the details and all the trimmings. She
has shopped and planned and cooked and set the table. She has
called together her family and extended her invitations beyond
the family to bring others to her generous table. She does all

this out of a real love for her family and as a keeper of tradition. Tradition, she knows, suffers for lack of the feminine touch. This is her gift and blessing. Without the women in a family, traditions might not even survive. So she is willing to give it her all . . . until she realizes that her gathered brood sits in front of the television, hooting and shouting at the game.

"The game" is the masculine world's solution to finding itself at home with Mother. They are uncomfortable with her on some level. They defend. They will gather all the masculine strength they can muster and soak it up from off the screen. They will escape relationship if they can manage it and immerse themselves in collective masculine sweat and noise. The frenetic voice of the sports announcer keeps at his incessant, high-pitched commentary, while the viewers beat on the arms of their easy chairs. They roar and groan.

Suddenly aware that she is being taken for granted in the

kitchen and that the feast is upstaged by some loud ball game, this woman is now fully capable of casting a dark spell over the festivities. Before she fully realizes it, her blessings may reverse themselves and cast a pall over the whole atmosphere. Things go wrong when we fail to deal with hurt feelings.

Daughter of a Negative Mother

As daughters of a forgotten goddess, we suffer from a negative mother complex. Briar Rose has stolen away affection and attention from her own mother and, through displaced anger, the mother turns to wounding her own daughter. When a daughter suffers from a negative mother complex her own anger may result in righteous demanding that sounds particularly primal. The lack of maternal feeling, the warmth, the tender attention and affirmation that were her due as a child may continue to cause her to be so hungry, so needy, that she will be touchy, feeling hurt, suspicious and neglected at every turn. Her sense of worth was so eroded that anger and hurt contaminate many of her relationships.

We all notice aspects of that in ourselves when we are irritated because our husbands or colleagues have different viewpoints from our own. Or perhaps we catalogue every slight, real or imagined, that has come our way—from the neighbors, the relatives, the in-laws, the staff, even history!—and can remember verbatim, and to the date, who was guilty of what slight or omission. Our store of facts, dates and statistics becomes a growing burden for us to carry because we haven't yet learned to translate all that data into wisdom.

The rage of the forgotten goddess passed along to daughters is really the same appeal for recognition and for love, but presented so that it may drive away exactly what a woman needs most.

The Ignored Feminine in the Man

And the man, living his life in a totally exterior, extroverted manner, neglects his inner tender, feeling, creative, relational side. He conducts his life in a practical but rigid way, he is unfeelingly "just." He is punitive, hard-edged, merciless, fanatically competitive, driven, or righteous and demanding. He also calls down the wrath of his forgotten feminine. She invades him with an irrational possession which manifests itself in withdrawal, pouting, a licking of wounds, a flurry of accusations, accusations of neglect, an unspoken craving for nurture, an inclination to plot revenge, and the projections of that witch onto any woman who might just cross his path.

Perhaps he comes home to see his daughters or his sons telling stories about their day to their mother with enthusiasm and delight. He interrupts. He breaks into the communication and would rather destroy it than engage the fact that he just walked into an intimate, happy exchange . . . and he can't remember when one of his kids ever opened up to him like that. He feels left out. Unimportant. Taken for granted. Useful only for paying the bills! It's as if they've got some secret understanding among them that excludes him. "Why the hell haven't you changed that tire on the Chevy like I told you?" he bellows— apropos of nothing. But destructive of everything.

When the golden plates are in short supply, we can expect all hell to break loose at the party.

The Goddess Must Evolve into What Is More Human

In myths, the ancient mother-goddesses, not unlike the forgotten goddess of our story, were jealous and rejecting of their own human incarnations on earth. Their daughter-goddesses were just like them—identical—and yet are progressing toward a new, more human, feminine existence. The mother-goddesses were primal, boiling jumbles of elemental, emotional, feminine reactions—all jealousies and spite and cunning in their plots— but they were also all passionate and fertile, generous without stint and nourishing to all who needed them. The mother-goddesses were as raw and direct as Mother Nature herself. The emerging daughters became more human, reflective, passionate but less impulsive, disciplined, clear-eyed and steady. But first they had to suffer.

If the evolution, the metamorphosis, of the emerging feminine incarnations of the goddess provides any chart for the emerging culture, the women's movement may continue to unfold a new kind of differentiated woman, conscious, passionately alive, at home in her skin, aware of her unique gifts, proud of her feminine nature, devotedly civilizing of the feminine aspect of her men, and alive to feminine value wherever it appears. But first we endure pain.

In the business of becoming human and conscious and aware of our profound responsibility to contribute to this global family into which we were born, we must invite into our field of awareness that which lurks waiting in the wings. That is why in a Jungian analysis one learns to meet head-on the types that people the shadowed corners of one's unconscious and haul them up into the light of day. There, invited, heard, embraced and integrated into the whole "party" of one's psychic constellation, they will bless rather than curse us. The incorporation and humanizing of archetypal power into our consciousness are social, moral and religious acts.

Chapter 20

THE DIVINE INCARNATE

We seem still to be groping to discover a satisfactory way to comprehend or gain access to the feminine aspect of the Godhead, but for all that the wholeness of God as father/mother is no invention of the twentieth century. The mother aspect of God is well described by the prophet Hosea, for instance, and we learn that this beneficent mother, too, will turn vengeful if sacrifices are burned before other gods:

> When Israel was a child I loved him,
> and I called my son out of Egypt.
> But the more I called to them,
> the further they went from me;
> they have offered sacrifice to the Baals
> and set their offerings smoking before the idols.
> I myself taught Ephraim to walk,
> I took them in my arms;
> yet they have not understood
> that I was the one looking after them.
> I led them with reins of kindness,
> with leading-strings of love.
> I was like someone who lifts an infant
> close against his cheek;

stooping down to him I gave him his food.
They will have to go back to Egypt,
Assyria must be their king,
because they have refused to return to me.
The sword will rage through their towns,
wiping out their children,
glutting itself inside their fortresses. (Hosea 11:1–6.)

These are days of a renewed and yet unfolding vision of the relationship of the feminine in the divine. The forgotten feminine is straining to be recognized. But in the mystery of the incarnation God becomes human in the person of his son Jesus, the God/man. And, for all that, Jesus too, must suffer.

Mary, Virgin/Mother

Mary, the Virgin/Mother of God, has so far been the human face (albeit, in our culture, the plaster-white face) of a feminine being, invited to be seated in the divine realm, as "seat of Wisdom," as human and as woman, and precisely *not as goddess*. The Catholic dogma of her bodily assumption into the heavens is a clear—if still generally unconscious—invitation and acceptance of the human and the feminine as equal to and worthy partner of the divine.

The story of Mary's assumption into heaven was regarded as a holy legend and a tradition from the early centuries of Christianity. And the celebration of this feast in the midst of summer's fruitful season is most likely the Christian evolution—conscious or unconscious makes little difference—of the early fertility goddess celebrations. What is worthy of notice here is that the evolution of consciousness has allowed the goddess tradition to become incarnate in a fully human successor, in Mary, as Virgin/Mother of God.

The proclamation in 1950 of Mary's assumption into heaven as dogma, and true to Jung's predictions at the time, was the harbinger of an important new age for the feminine. Springing out of popular piety and the visionary dream world of the patriarchal Church, this Catholic dogma offers a rich, symbolic language for the age of feminine value and the birth of new feminine energies wherever they are found.

It is as though the patriarchal Church had scared up another place setting after all and invited in what was waiting in the shadows. With Mary's bodily assumption into heaven, we can understand that the earth is in heaven. Having made the conscious invitation to the feminine in the personhood of Mary, the Church now seems caught by its several implications: woman, mother, the feminine, the human, the forgotten, sexuality, the earthy, the bodily, matter, nature, our human experiences, the very stuff of which we are made and on which we plant our feet, are worthy and equally valued—even though different from the divine.

The mystery of the assumption of Mary into the spirit realm of the heavens is the mystery of the incarnation—of God-with-us—in reverse. In the incarnation, heaven and earth, spirit and matter, were married and produced the God/man, Jesus. The mystery of the assumption seems to say: If you still haven't understood the profound principle of God-with-us, then reverse the story and see us-with-God. The assumption of Mary, who is human and one of us, brings all of us as human and of this earth to heaven. Heaven and earth are meant to be one. It seems that God and humankind ache to heal the dreadful split that holds us apart.

The women mystics had no trouble contemplating this union of heaven and earth. They also engaged it as a divinely erotic union. Sexuality and biological generativity had their part in the holy paradox that makes Mary the Virgin/Mother and all humankind the gracious womb of God's passionate love.

> Hail, noble maiden
> shining
> and pure,
> thou, bright plaything;
> thou, the embodiment of holiness
> which so gladdens God.
>
> Infused in you
> was heaven's potion
> which holy word
> took flesh inside you.

Thou, shining lily,
was known by God before
all other creatures.

O most beautiful,
most dulcet one
whom God found so delectable!
Enfolded in his passionate embrace
he implanted in you his own son
so that his son might suckle you.

Thus as your womb
became a home to joy
the whole symphony of heaven
sounded forth from you
for you, a virgin, bore God's own son
and in your purity you radiated God.

Inside your body you have known ecstasy
as grassland is washed with dew
and radiates its freshness:
so it has been with you,
O mother of all rapture.

Now let the whole sacred assembly
flush with delight
and sound forth in one song
for the most sweet Virgin,
Mary, worthy of all praise,
mother of our God. Amen. (Hildegard of Bingen, 1179.)

Holy Wisdom, the feminine principle of the Godhead, was
not thrown out of heaven to be trapped in matter—as the Gnos-
tics wanted to explain it. Holy Wisdom is made incarnate in
each of us humans as we evolve: like frogs out of the waters
of the unconscious, we take our first steps onto the shore of
consciousness, wholeness and holiness.

The Black Madonna

The dark and ancient face of the archetypal mother is the aspect
of the feminine that has, most particularly, still no place setting
in the organizational Church. The primal feminine is also dark,
mysterious, elusive and difficult to define and remains too messy

an issue for a rational, sunlit consciousness. Our intelligence has little patience with the ambiguous. We want to ignore what we don't know how to understand. Or we choose to invite to the party only what has been bleached of her dark richness and is rendered bland, innocuous, and nonthreatening.

Poland, Germany, Switzerland, Italy, Spain, Mexico, Brazil . . . these countries have a very strong, very old, folk relationship to Mary and they do not deal only with her light and bright side but recognize, on some primal level, her powerful, earthy darkness. Each of those countries has honored for centuries a fruitful virgin who is black and miraculous, and her dark and arresting image can be found in pilgrim shrines throughout Europe and the third world.

The Church as Mother

"Mother Church" is an image on the decline. Certainly in her poetic, nurturing, symbolic aspect, the Church is feminine and maternal. She has all the power of a Great Mother. Her symbols are feminine. At her center is the honored and blessed womb —the font of living water—out of which her children are reborn and through which they are initiated into her large family. She feeds her children at a generous table the living bread of eternal life and the cup of salvation. She uses only the simple signs of ashes, water, fire, bread, wine, story . . . earthy signs made sacred by their use. She guides her children with "leading strings of love" and nourishes through sacrament and sacramentals, watching over their every human developmental evolution and encouraging them, first of all, to be fully human and humble. She blesses and affirms the human experiences of birth, life, adolescent initiation, marriage, churchly dedication, failure and reconciliation, death and finally ultimate transformation, because she knows that it will be through our humanness that we come to touch something of the ineffable Mystery. She cares about our human seasons and cycles, and earth's seasons and cycles, matching them with her own seasons in helping her children celebrate the mysteries of their development toward healing and holiness. Despite everything, despite every patriarchal manifestation, this maternal aspect of church has silently always been there.

The Forgotten Goddess in a Masculine Organization

A masculine, hierarchical system of rules, of the intellectual, of control and organization—such as in the clerical class system of the Roman Catholic Church—seems, too often, to obscure its own richly feminine symbolism and sacramental poetry. As a hierarchical system, it seems arrested in its own power structures and chokes on grace even as it hopes to be the facilitator of graces. It seems ill at ease with its own feminine nature and has little room for the blessing of women. It leaves the rich gifts of women—and the laity as well—out of the mix. Thus it risks losing a renewed, lively fruitfulness as the price paid for organizational efficiency, power—or whatever its excuse.

It risks hearing only the outrage of women scorned and misses out on the blessings which are uniquely feminine and long awaited. Such a system is in danger of missing its chance at waking the valuable feminine that will bring back life and holiness to an entire culture.

The Church as Mother, with its richly feminine sacramentality and symbolic life, may simply be too archetypally feminine, too much the Great Mother, for a masculine hierarchy to—I don't know—to handle? To love? Is it possible that the masculine, hierarchical system has a mother complex of such proportions that it is paralyzed with fear of her? Could it be that the virility surrounding Mother Church still needs development and strengthening before it can admit the feminine gifts of women? What does it mean that laymen do not flock to church as women do—or mostly come when brought by women or when they have a special role? Why is the clergy class in the Catholic Church waning, even as the Church itself grows in numbers? How is it that women, ordained or not, still have such passionate interest in helping to keep that ship afloat? . . . And have such faith that it will float?

Two Catholic women, one a nun, an Episcopal priest and

his wife and a woman priest of the same church invited me for dinner one evening. All five of these people were very good friends and ecumenically generous, lively and involved with one another. We covered any number of topics as the dinner progressed. We worried over the religious and moral crisis of the times. We complained to each other about the problems in the Episcopal Church and the problems in the Catholic Church. When we came to the issue of declining vocations in the Catholic Church, one of the Catholic women declared with considerable impatience: "Things would be resolved if they just allowed a married clergy!"

The priest's wife countered: "We already tried that. Why not ask us how it works?" She crossed her eyes at her husband. We laughed. And we worked our way around to the issue of women's role in the Church, which caused the Catholic nun to sigh and say: "They should just ordain women and everything would be improved."

The woman priest replied: "We already tried that. Why not ask us how it works?" And she crossed her eyes at her rector. We laughed again. Naturally this led to the problem of a masculine hierarchical class system, and both Catholic women, putting down their forks almost in unison, declared: "Perhaps we'd be a lot better off without a Pope!"

And a whole chorus replied: "We already tried that. You ought to ask us how it works."

Though Judaism is hardly free of anti-woman sentiments, it carries a somewhat easier respect for women and enjoys and blesses sexuality. It is counted a mitzvah for husband and wife to make love on the Sabbath. And Sabbath ceremonies are begun by the Jewish woman as she gives the Great Blessing and lights the Sabbath candles. How curious that the Christian eucharistic feast, which is firmly rooted in the Hebrew berakah and the yearly seder supper, has so fully expunged any vestige of the woman's original role as presider (priest) and server (deacon). That there "were no women at the Last Supper" is hardly the issue—it has been the heresy-tainted Church that could produce (significantly) "only twelve plates."

The male, hierarchical system of the Church is not the only place where the feminine value or "the goddess" is crying for attention. For even as women are indeed waking up to themselves in gladness and healing and personhood there are serious issues which are forgotten in our whole culture and to which this civilization must wake. Issues of death and aging, of poverty, of ruined children, of the horror of wars, of a raped ecosystem—all these are realities and aspects of the goddess who has been blocked from attending the feast. These critical issues are the results of masculine governing systems that have forgotten feminine values. Furthermore, they are just as much the issues of women who have become imprisoned in masculine values—and of men who have ignored or forgotten to attend to the vulnerable, feeling, relational aspects of their own natures.

The feminine value, when it is left out, is rather like yeast left out of the bread mixture. The fermentation will take place in a wild, uncontained place while the bread suffers the lack of leavening: it becomes dense and hard, dry and dead. But when the yeast is incorporated into the dough, it grows in warmth and moisture. It is mysteriously alive and quickened. Mixed into the dough, yeast brings life and leavening and growth.

Chapter 21

CURSES AND
BLESSINGS

The Curse as Blessing in Disguise

We pick through the layered symbols of this story as an
archaeologist sifts through layers of civilization, trying to
read the signs and delineate the layers. The oldest, deepest
layers are archetypal and primal and tell us the conditions
that belong to us all. Successive layers bear the influence of
the oldest layer. Primally/religiously—collectively—
historically—culturally—familially—personally, we tally
striations of curses and blessings that are the very ground
of our being and find them repeated or redeemed all the
way up into a layer of our own personal experiences.

We sift through the blessings bestowed on the princess
and come to wonder if there was not some deeper, even
necessary reason why one blessing should be omitted. The
English divine and poet George Herbert wrote a piece that
has God, at creation, pouring out a "glasse of blessings" on
humankind: ". . . beautie flow'd, then wisdom, honour,
pleasure"; and then God stops the flow midstream and de-
cides to reserve the final grace: rest. God says that should

he "bestow this jewell also on My creature,/He would adore my gifts instead of Me,/And rest in Nature, not the God of Nature: So both should losers be." Having all the blessings—save one—will make us rich but restless: ". . . rich and wearie, that at least,/If goodnesses lead him not, yet wearinesse/May tosse him to My breast."

The blessings of strength, wisdom, honor, beauty, pleasure are still not complete knowledge. Still omitted is what is dark, frightening, elusive, hidden—all that is yet unknown—all of which is just as much a part of the human soul. All of it, every bit of it, we want to unite and, as Herbert goes on to say, "Contract into a span," and "make as One Thing on the breast of God."

Writing on George Herbert's poem, R. H. Blyth points out that God's breast is all things united as One Thing. Somehow, not quite "having it all" creates in us the restlessness that is our call to God, to a whole truth, to beatitude and a lively peace.

Fundamental to human nature, then, is this restless desire for something more and something deeply real.

The Blessing of Restlessness as the Seed of Revolution

The blessing of "rest," then, may not just be the gift *not* given, but might be seen as "the *blessing* of *restlessness*." Or the blessing-turned-curse is a "blessing in disguise." In the early stages of the recent feminist movement, in a whole new wave of awareness, women began to wake up to an entire history of neglect and exclusion, of repression or abuse. Aroused with unrest, women charged into the fray, wielding pitchforks of anger and indignation. In some ways this was the determination of the goddess to see that sacrifices would again be offered on her altar, or the rage of the Wise Woman who knows she has a blessing to bring, if she were just invited to bestow it. She knows her own value and that she has a rightful place at the feasting table.

The early movement arose out of a vision of reality and was fired with enough restless determination and momentum to begin a change, indeed, to change the course of history. It is a determination that will not allow women to be caught sleeping or handless again. The women's movement has succeeded in getting the attention of everyone at the party. "Henceforth, all generations shall call me blessed."

Fury and rage from a forgotten goddess supply the momentum necessary for a radical change when things have gotten stuck for far too long. The energies of the forgotten goddess have the ability to make a whole society restless until the doors are thrown open in a spirit of inclusiveness and all who are in any way disenfranchised are invited to the feast. The lowly will be raised up from the dunghill. The rich must give place to the poor. The hungry will get their fill. Every feminine value which has been repressed, along with women themselves, must be invited to this feast.

Women will be restless to gain personal autonomy and receive the dignity due their personhood. But the energy cannot subside or the vision fade with the first successes gained for the personal female ego, here or there.

The Wise Woman, retrieving her place at the table, must bring along her restlessness. And with that, every aspect of the feminine value that the whole culture has excluded from the party. Her wisdom will not only be a closed realm of knowledge accumulated for its own sake intellectually but a wisdom which is knowledge lived—a union of thought and life.

Knowing who we are, clearly, as women, as Wise Women with a very special gift and blessing to bestow—with a gift so long forgotten that we have yet to recognize it fully ourselves—is a calling larger than we have yet wholly realized. We will be restless until we have "contracted into a span" all loose ends and made them as One Thing. "Our hearts are restless until they rest in Thee."

Chapter 22

THE EMERGING
FEMININE

Sexuality

The new, emerging feminine, in the person of the little princess, is the cause of both joy and blessing, but also the cause of jealousy and a threat to the old, established order. Wisdom in this kingdom abounds. Blessings flow freely. But the thirteenth goddess also represents that quality, both personal and cultural, which we have managed to govern and control or even constrict and abuse until this moment.

This is a goddess of enormous power, of blessing and of danger. Collectively we haven't quite known what to do with her. We have tried to ignore her officially by surrounding her with taboo: for she also represents sexuality. The power of sexuality—its potential for new life, for passion, for destruction, for joy, for religious experience—has been regulated and surrounded with forms to contain it, to sanctify it, to dispose of it and to protect it from becoming commonplace and ordinary. That something with such high voltage and beauty should be called sacrament and conducted through the transformer of sacramental rites and rules, on the one hand, makes perfect sense and is sheer wisdom.

Safe Sex

Sex is like fire. A fire is a warming and comforting energy. It draws people to it—fascinates, delights, awes. But if the fire is to serve us safely and not destroy us, it needs its own place within which to be contained and controlled. The same fire, built four feet outside the fireplace and in the center of the living-room rug, is a totally different kind of fire. It does the very opposite of bringing comfort and joy. So powerful is our sexuality that someone once told me she thought the phrase "safe sex" was a contradiction in terms—an oxymoron on the order of "jumbo shrimp."

Small wonder that the father in our story, upon hearing that his beloved daughter is condemned to a deathlike sleep on the occasion of her first bleeding, sends out the order that all spinning wheels and spindles in the entire kingdom should be destroyed. A sexual experience can cause a blooming young girl to become arrested in her development. It could even destroy her on some level. Something in her will either go to sleep or die. In one sense, he does exactly the right thing for his daughter. He restricts and confines the sexual experience in order to protect her. Parents do not do their youngsters a service by allowing into the household all the powerful sexual stimulation that the culture pours out through the media, for instance. Children are overstimulated sexually at a younger and younger age. They are deprived of a healthy latency. Their experimentations often wound them seriously. They become more vulnerable to abuse at the hands of adults who are immature, and sexuality is being leached of its mystery. Rules and restrictions are perfectly in order.

Sinful Sex

On the other hand—and if we are to push the image into a negative balance—if the father (or even the Holy Father) sends out the message to his beloved daughter that becoming a sexually mature woman is dangerous, if not flat out forbidden—that sexuality is something to be feared and avoided and he will do everything in his power to control, supervise, restrict, admonish, forewarn, forbid, interrogate, intrude, suppress, even banish it from the kingdom forever and ever—his message is exaggerated and is also a lie. If the father, or the authority, can love his daughter and approve of her only so long as she remains an innocent baby, his preoccupation with her becoming sexually mature tells us plenty about his own sexual feelings for her, which he fears, and thus denies and represses.

To become sexually mature is a holy and precarious developmental task. Even the occasion of her first bleeding is wound enough in any young girl-becoming-a-woman, for her to mourn lost innocence and her lost childhood. Mourning that loss is appropriate to her developmental task. Adolescence, whether for girls or boys, is a delicate and important period of transition when young people are easily wounded further, and too often unnaturally arrested or painfully afflicted with the sexual immaturities of their parents and their society.

Secret Sex

And, with that, such a powerful goddess will not pack her bags and go off in search of a new cause. She will just retire behind locked doors. The King, in fact, has unwittingly just set the powerful goddess up for business in a tower on his own grounds. There she will wield tremendous power, functioning autonomously and having at her disposal everything she needs to attract the girl. For nothing attracts quite so unfailingly as the forbidden, the hidden and the locked.

In a more exaggerated situation, when a man is not on good terms with his feminine side and has an immature sexuality or harbors incestuous fantasies, his problems may be passed on to his daughter for her to resolve. We could say that he leaves his secret problems locked away for his daughter to find and to spin out for him.

> *Then it happened that on the very day of her fifteenth birthday the King and Queen were not at home. The maiden was left in the large castle quite alone.*

Her parents, probably preoccupied and struggling to create a mature and loving relationship themselves, "go out" on their daughter or leave her to be alone on some emotional level. And the young princess will venture into her adolescence, gathering information in her own way.

The fairy tale seems to suggest that sooner or later the girl will bleed. Sooner or later, all of us also need to know the secrets we have not known before. We will take the opportunity, while the parents are out to lunch, to search in all the drawers and closets, try on all of Mother's clothes, go through her purse, peek into the shelves of the bedside stand, and eventually find the mysterious stairway to the forgotten tower and unlock the forbidden door.

Chapter 23

ENTERING
WOMEN'S MYSTERIES

At last she came to an old tower. She climbed the winding stone steps until she reached a little door. A rusty key was in the lock, and when she turned the key the door sprang open onto a tiny little room. In the room sat an old woman with a spindle, busily spinning her flax.

Briar Rose comes upon the old woman waiting for her and, with that, she has entered the world of mysteries where the curse, and indeed the blessing, of women is passed down the ages from Eve to the grandmothers, to the mothers, to the daughters.

There is a mystical connection between female initiation rites, sexuality and spinning. In many cultures, even into the twentieth century among peoples long since Christianized, we find puberty and prenuptial rituals that contain fragments of a forgotten mystery. In some puberty rites girls during a period of seclusion learn ritual songs and dances and most specifically the feminine skills of spinning and weaving. The symbolism of these crafts is significant since they are raised in myth and meaning to a position of

explaining the world: the moon "spins" time and "weaves" human lives. And the Goddesses of Destiny were spinners as well. Only in darkness and in secret can time and destiny be spun out. So spinning was seen as women's work, a magically perilous craft, often to be carried out only in special houses and during particular periods and certain hours. The power, the universality of spinning and its association with women's initiation rites would seem to indicate that we are dealing with a very old religious experience—a preeminent feminine mystery, one that is basic to the experience of women's souls.

We might also say that the parents of Briar Rose have removed themselves on a personal level and turned their daughter over to the rites of initiation which can only be presented by the archetypal old woman who knows the secret meaning of what is a natural and visible sign.

The old mother sits waiting in the tower and slowly, silently nodding, she treads her spinning wheel. Very likely she is the Wise Woman and displaced mother who was excluded from the great feast years ago. Long since, she has lost track of how and where her feelings were so hurt. And from this secret place she is condemned to pass her wound along, to keep on hurting whatever is new and blooming.

At one time, whatever was lively, passionate, instinctive, creative or irrational about her own nature may have been danced and sung and played out in orgiastic rituals which reversed all modesty into exhibitionism. The laws were suspended and the rites were meant to recreate a state of absolute spontaneity for a ritualized period of time. But now all has been locked up in that civilizing convention called the tower. So outwardly her manner is contained and civilized, but inwardly she is rankled to the heart. Deep down, where no one sees, she functions on the principle of an "eye for an eye." She still knows how to pay one back and still gets even with the world.

One day—in a hundred years perhaps—her rancor will be redeemed by a new, humanized feminine element that is willing, even in the midst of legitimate resentment, to pay the price, to die a little to those demands for justification.

When the Spindle Makes Its Point

The woman is spinning at her wheel, from which extends the fateful spindle. The spindle is the rod around which the thread is wound as it is drawn from the raw flax on the distaff. It is the phallic aspect in spinning which, in our story, is also capable of pricking and wounding the girl. The witch uses needles to pierce the image of someone she or he intends to harm or paralyze. A woman's masculine side, and the feminine side of a man, are more likely to use sharp words, to "make a point," or to "look daggers." It is feminine aggression with subtle but fatal aim. The spindle pierces where the other is most vulnerable and stings or even kills something in the one attacked.

In fairy tales a prince may slash with his sword, but the weapon of the woman is needle-fine. The spindle, like the distaff, is a symbol for the "mother's side of the family," or the feminine, and is often associated with both wise old women and witches.

An Initiation by Witches and Wise Women

The feminine images and healing of the Handless Maiden in our last story seem to be in direct contrast to the feminine images and healing of Briar Rose.

We learned that the Handless Maiden suffered much at the hands of a negative father, and she is at first rendered dependent on men and in awe of men and masculine principles. But her woundedness is finally healed, not by the masculine, but by the redeeming feminine principle. Though not very effectual, her mothers are basically benign, she has wonderful feminine guides on her road to healing, and she is surrounded by the rich, feminine images of moonlight and pear orchards and the healing forest. Finally she retreats into her deepest feminine place. And through coming to know her own feminine value, and with the grace of God, she heals herself. The Handless Maiden's initiation into adulthood seems rich and reassuring with its clearly positive, feminine imagery.

A Briar Rose, however, suffers a terrible wound because of her too close attachment to a father and her ambivalent relationships to positive and negative mothers—all Wise Women, to be sure—one of whom turns vengeful. A father's immature sexuality (which in magnified cases includes sexual improprieties), or a seduction by a patriarchal culture, or a seduction by the masculine values of intellectualization, competition, production and the like, causes a Briar Rose to be delivered over to the jealous and death-dealing mother who will ultimately freeze her feminine development and imprison her inside a masculine attitude.

A DEATH-DEALING MOTHER

If a woman has a negative mother complex (which need not be her personal mother, but more the archetype of a negative mother) or was raised on the borrowed masculine opinions of the women who surrounded her as she was growing, she will be well educated in the world of shoulds and oughts. The positive masculine values of education, knowledge, rules, manners, justice, independence, competition are highly regarded principles trained into her with rigor. But even if such positive values are filtered down to her through the hard-bitten and sharp judgmentalism and competition of her mother's own ambitions, the daughter's genuine feelings and primary feminine values may not be honored and her soul may not be nurtured in a healthy way.

Beside all the ways in which a mother may control, instruct and limit her daughter in appearance and behavior, she can also limit her daughter emotionally by her masculinized measures of success and competence. She measures her daughter against masculine values and does not see her for herself. Competition, for instance, is so threatening to many women that they do not face it with consciousness or with a sense of personal value, but rather avoid it on the outside—to worship, instead, male figures of authority. But inside the competition continues to stew and simmer as a jealousy of other women who, a woman fears, are more successful than she.

We could say that the negative mother, who herself has suffered years of oppression, banishment or lack of appreciation —who is a mass of unfelt feelings and an unlived life—resides in a prison tower of masculine principles and wants the young princess to take her place. She is secretly jealous of the young girl's youth and beauty and the life she has ahead of her. She is jealous of her freedom. So a negative mother attitude passes along her own fate to the next generation.

This is especially well illustrated by the jealous, undifferentiated mother of Snow White, who disguises herself as a harmless peddler woman and seduces Snow White into eating a poisoned apple—an apple that was Adam's and that she has polished up again for the next Eve.

The apple may mean not just sexual knowledge but knowledge as a defensive intellectualization. This knowledge is so tempting that the daughter cannot resist—but it is knowledge tainted with the negative mother's poisoned opinions about this life and this world.

When Adam's apple gets caught in a girl's throat, she cannot breathe in the spirit or be inspired because she has aspirated the apple. Whatever secondhand values of shoulds and oughts the mother feeds the girl—good behavior, proper responses, how to dress and be pretty, to be the top of the class, what to excel in, whom to date, how to judge, how to compete, any hard, defensive, intellectualized attitudes—these stick in the daughter's throat and her authentic feelings and her feminine feelings are immobilized. Snow White, pale, beautiful and untouchable, sleeps the sleep of the dead in a glass coffin.

And her sister, Briar Rose, blessed though she was with a dozen blessings by the Wise Women of her kingdom, seems unable to withstand the power of the forgotten mother who waits for her in jealousy, determined to seek revenge. It will cause Briar Rose to become immobilized in turn. She is destined to fall asleep in the negative mother's masculine tower.

When a young woman is wounded by her parental complexes she may become unapproachable, untouchable, under glass, or thorny on her feeling side. Her abilities in relationship are impaired, confused, uncertain or simply dealt with in an unfeeling or uncaring way.

A couple had six daughters. Each time another girl was born, the parents felt deeply disappointed that they still had no son. The mother admitted, one time, feelings of guilt—and her husband agreed: she didn't "think the right thoughts at the moment of conception" which caused "a chemical imbalance." This "imbalance" never allowed them to have a son. The daughters shared in the guilt, but it was deeply unconscious. One of these daughters, most particularly, was destined to make reparation: she was groomed by her parents, but especially by her mother, from an early age to become a physician like the mother's brother. It seemed everything the girl undertook was directed to that end. The young woman is now in medical school. She is very intelligent. She is also very unapproachable and distant. Cold. Beautiful. And bulimic.

THE WOMEN OF WISDOM AND EMPOWERMENT

Like every aspect of a dream, so too every symbol and image in a fairy tale must be turned over in our hands, because the image always has two sides and we must admit them both into our view.

For we have to remember that Briar Rose was, indeed, also blessed by a dozen Wise Women. Women can be aware of the uniquely feminine power that they pass along to the younger generation of women coming behind them. Many know how to share generously and with nurture the mysteries of womanhood and feminine values. While the spindle may wound, the act of spinning is also a "feminine art." Beyond the spinning of plots or webs to entrap, the symbolism of spinning also has its rich, positive meaning.

Spinning an Atmosphere as a Holy Art

To spin also means to follow your fantasy or to "follow a thread" as far as it can take you. A storyteller "spins us a yarn." A mother, knitting for her unborn baby, removes herself from the rushed work of the modern world and, sitting back, is likely to allow her mind to slip into that quiet state in which she spins out her fantasies for her child. Today, we might find little cause to knit booties for a baby when we can buy them more easily. But knitting for a baby has less to do with the practicalities of keeping his feet warm and more to do with a very important feminine inner activity: the spinning out of feeling and right fantasy for the child.

Von Franz is quite passionate about the value of such activity, especially for modern women: a woman has great power to create an atmosphere—most especially for her household and family. She must not overvalue or undervalue her children but trust and entrust them with realistic and loving expectations that will lead to their healthy development and autonomy.

I don't know where a modern, busy woman "spins her family into existence," but it may well be in the preservation and creation of family traditions which enrich her family. If she spins for her family a right feeling tone and value, she nourishes herself and all of them at their deepest and most vital level.

My own mother, as one form of the spinning she did for us, kept a book for each of her children in which she wrote to us and explained us to ourselves. The books were our own written history, spun out as our mother "imagined us through" our growing years. Sometimes one could see clearly where her ideas for us clashed with our ideas about ourselves. But her gesture in writing to us so illumined and delighted us, both as we grew and especially as we read those books today, that some of us made of it a tradition and keep books for each of our children in their turn. My husband and I both kept and wrote in these books for over twenty years. With ceremony and ritual, we present these journals and accountings to each of our children on his or her college graduation day.

I remember when we presented our oldest child with his book. Peter, all trussed up in a suit and tie, as we were rarely likely to see him, reigned at the head of the festive table. When he received the book, he opened it quietly and began to leaf through it and read bits in silence. Then he shared a line with us all. Some things he read caused us to hoot and laugh with delight—especially those wonderful, goofy things little kids tell their parents. Other samplings caused a bit of hard swallowing and filled eyes. Then he read us something I had written when he was five. "Peter, you're a frustrating dawdler! I've been trying to teach you to get on with dressing yourself in the mornings and, when I come in to check on you, you are lost in your daydreams. Today I set a little ticking timer on your dresser and explained that you could dream all you want, but when the pointer reaches to the top of the cycle, it will 'ding.' The 'ding' means that you must be finished dressing—shoes and all! Later, passing down the hall, I heard the timer go off, poked my head in, and there, with a frantic start, you were scrambling to find your shoes. Hardest of all is for you to get your shoes on. I swear, Peter, if I don't put them on for you, you'll go to *college* barefoot! But, for all that, you love to name all the salt water fish on the poster that hangs in your room." Then Peter, the marine biologist, looked up at all of us and grinned. "Funniest thing," he said, and slowly from under the table he drew up one foot and displayed it in all its bareness.

Friends of ours, present at that same graduation dinner, had laughed and cried with the lot of us. When they were expecting their first baby some years later, they began a journal for her. They wrote to their little daughter every day while she was still in utero. And still they write to her, about her and about themselves, their dreams for her, this world that they are trying to make a better place. It clarifies their own resolve and sharpens a vision for their little girl. The father told me only recently that he's "become addicted to writing in this book." At this rate, he will speak volumes. For a father's feminine side can spin nourishment for his child as much as any mother can. And much of this process of his "spinning the child into life" happens, indeed, before the little one is even born.

Another father, awaiting the birth of his son, found the traditionally "feminine skills" of crocheting and weaving to be exactly right and the best way he could prepare himself for the child's arrival. He crocheted a large rag rug for the baby's room and then he wove an intricate blanket on a primitive loom which he built by reading books on Native American weaving. He also built the child a sturdy wooden train, put together with beautiful, different woods. All this he did between teaching his law classes at the university. And when their son was born, the baby went to classes with his papa, three days a week, and slept in a little basket by the podium.

Mahatma Gandhi was also convinced of the calming, meditative efficacy of spinning—literally spinning. As the industrial world flooded into India, Gandhi urged—perhaps to keep hold of some thread of the old Indian ways—that each person spend time at his or her spinning wheel daily and provide the thread and the cloth for their own clothing. He saw it as an activity both practical and religious. I imagine he wanted Indians to spin their nation into peace and healing.

As a Religious Exercise

To "follow a thread" or a "train of thought" can also be seen as a spiritual exercise and an opportunity for religious insight. Catch a random thought that "comes to you out of nowhere," or take between thumb and finger a passage from Scripture,

and then in faith and hope,
tie
one end down
firmly . . .
follow its lead
trusting
splicing in
following
with fingertips
through all its vicissitudes
consequences
down the hallways of its joys
and its terrors
snap
return
to the interruption
the snarl
know it and name it
feel its feelings
follow them
to where fear throws up a wall
builds blockage
distraction
from the flow
to lead you away
and yet,
stay with it
remain
with the point of interruption
weep it out
until you experience
a breakthrough.
There, pick up the thread again
and be led
from flax to thread
to the holy face
to Mystery.

Holy spinning is to give up ego control and trust that God
has something new to show us if we will follow a lead all the
way to its end.

The power and importance of the feminine imagination are
graphic in the writings of the mystics who followed a thread
of thought into the place of mystery. Their writings are a

wholly feminine theology—allowed, even encouraged—in their own time.

St. Gertrud, Mystic and Spinner

My own patron saint, Gertrud of Nivelles, is depicted in sacred imagery with a spindle or spinning wheel—and with a mouse. She was a mystic and the abbess of a medieval convent. Legend tells us that all winter long she and her fellow sisters would spin flax while they spoke of God and holy things. It happened, often, that they were quite rapt in meditation and in Gertrud's spiritual exercises and they lost track of time. One day Gertrud and her sisterhood apparently had gotten rather far afield again and while they were still lost in prayer and meditation—in holy spinning—a fat field mouse scurried into the room along the skirting boards, darted to where Gertrud was spinning and gnawed the holy woman's thread in two.

With a suddenness, the interruption brings Gertrud down to earth: She recognizes the mouse is in from the fields—which brings her to consider the fields—which brings her to the realization that winter is past, the snows are melted, springtime has arrived and the fields lie ready to be plowed and planted. There is no time to be wasted! The prescribed ritual time for spinning has probably come to an end. Gertrud, brought back to the holy earth beneath her feet, hurries the sisters away from their spinning into the fields to repeat a new cycle of women's mysteries: they go out to plow and plant the fields with new flax.

Gertrud's feast day falls in springtime, just days before the equinox, and she is called "the first bride of spring." Hers is the day traditionally set aside for the blessing of seed and plowed fields. She and her sisters were some of the early Christians associated with the pagan fertility goddesses, for flax is also associated with fertility, planted by women and spun and woven by them. In parts of Europe, in the autumn when the flax is harvested and readied for spinning, you can find the distaff wound with a hank of fine flax and set out in celebration of the fruitful season's end.

The Sacred Imagination

If women have not developed a true feminine identity, if they feel inferior, abused, unappreciated and unfulfilled, then spinning together is little more than the spinning of webs and plots or destructive gossip and jealousy. But when women are aware of their unique blessings, and celebrate their gifts from the Wise Women, they "spin together" in feeling and wisdom. This kind of sisterhood as a special feminine mystique has always been a possibility in the realm of women's experience. A true sisterhood is possible when each has developed an identity founded on her deepest feminine value. When each Briar Rose has waked up to herself as whole and autonomous, as gifted and wise, she is no longer passive but vulnerable and authentic. She can share with others her own reality. The sisterhood will be one of women who are not self-righteous but self-knowing. And knowing who they are, they become self-transcendent.

Today, women sharing with women, while it has been rediscovered as a rich value, is also quickly becoming more and more a luxury in a world where everyone is drawn away into the work force to earn a separate living. But "sisterhood" is a value that needs recognition—a feminine value in a patriarchal world. Knowledge and masculine values—thinking and scholarship, information, statistics, data, education—need not be secondhand values but the rightful realm of women who spin them together with that wisdom which is uniquely their own gift. Wisdom is that which transforms knowledge to the benefit of humanity. It infuses meaning and purpose.

Because of the blessings of her Wise Women, a Briar Rose has the gift to transform and is transforming the whole culture around her. Wisdom is the feminine contribution (which both men and women can give) to a world grown too heavily patriarchal. Wherever women develop a better self-esteem and have ways to honor and share their special talents, a more human evolution is taking place. There is sharing among women today in which the thread of a new fantasy for the role of the feminine is diligently being spun out. Women imagining are bringing beauty and art and ritual and a theology from a deep inner source where springs a grace that is not alien but deeply familiar.

Chapter 24

GRASPING
THE SPINDLE

"Good day, old mother," said the King's daughter. "What are you doing there?" "I am spinning," said the old woman, nodding. "What is that thing that rattles around so merrily?" asked the girl, and wanting to spin too, she reached out to grasp hold of the spindle.

Briar Rose reaches out her hand to grasp her experience—to take hold of her own fate. She takes into her own hands what fate contributes toward her personal autonomy. Hardly has she grasped the spindle in her hand than she pricks herself.

While we may have been shocked at the graphic symbolism of the Handless Maiden's brutal mutilation, the wound that Briar Rose receives in this story is at least as serious, perhaps worse. The story portrays her wounding as a simple prick to the finger, but its consequences are profound and affect not only the hero but the entire kingdom: the whole culture and all creation suffer with her.

The Wound of Lost Childhood

At the simplest level, a young girl at the experience of her first bleeding suffers the wound of lost childhood and no longer has a place in the garden of her innocent girlhood. She is no longer just the happy daughter of earth's mother, picking narcissi with her girl friends in the field. She will need to sort out the matter of being a sexual woman, and often she will retire into herself for a time and "sleep" until she is ready to meet men.

Certainly, many parents of adolescents, girls or boys, observe that their children spend as much time sleeping and napping again as they did when they were babies. Who knows what raveled sleeves of care are being knit up again? For a Briar Rose, this retirement into herself can be a healthy reaction, a way to assimilate her new reality and a way to avoid sexual experience which, if it comes before she is sufficiently mature, will be destructive and could put her to sleep for a very much longer time.

A father once told me his worry for his sixteen-year-old daughter. She did not often go out on weekends with her class-mates and she did not date. He was concerned that she was missing out on all the fun that "kids that age should be having." The girl, who had "grown a little plump," was very pretty, naturally quiet and much preferred to stay at home. She had set up a table with an elaborate jigsaw puzzle in the corner of the living room and spent hours there working in wordless silence. With considerable consternation the father told me that he tried to force her "to go out and have fun—that only old ladies in retirement homes did puzzles." But the girl, often moved to tears, would not.

The father needed reassurance. His daughter was not some sort of maladjusted teenager missing out on life; rather, she had discovered a way to protect herself behind a little layer of pad-ding and was trying to "puzzle out" this new womanhood that she had just entered. Actually, her process was not unlike that of the "old ladies in retirement homes," whose task it is to work out an integrated picture of their whole lives. If he en-couraged her and trusted her natural method of making a tran-sition, he would help her. She actually needed to "miss out on life" until she was ready to live it. Though the father meant the very best for her, to treat his daughter with intense, anxious concern was to define her as odd or inadequate and could easily be harmful to her natural rhythm of development.

A Disruption of the Incest Taboo

On a magnified and more intense level, the wound that a Briar Rose might suffer could be the psychic and emotional consequences of a disruption of the incest taboo. A father (or a stepfather, relative or friend) who does not address and heal his own sexual woundedness or immaturity is quite capable of affecting or arresting the daughter's healthy development.

When such a man teases the girl about her sexual development and shows a clumsy and unfeeling interest, he wounds her. In her vulnerability, it doesn't take much to paralyze her on some level. Some fathers are inappropriate—pinching and poking and thinking this is "all in good fun," when it is not. His teasing is hostile wounding and is out of place.

Most serious is the wound of sexual abuse. This is sexual experience which, like the poisoned apple offered to Snow White, is simply too much to swallow and so becomes lodged in the girl's throat. Unable to process what has happened, and unable to spit it back out, the girl falls asleep to some aspect of her own femininity and sexuality. In Snow White's situation, she can only exist as one dead, in a glass coffin. And Briar Rose must sleep as one who is dead for one hundred years in a tower.

So this prick to the finger (or this bite of Adam's apple) can be understood not only as the natural wound of first bleeding but as the wound inflicted on the daughter by her father, or by a father figure. This comes about because of the man's own sexual immaturity and is allowed through the unconscious complicity of the negative mother, who passes along the apple through her own poisoned relationship, or who "allows" the spindle to wound by inattention.

Because the wound does not result in a brief retirement into herself, but in an archetypal deathlike sleep of one hundred years, one has to take into account the possibility of a broken taboo on some level, if not on the literal one. The consequence of Briar Rose's wound affects her life, her household and the entire kingdom/community in which she lives her life. Essentially, the kingdom is now as desperate as it was at the beginning of the story, when it was barren. Maybe it is even worse.

The Wounding Cultural Attitude

So we will have to look at the story on another level—as concerned with the patriarchy's psychic wounding of women and of the feminine, that history of devastating effects on women which are capable of laying waste the whole kingdom and culture.

A BIOLOGICAL PSYCHOLOGY

Freud's observation that women are wounded men—castrated and hence imperfect—reflects not only his personal misperception but the perverse reading by an entire culture. Freud's concept of the feminine is built on what a woman "lacks" and hence his whole psychology, based on a physical perception, does not recognize the psyche as an autonomous element in itself. It is based on the biology of the female and implies that *anatomy determines destiny*. He founds his woman's psychology on what is defined as already wounded and incomplete.

When girls are raised, or women regarded, as damaged goods, that attitude alone is dreadfully wounding to them and to their sense of feminine worth. Thus defined, women have too often participated in the prevailing cultural bias, favoring their sons in subtle ways over their daughters by simply not believing in their own worth.

A CULTURAL PSYCHOLOGY

Naturally, once women realized the injustice of determining a woman's nature by a distorted understanding of her anatomy, or by defining her as intrinsically dependent and passive, there arose the movement to liberate women from what was defined as *an inferior cultural position*. Women, culturally shaped and psychically defined by a male tradition, needed a redefinition. So the initial impulse of the women's movement was to claim that there was *no real difference between men and women*, other than what unjust standards created.

That early reaction to the misunderstanding of women, however, retained the basic concept that *feminine value*, though it did indeed not belong to women alone, was intrinsically inferior. If women were equal to men, then they had better be competitive, striving, productive alongside them—and in the same patriarchal system. The new value judgment only reflected the same old chauvinist definition by agreeing that (though women were now equal) the feminine value—whatever was interior, qualitative, poetic, etc.—was itself, if not flawed, of lesser importance and unequal.

How might that prejudice play itself out? Culturally, we still get hung up on the notion that "drudgery" should be removed from the life of women. We press ourselves to join in the workplace and give ourselves over to production (masculine value) and reserve home (the symbolic center of the feminine) as the place where we enact our passive consumption.

Physical work and the use of the body, now defined as "drudgery," is relegated to the next minorities "below us"— from day care workers to gardeners. Often, we deny ourselves the pleasure of physical work and human interaction. Our work becomes "disembodied," mechanized, technical and often lonely. By entering the value system of producers, we become accomplices in the patriarchal culture that exploits, and by inattention we "allow" the taboo to be broken in the irreparable rape and plunder of the natural world.

A Psychology of the Feminine That Heals

To understand feminine value as equal and "other" is prerequisite to the constant process of reconciling polarities within us and around us. For the polarities which we see and struggle to reconcile are not simply biologically or culturally determined. They are not just problems "that men have inflicted on women." They are something much deeper. For masculine and feminine reside as archetypes in the unconscious. And it is the reality of the autonomous unconscious which influences persons at least as much as does biology or culture.

Until we build up the self out of the constant process of encountering otherness—a process which describes personal wholeness and healing as possible only through the full aware-ness of both masculine and feminine values in the achievement of personhood—we will continue to be at odds within ourselves and with one another. We will continue to give greater im-portance or superiority to the masculine power of action and production. We will be unable to construct between women and men as equal partners a new and creative relationship which is the concrete expression of an inner synthesis of the masculine and feminine psyches.

Forgotten because we find it hard to see and measure, im-prisoned because we fear it, misunderstood because we have forgotten how to translate its meaning as it expresses itself through our emotional responses and our personal and cultural behavior patterns, it is feminine consciousness itself that sleeps in the tower.

Only slowly are women waking up to their own feminine natures and the *nature of the feminine* that is our common ground. With that, women will take responsibility along with men for the renewal of the culture. *And men will not take all the blame for everything that went wrong in the world.* For it is neither sex who is the enemy but our mutual and protracted immaturity.

Slowly—and there is little time left—as a culture we must encounter and reconcile "the other" as we have all mistreated her value, ignored her limitations and destroyed her integrity in one another, in the natural world and in society.

Chapter 25

DRAWING BLOOD

In many cultures and ages the blood of menstruation has mystified and frightened men. If men bleed, after all, it means a true wound—a minor castration, or even the threat of death. But for a woman to shed blood, which should give life, is hard for men (or even the masculine mentality) to grasp. This cultural view of menstruation may have been an additional factor in the incest taboo, since men were to stay away from women when they bled. And many societies still seclude women during their periods, suggesting that it is for the safety of men rather than the health of women.

In the Western world we, too, have a conflicted attitude toward menstruation. Without even thinking of the story of Briar Rose or remembering Eve's fate in Genesis before her, women may call their monthly cycle "the curse" and see it as a punishment or an evil spell cast on women.

Old cookbooks warned the housewife not to undertake cooking certain recipes "while she is having her days," for milk and eggs would curdle and the jam would not jell. A friend tells me that her mother forbade her to water or touch the houseplants during her periods because the plants would certainly die. In a certain province in India, menstrual blood is considered polluting and women are segregated and fed inferior food or old leftovers during their periods. We want to think of menstruation as purely negative.

But perhaps we should view these rites of segregation as responses to necessity as much as to culture. *Segregating* women and *devaluing* women need not be the same thing. Power works two ways: menstruation means that something dies, but it can also mean healing and cleansing. Previously anthropologists, perhaps not intentionally, focused on the negative aspects of menstruation in other cultures as a devaluation of women, but they were probably victims of our Western attitude that is uncomfortable with ambiguity. Once we adopt negative attitudes, we unconsciously ignore positive ones because we don't want to believe that something can be both bad and good, both empowering and degrading.

For in some Eastern societies menstruation, while it is thought to be polluting, is simultaneously held to be purifying: it is a sacred power that cures and connects women to all the cycles in nature that renew life. Like rain that refreshes the land and allows seed to be sown, menstrual blood is believed to cleanse women and make them fertile as their cycles begin again. Therefore, isolating the women was based on complex and sensitive realities.

A Rite for PMS

I have a friend who had recurrent bouts of disabling depression or dark moods. Sometimes she harped and railed at her family. She burned what she cooked. She was certain that her husband would soon have them all in the poorhouse and that her family would come to ruin. Often, because of her anxiety, the family pulled back. After a while things would return to normal again, and all was fine. Until the next round of darkness overcame her. Before long, she'd share with me a new installment of impending doom: all her appliances were on the fritz, the dog ran away, and since she'd forgotten her credit card at the gas station their account would now certainly be drained. Each month this anguish crept up on her and overcame her until, finally, she noticed a pattern: her period followed promptly.

She taught me something about this syndrome that some women suffer. We talked about it over tea one day and laughed and cried about the fate of women. And then, struck by what I'd read about the Indian women and their periodic segregation, I asked my friend if her cycles were regular. Indeed they were—utterly predictable. So why let PMS creep up on you and surprise you from behind? Why risk being banished from the family psychologically for incompetence or a dreadful mood? Why not *circle* that date each month and approach those days with both eyes open? "Seize the spindle!" one could say.

Menstruation may have little to do with "pollution" in a literal sense, but these women in India, I felt, were on to something: certainly my friend seemed to "pollute the atmosphere" on some level—burning the food and spoiling all the family relationships. So perhaps she could circle the date, know when it was approaching and embrace it with ritual recognition.

My friend, then, did devise a ritual for herself. When cooking dinner, over the weeks, she doubled several of her menus. She stowed away half in the freezer in ready-to-reheat portions. She stocked the fridge and pantry. And then she announced to her tribe that in two days she would be out of commission and not to be spoken to. She would be taking, not a sick day, but a well day—a day to be quiet and on her own. She segregated herself from her family by *choice* and settled into bed with a thermos of soup, a pile of pillows and a delicious novel or book of poetry. Each month it became a time to look after herself— a time to look inward and to repair on every level—truly, a well day.

Understanding this about oneself means that a woman need not define herself as "bitchy" or that the world should seek to escape her "pollutions," but rather that she is the one to remove herself from harm's way. She creates a ritual way to recognize and honor her condition as a certain interior *vulnerability* that deserves protection. Like a woman on retreat, she can reemerge when the going is clear again. Like the moon, she can swell and fade and vanish and reappear in rhythm.

My friend didn't mention her PMS again until recently when

she learned that she was entering an early menopause. She was in mourning. It was too early an end to a wonderful cycle of marking time, of caring for herself, of honoring what was feminine in herself. "I got to loving that time alone. I loved having a ritual way to know and nurture myself. I need to devise a ceremony that addresses my next 'phase'!"

"Ahha!" says another friend of mine, hearing that story. "I just figured out why every computer I touched at work today got hopelessly fouled up! Seems I could use a little time by myself—a well day."

One step on the way to healing is to "grasp the spindle"—to accept our biology, and value, even enjoy, what our feminine cycles reflect about the feminine nature in the soul.

Ritual Initiation for Women

Our culture is sadly lacking in rituals or ceremonies that can surround and make safe and sacred the vulnerable times of our transitions. Transitions are dangerous moments because we are about to enter into a new and yet unknown phase of our development and our inclination is to regress, rather than risk going forward. Like a snake that outgrows its skin and must shed it, we emerge, soft and shiny, vulnerable and afraid. We are ready to strike at anything in self-defense. But, unlike the snake, we sometimes try to regress. We want to go back to what we knew and were comfortable with. We wrap ourselves in the brittle fragments of our past and are foolish for trying to feel safe again as we once did.

For a long time, as my own children were growing, I wondered how we might create rituals for them as they entered adolescence. We had indeed made a ritual at birthdays broader than just increasing the number of candles on a cake. The birthday child received two envelopes on that day, one marked "New Privilege" and one marked "New Responsibility." At six, you might pick out your own new bedspread. And at six you made your own bed each morning. The ceremony made graphic and real the subtle evolutions into maturity that birthdays marked and taught that privilege and responsibility were the matching hallmarks of growing up. But I was sad that our society didn't have any strong, collective rites of initiation which, by virtue of some archetypal universality, would be filled with power and mystery and carry them over that precarious bridge to a new beginning of privilege and responsibility in young adulthood.

All three of our children were fascinated with the myths and rituals of Native Americans and we often visited museums to learn what we could. The girls were especially taken by one exhibit where the puberty rites of a tribe of young Indian girls were depicted in photos. The initiates were surrounded by their sisters and mothers and grandmothers. They danced, they fasted, they chanted, they burned sweet grass. They told their stories and kept their secrets. Finally there was a painful, ritual wounding or marking that set the girls apart and signed them over into the world of women.

Then came a time when our daughters longed to have their ears pierced "like all the kids at school." I wasn't terribly happy about pierced ears. Somewhere early, it had been put into my head that women with pierced ears were just "a step away from being wild women." It seems I'd never questioned that. So *little* girls with pierced ears, well, that would be giving them a head start in wildness. Hence, for now, pierced ears were definitely out of the question. But—I seized on the symbol!

We conferred and came to the decision that when the girls had their first periods we would make a great ceremony. We, too, would sing and dance, tell stories and keep secrets, laugh and cry—and they would feel the frightful prick of a sharp needle in their ears and have them pierced. Then we would have a fine feast. Well, these two little girls couldn't *wait* until they had their periods.

A friend, with whom I shared the concept, passes along the experience she had with two of her daughters and the ceremonies for their initiation into womanhood.

When Kara came to me and announced the good news, we were both very excited and happy. We laughed and we hugged and we went off for private talks and covered every eventuality all over again. We made a calendar. I told her my own stories and I told her the sun and moon myths. When she was ready, she announced the good news to her daddy and her little sisters, she even invited her best girl friend to the ceremonies, and we all trooped over to the disconsonant setting of a shopping center and stood in a solemn circle around her as a bewildered lady in a white coat pierced her ears. Her friend threw her arms around her neck and said, "Let me be the first to congratulate you!" and we all followed with hugs and kisses and led her away, pink-eared and glowing with dignity, to a special supper. She was ear-marked, and her little sisters looked on with pride and longing. "Does it hurt, Kar? Very much?" "Sure. It hurts. But it's *supposed* to."

When it was Britta's turn, however, she surprised us with a totally different attitude. "Look," she said, "Mom, I think this is the day for me to be ear-marked, *but* I do not want to tell Dad and the others, I'd much rather *you* explained it to them. *Neither* will I have this whole family coming with me while I get my ears pierced. That's *private*. But I guess you'll have to drive me down, and I guess you can make me the festive meal—you know what I love best . . ." and she proceeded to give me my instructions.

We put together what she needed. We drove to town together. We talked. There must have been a story along the way, but I remember mostly that I couldn't cheer her up— and that I was instructed to look nonchalant and disinterested while the woman did her ears. I was really confused about what was going on here and I couldn't understand why this wasn't coming off with all the joy and celebration we'd experienced with Kara.

At home, I prepared the meal and we ate together with a rather cautious rejoicing. The announcement to the rest of the family was simply Britta's gold buttons in her rosy ears. As soon as the meal was ended, Britta fled down the hall to the back bedroom and called me to come. "*Look*, Mom"— she had her hands on her hips and tears in her eyes—"I appreciate the meal and all your help, but I think this *whole* thing has been *highly* overrated! It's a *mess!* And you think this is something to *celebrate?* I *hate* periods—period!" Floods of tears.

I couldn't figure out what the problem was or comprehend this avalanche of woe, this litany of the disadvantages of "what *you*, Mom, call the '*privilege* of being a woman now.'" I nodded, swallowed and asked her to hang on a minute. I'd be right back. I needed to do something or other—and I slipped out of the room a moment to gather my wits and remember what we had talked about once regarding ceremonies and such. This one wasn't going well. She thought it was all a big mess—like some disease I'd given her! She hated it!

Then I remembered that principle we'd spoken of, that "you heal the feminine wound not with the masculine but with more of the feminine." Now I understood. That meant that I was not to balance out her despair with rationalities—with intelligent counters—with trying to get her to "look at the bright side." Clearly the prick of the ear ceremony hadn't been painful enough to engage the fullness of the pain she was feeling much deeper. I needed to validate those sad and angry feelings and enter into the darkness with her. I needed to agree with her and hear her out. In fact I could even add to her list of woes factors that she probably hadn't even thought of yet, realities which, in my preparing her, I had glossed over or downplayed.

So I reentered the room, saying, "Where were we now? Oh yes." And I began agreeing. "It *is* a mess, Britta, a real mess, and sometimes you get stains on your clothes—you get up from your chair and have a big *blot* on the back of your skirt and you won't even know it and the boys may even snicker and a *grown man* even told me once that I'd 'sat in the strawberries!'—you know what he meant—and you'll probably feel bloated sometimes and look pale and pasty and some people get cramps and ache a little and it happens *every* month of the *whole* year and every *year* until you're at least fifty-*three!*" I came up for air. "You'll never, never get to be a little girl anymore.

"Oh, Britts, isn't it sad? You'll never be a little girl again . . . our little puckish one . . . it's the little girl . . . who's gone . . ." I felt really sad! We both cried and then she put that slender little hand of hers on my arm and said hoarsely, "You know, Mom? It's okay. It will be fine. I can handle being a grownup. Thanks." I never heard another complaint.

That's the thing about ambiguity. It's very difficult to hold opposing concepts in the same place. We'd thought the initiation could be all beautiful and positive—without too much pain. But a power works two ways: menstruation means healing and enhancing, but it also means a death. The loss of girlhood is bittersweet.

And the core of any celebration will contain what is both

bitter and sweet. Another friend made a ceremony for her daughter. The two of them made a lovely new dress for the girl's doll. Then they wrapped the doll in tissues and ritually buried her in the bottom of a big, old chest. The young girl's favorite plant was the calla lily. They planted a calla together in the corner of the garden while the little brother looked on. Later, the little fellow, visiting at the neighbors', said, "I have to hurry home now. We're having a big feast tonight because my sister is blooming."

Ceremony needs to be big enough to acknowledge contradiction and allow ambiguities. When we are touched with a mystery we will find ourselves at the point of paradox because we have seen a whole truth. Initiation into women's mysteries is both curse and blessing.

Chapter 26

THE TOWER

As a Protection of Value

> *In that very moment when she felt the prick, she fell down upon a couch that stood there and slept a deep, deep sleep. This sleep, like a cloud, spread over the whole court and the whole court slept with her. . . . Slowly, around and about the whole castle, there began to grow a curious hedge of thorns.*

Briar Rose, the blooming daughter of our story, is stopped mid-blossom. She bleeds and falls promptly into a dead sleep at the center of the old tower. The tower has ambiguous meanings, good ones and bad ones. Unlike the healing forest of the Handless Maiden, it is a cultural, man-made structure. As a protective holding area for the sleeping princess, it offers the masculine rules of convention and society, of patriarchal values and opinions, of rules and education. This is to keep her safe and valued until the time is ripe for her to awaken.

Archetypally, masculine power faces outside and deals with the extroverted activities of the outer world. Feminine power looks inward and cares for the things of the inner

world. When a man is in right relationship to his inner feminine, she is in charge of the inner world, of the psyche, and is to feed, inspire, animate and bring feeling and meaning to the way in which he relates to the outer world.

This same structure has been adopted as a literal principle of behavior between men and women in many cultures, most especially in Eastern societies. In India the power of the inner, feminine world is seen as a great value—even more important than the value of the outer, masculine world. That is why Eastern thought and philosophy are soaked in feminine value which is interior in nature, symbolic, ceremonial and religious.

Until the superimposition of Western values, the woman in some Eastern societies was absolved of the vicissitudes of the bustling outer world and had no part in its responsibilities or destiny. She was "protected" so that she might nourish the greater value, the inner world of ceremony, of ritual, of feeling and relatedness. It was her role to spin a rich atmosphere for the family to grow in. With the inner world given the greater value, Eastern religions, their ceremonies and rituals blossomed—while, in some Eastern societies, the practicalities of the outside world seem hardly to work at all.

The Tower as Cage

Push the principle of protecting the inner value too far, or interpret it too literally, and it flips over to its opposite: women lose the dignity of their position as keepers of the dream world. They are imprisoned at home, the possessions of their men, the drudges of the household, and powerless over their own fate. The tower, which was meant to protect and incubate and integrate, has been gradually recast to stress domination, power and wealth.

It would seem that to forget or leave out the Wise Woman is one great folly. The other is to trap or imprison the princess to your use:

> How sweet I roamed from field to field
>   And tasted all the summer's pride,
> Till I the prince of love beheld,
>   Who in the sunny beams did glide.
>
> He showed me lilies for my hair,
>   And blushing roses for my brow;
> He led me through his gardens fair,
>   Where all his golden pleasures grow.
>
> With sweet May dews my wings were wet,
>   And Phoebus fired my vocal rage.
> He caught me in his silken net,
>   And shut me in his golden cage.
>
> He loves to sit and hear me sing,
>   Then laughing sports and plays with me—
> Then stretches out my golden wing,
>   And mocks my loss of liberty. (William Blake, VIII Song.)

The Tower as Marker of Values

The Western world reverses exactly the value of inner and outer. The outer world is seen as the more valuable. Business flourishes, telephones work, planes and buses run on time, the mail is delivered and fresh produce arrives in the market daily. The outer world, in fact, has been so highly prized and so much energy has been pumped into it that the inner world, or the value of the feminine and all that is religious and symbolic and relational, may be forgotten or even left for dead. Above all, the story seems to warn our culture that we have become so exterior in our values that we have forgotten and repressed the inner value.

The tower is a great cultural phallus. In our Western cities, it no longer marks the place of religion as did the church steeple at the center of the city. Rather the towering skyscrapers of the city are what mark the religions of a consumer society.

The masculine value of rationality and intellect can overreach itself. While rationality can probe our actions and make valuable distinctions, while it can show us how we can be happy, it can also replace religious functioning by fooling us into the belief that it understands life. It replaces the valid function of the poetic by replacing imagination and compassion. It denies fear. It walls back vulnerability. It insists on "justice" and "the principle of the thing" by usurping compassion. It is always right, but often at the wrong moment or in the wrong place. Overrationality can take life away and replace it with dry abstractions and dead concepts. The Zen expression for intellection is "grasses" or "briars."

If the tower and its briars were ever meant to protect the feminine value, then something seems amiss if the feminine keeps on sleeping in total passivity and the whole land lies in waste around her. We had thought ourselves happy, but we are not yet happy. Gradually we will come to notice that this efficient, spiny, man-made fortress is warding off relationship or an integration and is protecting a virtual corpse. We will notice that the land is in ruin, that the culture is paralyzed.

> The highways are deserted,
> no travellers use the roads.
> Treaties are broken, witnesses despised . . .
> The land mourns, it pines away,
> Lebanon is withered with shame,
> Sharon is a desert,
> Bashan and Carmel are stripped bare. (Isaiah 33:8–9.)

The full effect of the new spirit cannot reign free to revive the land until the sleeping princess heals and wakes. For, culturally, it is our raging pursuit of power that rapes the feminine. Not as women, not as men, not as community or policy or church will we wake to the new evolution until we free the feminine value. And as long as wealth and power are our motivations we will keep her walled up in the tower where she can ask no questions or cast doubt on the masculine value system of our culture.

The Tower as the Woman's Masculine Side

The tower in a woman's life is often the tower her father or her education built for her. To live out of that tower, to face the world from the vantage point of your father's fortress, may also be a worthy way to function. The world is coming to respect strong, independent women who can stand tall on their own. The skyscraper world, the corporate ladder, the ivory tower of academia, even the steeple on some churches, are rapidly becoming culturally acceptable as the province of women.

The Briar Rose in a woman is often especially capable and gifted in what has been culturally seen as a man's world. This is a special gift she has that her sister, the Handless Maiden, would never have been able to understand before her healing. A Briar Rose may be singularly at ease in the company of men as business associates and colleagues. Hearth and home may be, through choice, through fate or through inclination, considered a stifling world whose duties asphyxiate her. Or household and family are simply not the whole breadth of experience that would put her full talents to use and she is, now more than ever, able to integrate them both. She may be especially gifted in traditionally male disciplines—math, engineering, business, intellectual endeavors, law, religion as a scientific study or ministry, medicine or politics.

Women with a clear and strong masculine side know themselves and are not shy about engaging in what needs doing. If the feminine, which must be their first definition, hasn't been anesthetized, then such women may use their special talents to create their own lives and in dedication to heal the society around them. In politics, they often lobby for the aging, the dying, the poor, the sick, the care of children, of animals, of the earth, nature and the atmosphere—these have become, more than ever, the special province of women. A city councilwoman brings the farmers into town to sell their organically grown produce. A mayor makes recycling and land protection top priorities in her work. An astronaut who lives near me uses her training to teach peace at the university. A teacher involves her students and offers her spare time organizing for the approaching Habitat for Humanity project in town. Parish women in relay take turns working at a shelter for homeless teenagers. Others organize lessons in English for Salvadoran refugees.

Above all, this outside world can become a powerful one for the woman to inoculate with the feminine value, as long as she keeps the feminine value awake and is not seduced by the cultural bias that is contemptuous of the less showy feminine value. If she is not solely identified with ideas, statistics, action, achievements or power in the outer world, then the feminine, leavening properties of nurture, of receptivity, of conservation, of patient, steady education will bring to life whatever is her domain.

But at the historical moments when there is a balance to restore and we are compelled to make a change—call it liberation, call it *glasnost* or *aggiornamento*—the windows are opened for fresh air and the winds kick up dust. Change, though we are already well into it, is not always neat.

One of the dangers of our own time, as we women try to awaken our own value and grow back our hands—as we try to regain control over our own destinies—is the impulse to rush up the tower and clothe ourselves with the borrowed sheath of masculine value. Rather than "marrying" our masculine and feminine natures to become whole and autonomous, we may delude ourselves into believing that functioning out of a father's phallus is true autonomy. We do stand tall and alone. We do protect ourselves. We do function on some level in the Western world—certainly far better than we did when we were handless. But this seeming autonomy can also be a false or interim independence.

To rush from one inadequacy to its opposite form may indeed sometimes be necessary to wrench a personal or a cultural pattern out of its bed. But to settle for this variety of tower function as the whole of it is still to disregard the feminine values that animate a culture. It is simply an alternate variation of the father complex in action. The odds remain against feeling, empathy, wholeness. The tower is still a prison to the soul.

Sometimes a woman's tower functioning may be just another form of male supremacy. What is supreme now is her overregard for masculine value. She may have adopted a rationality which is only the thorny evolution of reason. Her manner is as exclusive as any men's club and it is the feminine that she excludes. A right relationship to her masculine side means that a woman must function in the world out of her central, feminine identity and know her inner masculine side as her guide. From his inner place, he will animate her life. He will nourish her words, her art, her skills that allow her to function well in the outer world. He will bring order to what is scattered and diffuse. Furthermore, he will allow her the spirit that infuses ordinary life with extraordinary meaning. The tower may be flashy, institutionalized boredom. The positive, *inner man*, however, once allowed to enter the fortress, will make the ordinary holy.

Briars of Intellection and Briars of Revenge

For we cannot overlook a warning that our story offers us: the tower of our heroine is also the phallic tower she inherited from that power man who wounded her. What is more, her mother complex has paralyzed her feminine value and left it petrified in an undeveloped state. Briar Rose has been stunted by the fatal prick of a spindle and now turns to the world a closed, stony face and thrusts out her own sharp thorns, thousands of them, that wound and lacerate anyone who threatens to come too near.

A Briar Rose, unlike a Handless Maiden, may want desperately not to be dependent on men; rather, she keeps them away and may sheathe herself in borrowed masculine attitudes to shore up her vulnerability or to fake her independence. Briar Rose's feminine nature, then (not just her hands as in the Handless Maiden's case), becomes totally unfeeling, from head to toe. That feminine part of her sleeps through a great segment of her life.

What may look like independence and autonomy may still be a tower to hide feelings of inferiority and hurt for which a Briar Rose may compensate by being disagreeable and thorny. Sharp-eyed, sharp-tongued: "I've never been good at taking garbage, especially from men." Or she may pad herself out in a cumbersome layer of fat or dress in bulky, dowdy clothes to protect what is sleeping in her.

Though she has fortified herself in masculine values, her past experience with men has taught her not to trust them. She will ward them off even as she challenges them, invites them, dares them, and may secretly wish for someone out there to be stronger than her bluff.

Sometimes she may be especially attracted to male institutions that flaunt their exclusion of women. She may see them as a personal challenge, as an inner sanctum she would like to penetrate and invade "just for the principle of the thing." She is very likely less interested in the place, the job or the people than in breaking the taboo.

Thorny defenses, prickly behaviors, a touchiness by which

she controls others, a hard, thick intellectualism, a lacerating, opinionated, attacking exterior belie her real vulnerability, which lies weak and waiting at the core of her being. Though she may be the last to admit it, and may even hotly deny it, deep down, very deep down, she longs for the relationships that are strong enough to wake her to life again and finally bring the roses to blooming.

In the Company of Women

A Briar Rose may surround herself with other women—wise women with blessings, when things go well. Behind convent walls she often found her haven and sometimes her healing. But it may also be true that the bitter experience of her negative mother may have sent her in a compulsive search for mothers who might heal her this time but who, more often than not, will be curiously compelled to repeat the negative wound she originally experienced. Before the fateful pattern is finally broken, her female therapist, her friend, her supervisor, her mother superior, is particularly challenged to break the spell and not get hung up on the thorns of her touchiness.

As Mother

As a mother herself, she must guard against passing on her own mother's destructive nature to her children. (Or as a teacher to her students, a manager to her employees.) She will need to watch herself, that she not lacerate what is feeling and delicate and growing in them with that thorny outgrowth of reason. Rationality dismisses feminine value as nonsense. She must guard against raising her children on her rationality, her borrowed masculine opinions and principles, crushing what is feminine in them, piercing growing egos, putting down the dependencies that are natural and necessary in growing children. The masculine tower from which she functions is her defense and she will overvalue all that it stands for—judgment, rules, education of the intellect, competition, independence—and she will want to imprison her children in the same false autonomy that traps her. It will take her own healing and consciousness for her to wake up to the fact that she has wounds that want to keep on giving.

As Wife or Partner to Men

As a wife, or in her companionship (or professional relationship) to men, when Briar Rose is wrapped in thorns, she may offer her men endless challenges to survive her deep, silent depressions and bouts of passivity, or her frequent inflictions of pain. Unclear about her hidden anger, she may drive her thorns, quite unwittingly, into every one of a man's vulnerable places—all the places where he is uncertain and in need of understanding. She is impatient with his weakness and may be quite willing to lacerate him with her righteous "observations." She is right. She is truly always right and will remind you of that. She can even use what is right and good information to wound and confuse and then she will rise up as the victor. With her foot on his chest, she is dead right.

Over and over, her man is repelled. Over and over, he is unable to get through to the best in her. She is too complicated for him. So he boils with a steady anger, or he just gives up like the suitors in the fairy tale—impaled on the thorns that cause one to "sleep"—to doze away behind his newspaper.

A friend says he finds when a woman is *depressed* she must go back and find where she is *angry*. Then she must learn *how* to express her anger. And when a man feels *angry* he must go back and find where he is *hurt*. Then he must learn how to *weep*.

As the Feminine Side of a Man

Briar Rose, as the manifestation of a man's feminine side, is also prone to a low-grade anger, to curmudgeonly behavior, or to lacerating and poisoned jabs. He will remember every injustice and flaunt his barbs. He can be so delicate and touchy and overly sensitive that he cannot interact with his women or he uses his touchiness to keep them away and tyrannizes people with his moods. He is invaded with a generalized discontent.

One may hotly argue his rights to the ownership of lethal weapons and guns, which have more to do with his defensive feelings about what he harbors out of his own sight: his weakness or vulnerability and his need of wounding weapons to validate his threatened masculinity.

Collectively, a community or a nation does the same thing by putting more energy into protective measures—night watchmen, supervisors, police protection—than into human services or even production. A nation may spend seventy-five percent of its budget on defense because it wants to protect a level of material well-being that its elites demand and is, in fact, reaching its limits.

So when the masculine elements of a society or the man himself are immature and afraid of feminine value, they may strut around showing their missiles—or drive around in trucks with gun racks, or trump their towers and flash whatever they own in hopes that theirs is the biggest.

Another man may just clam up in his idyllic ivory tower and become unreachable. He barricades himself behind his books, his statistics, his experiments, his terribly important work—but what is feeling and tender, relational and vulnerable, in him is buried under it all.

Or he may unwittingly choose to live in splendid isolation, daring—even begging—someone to be equal to him. Once there was a gifted man, creative, intelligent, who prized his efficiency and his clear, direct thinking. As an administrator he was an unquestionable success. He got things done promptly and perfectly. His office and surroundings were starkly elegant. Clean. Cold. Perfect. This man also had a powerful feminine side which was the basis for his very good taste, his clever verbal skills, his fine imagination and his gracious, polished manners.

When this same man was in a foul mood, however, he didn't pound the table and storm around—he became icily demanding, superior, critical and right. Impeccably and infallibly right.

With a few well-chosen words he could pierce, cleanly, coldly and devastatingly, any person who brought in his or her work which he found lacking in any manner.

With a single, well-aimed sting, he paralyzed his prey and wrapped this person deftly at the center of his web—all before his prey even knew there was a web or that he or she was anyone's prey. On the phone, a woman repeated a question and received a withering reply in clipped and mincing tones— if she would now listen to him, he would repeat himself once more. "But only once more—are you ready to listen this time?"

Many good people who worked for him in his department withered and left their encounters with this man bewildered about what really happened. They felt sliced into pieces, inept, stupid, childish—some said bumbling and clumsy; one said, "all thumbs—with fingerprints." Most said they felt uncannily *compelled*—and only with regard to him—to become inept and inefficient over and over again. They all felt hurt and angry. By the next encounter, they entered his presence afraid, or steaming with determination to stand up to him this time. But their boss treated these occasions as contests, which he always won, hands down, and coolly—his victim again defeated and licking wounds.

The people in the department, even though it made them feel guilty, talked about him. "Watch it! Himself is at it today!" They protected each other and compared their war wounds; they traded insights to see if they might crack his pattern of behavior. All the while, he reigned in his marbled suites in icy, splendid isolation.

Though women were the more likely to be caught in his thorns, men were not exempt. One day one of the men in the department received a curt and cold message accusing him, most unreasonably, of a delay with a report. The fellow was angry—very angry. He felt how much he wanted to go in there and blow up all over the map—tell that so-and-so where to hop it! But, owing to an incredible wisdom, he was also determined to be strong, kind and vulnerable.

He grabbed a friend and role-played several times how he would come into the boss's office, state his position clearly and honestly and also tell his boss how he felt when he was treated unfairly—that he was angry. But he would not blow up in an angry, generalized outburst and finally pay his boss back. He was determined that this time he was going to do this well: there would be no winners, but there would be no losers either. He practiced his "I" statements—never accusing his boss or calling him on what he did, but rather always going back to how he himself felt. This was an exercise, he figured, that both of them needed. He needed to present himself with strength, but not as the enemy. He was going to be large enough not to pay the man back—large enough not to have to win at this game.

He then sheathed himself in what he called his "imaginary, magic net." He covered himself from top to toe and closed it tightly at both ends. Inside this enclosure, he was clear, honest and not vindictive. He knew exactly who he was. His vision was not obscured and he was not hard or defensive. Anything that passed out of him and through this net would pass through a mesh of grace that made everything understanding and honest, fair and, yes, even kind. Any spears that would be hurled against him, any barbs or briars, could not enter and hurt him through this net. Barbs would remain his boss's problem and not his own.

The young man's consciousness—even the compassion he suddenly found in himself—allowed him to encounter his boss and, indeed, reach him as he could hardly have believed. He laughs and says that now he shares his magic net and its "user's manual" with his fellow staff members. They figure they all still have a way to go, but they are clearly on the way to making the briars bloom!

It is paramount to remember that when two people start pitching spears at each other—when two such Briar Roses have a "lovers' quarrel"—it can be a horrible, slashing, hurting thing that has no solution but for one of them to be strong enough to call a truce—*which is not rolling over and playing dead*. It is being strong enough to pass the test that a Briar Rose unwittingly offers the world, over and over again. *It means being strong enough—to die!* To die "on the inside."

The Art of Turning the Other Cheek

Every one of the thorns in which we wrap ourselves is tipped with the poison of revenge. And each thorn functions by its own law of "an eye for an eye"—a death for a death. We inherited the poisoned spines from the old woman who poisoned us and the father who built our tower. Though the rest of the kingdom has dried up, these thorns have continued to grow, thick and strong, for "one hundred years." Before those thorns can give way and open themselves to what is delicate and vulnerable, we must recognize that such a primal law of revenge is alive and well and growing strong even into the present age and into our own experience.

Clearly, we are not going to settle so easily for injury or injustice and just turn the other cheek. Jungian writer Helen Luke says:

> The first step is surely to rid ourselves of the idea that we have outgrown the law of "an eye for an eye." We have to expose the delusion that, to forgive our enemies in accord with Christian ethic, it is only necessary to behave in an outwardly civilized manner, without bothering about what our repressed fury is doing. Every time we are hurt or angry or resentful toward a person, a circumstance or even a material thing, a desire to inflict an equivalent hurt is born, however unconscious we may be of it. We have suffered a little death and the desire to kill follows, for it is the nature of the psyche to seek always a restored balance. (*Woman Earth and Spirit*, pp. 98–99.)

Better, says Luke, to have a blazing row than to think you can come to any such easy settlement. A *true* "turning of the other cheek" is first to recognize our primal drive to pay back every hurt and then to willingly accept "the necessary death within our selves." To take on a death in this way, says Luke, is the only way to prevent inflicting it on the other—consciously or unconsciously.

Our story seems to tell us that the forgotten goddess's compulsion for revenge, her law of a death for a death, can be redeemed only by the new woman, Briar Rose, whose very woundedness will eventually prove redeeming. *The wounded woman herself redeems the ones who wounded her. The wounded feminine value redeems the whole kingdom and culture.*

As wounded women, we will have to recognize the fact that the other one's guilt is also, in a deep sense, our own. We finally grasped that spindle to ourselves. And so we must also agree, as Luke says, even as we suffer legitimate resentment, "to pay the price, to die a little to the demand for justification and immunity."

It seems that Briar Rose is required to be exactly what we defined her as incapable of being. The unconscious conscious one. As in the variation of the Handless Maiden story, where the hero, to save her child from drowning in the river, is required to grab him, but with her stumps, so now Briar Rose in all her passivity and weakness is required to be strong enough to pay a price and die on the right level. She who sleeps is to wake up to a death.

Chapter 27

THE TOWER AS COFFIN
AND NUPTIAL BED

Touch Me, Touch Me Not

. . . the sun is shrunk, the heavens are shrunk
Away into the far remote; and the trees & mountains withered
Into indefinite cloudy shadows in darkness & separation.
By invisible hatreds adjoined, they seem remote and separate
From each other; and yet are a mighty polypus in the deep.
As the mistletoe grows on the oak, so Albion's tree on
      eternity. Lo,
He who will not commingle in love, must be adjoined by hate!
(William Blake, *Jerusalem, the Emanation of the Giant Albion*.)

The polypus clings to its stone as the sacred mistletoe clutches a tree—as briars embrace the tower. It is a parasite with poison in its tentacles. Blake makes the poisonous polypus and the spreading, clutching Tree of Mystery a single entity. And so, it seems, is every symbol in our story: a partnership of bitter and sweet. Of curse and blessing. Of attraction and repulsion. Of rose and thorn. Of life and death.

From her father, Briar Rose learned early that being a sexually mature woman was life threatening. "She's cute now, but just wait till she's fifteen! Burn all the spinning wheels in the kingdom!" How else can she maintain her beauty and innocent youth and avoid death but by "Rooting over with/ thorns and stems/The buried soul and all its gems"? (Blake, *The Everlasting Gospel.*)

In a narcissistic withdrawal she retreats into chilly isolation, behind glass, under thorn, into her head, in her manner of dress, behind a mask, playing dead. Briar Rose is fascinated with death. And denies death.

> We thought her dying when she slept,
> And sleeping when she died.
>   (Thomas Hood, *The Death-Bed.*)

There are other interesting variations of the Briar Rose story that tell us how invasive that deathlike sleep can be in a Briar Rose's life. When the princess in one of these stories gets a fateful splinter of flax caught under her fingernail, she falls "dead upon the ground." Her father places her seated on a velvet chair in the castle, locks the door on her, on the memory, and leaves forever. Years later a young king goes falconing. He wanders into the wood that has grown up around the castle. The falcon flies into a window of the abandoned castle and the king goes in to retrieve it. There he finds the beautiful princess asleep. Nothing wakes her. But he is so taken with her beauty that he makes love to her and then goes off and forgets about her. Still she sleeps. Nine months later she gives birth to twins. She keeps on sleeping! The babies crawl all over her and nurse—while she sleeps. One day, when one of the babies cannot find her breast, he sucks on her finger and draws out the fateful splinter, whereupon the princess finally wakes up. Her trials, however, have only begun, for the story then continues in a manner very similar to the Handless Maiden story.

Sometimes a girl/woman sleeps through her father relationship, through her coming of age, through her courtship and wedding, through her sexual experience, her giving birth to children, all the developmental stages of her growing womanhood, all the religious experiences that belong especially to feminine spirituality—all the experiences that might wake and heal her are lost—that is, until *the time is right for her*. Then she wakes up one day to her body, as receiver and giver of life and food, love and care.

> Food is shut in within our bodies as in a very beautiful purse. When necessity calls, the purse opens and then shuts again, in the most fitting way. And it is God who does this. (Dame Julian of Norwich.)

For a Briar Rose, this second version of the story tells us, sexual and spiritual maturity will come in discovering the physical, passionate, sexual, caring, creative, and life-giving part of herself. Like her sister, the Handless Maiden, who receives back feeling hands for having felt for her child, so Briar Rose learns that, in giving life, she also receives it. Suddenly she is awake to everything and everyone with a passionate love and concern and sees all that needs her care and containment. She discovers the holy sacramentality of her own body and blood. As *mater,* on whatever level, she comes to see the holiness of all matter.

But the process of waking may also wake her to all the painful experiences that caused her to sleep so long in the first place.

Numbing

Children cannot process painful experiences. They repress and anesthetize feelings which are too dreadful to live with, in order to have the energies they need to deal with the daily problems in life. Painful experiences, however, never die; they lie dormant in the unconscious and wait. One day, especially at crucial developmental junctures, they will resurface to be dealt with again.

We can deal with these painful issues in two ways: through neurotic symptoms and behaviors which are a vain attempt to put the issues to sleep again. Or we can recall them, choosing to suffer their reality with consciousness.

Sometimes the numbing sleep of an adolescent is expressed in suicide attempts. She does something to herself, denying the possibility that this sleep may be permanent, and thinks only to "sleep through" some issues that she doesn't know how to address or that she inherited from her mother's unlived life. Too sensitive to the father's sexual feelings, she may become an actual victim of sexual molestation. How can she survive such pain but by not feeling it, not feeling anything at all?

Sometimes a Briar Rose and her mother may develop an uncanny fusion that causes them to become undifferentiated. Their sexual feelings merge. The mother is in love with the daughter's boyfriend. Or the daughter is delivered to the father's sexual energies. A Briar Rose may be drawn into a compulsive promiscuity by which she asks, "Am I alive?" and repeats and repeats the father's wound to see if this time it will no longer kill but wake her. Or perhaps she will try to look like a pure, acceptable snowdrop. Acceptable, but under glass. Or a goddess, so superior that she is out of reach. Or a living image of the man's perfect inner feminine, arrested in youth—denying age and death.

A Briar Rose may also feel that she must never die. Obsessed with removing her wrinkles and fretting about her graying hair, she says that she is still young. She may become addicted to cosmetics or cosmetic surgery. She finds herself acceptable only as the eternal spring. She cannot die, because she has not yet lived. Her body is something to control and pinch and punish, and fear and criticize and be obsessed with—and not the worthy, ever changing housing of her spirit. Or she may invest all her energies in her adolescent daughter, living through her, contaminating the daughter's development with her own unlived life. With that, the cycle is continued, theme and variation, in the daughter.

If the adolescent is not helped to get to the bottom of her fear and despair and to suffer it consciously, she can do untold harm to herself and her surroundings, only to store up the pain for its reemergence later. She may dance with death and ward it off by pursuing hobbies—or careers, later—where she can look death in the face. Anything from riding with a motorcycle gang to thinking about a career in medicine. If the career does not become the framework for her own healing, she may repeat the suicide attempts at crucial intervals of her development or become seriously depressed.

In a "worst case scenario," the adolescent, overwhelmed by painful experiences and the current deep feelings of her adolescent transformation, may look for the sleep of a Briar Rose, courting death by inching toward it. She wants to avoid suffering. She wants no insight, just the pure, chilled, clicking of her mind. No feelings but the airy lightness of being. No responsibility for what she is becoming, just the thrill of the driest abstraction. She seeks out a style of living which is nearly nonliving. She flirts with death.

In love with the beauty of death, she will wear black and whiten her face and think herself beautiful, a body arrested in snow-white, bloodless perfection. She must not bleed. It was forbidden. Perfect grades, perfect mind, perfect clothes, perfect fingernails, perfect taste, perfect foods—that she will not eat herself—perfect control. Perfectly passive. A goddess, exquisite, shimmering, a transparent skeleton under glass. Perfect. Perfectly dead.

Black clothes and a white face, sunken cheeks and green around the eyes, the look of death warmed over is a "fashion statement." A tall, sleek, knife-sharp woman leaned over her white daughter—mirror image of herself: "Just a few more pounds off and your cheekbones will be perfect. When we get you out of this hospital we'll bring you back to the agency in Milan." Bones. Stretched skin over bones. The child was all feeding tubes and bones.

> Forgive us our trespasses as we forgive those who trespass against us.

> At some point . . . (the boys) dreamed of . . . buying Snow-White from the dwarfs; we (the girls) aspired to become that object of every necrophiliac's lust—the innocent, *victimized* Sleeping Beauty, beauteous lump of ultimate, sleeping good. Despite ourselves, sometimes knowing, unwilling, unable to do otherwise, we act out the roles we were taught. (Andrea Dworkin, as quoted by Jack Zipes in *Fairy Tales and the Art of Subversion*. New York: Methuen, 1983.)

While Dworkin says the fairy tale world taught us our roles—and I add that being weaned on Disney's romantic kitsch certainly didn't help us—to see fairy tales as merely the conscious concoction of a culture designed to form little girls into a certain kind of oppressed woman is too simplistic and, frankly, paranoid. It is to forget the question: and what unconscious source feeds storytellers their symbolic language? Why the same themes over and over and in almost every culture?

But to recognize in the fairy tale a truth so old about our human developmental cycles that it can only be traced in myth and symbol is to know that the ancient stories also are capable of warning us about the spells we tend to fall under, the places we get stuck and the heroic deeds we must perform in growing up that will break the spells and set us free. We ourselves taught the fairy tales to speak out about our oldest nature. We, in telling our stories, beg the stories to feed back to us some meaning and salvation.

The Hundred Years of Solitude

The Gospel feeds us meaning. It uses nature to tell us of our human nature: "Unless a grain of wheat dies, itself remains alone." And yet, in nature, there are seeds and spores that "sleep"—even for thousands of years—waiting until the conditions are right to burst again into life. The therapist knows the wisdom of the "therapeutic silence." Nothing seems to be happening. Nothing can be applied from the outside. One does not pick at the shell of a hatching chick. Sleep, darkness, containment, formation have their own season.

She Who Must Die

It is a narrow line we walk between "being the victim" and "taking up our cross." We can just lean back and go unconscious, or we can stretch out arms to put the old person and her doings to death and rise as a new being because we recognize that we are made in the image of God. The cross is paradox, bitter and sweet. Fasting can be the spiritual exercise that alters consciousness and sharpens the mind. It can become a religious experience in its own right. And it can kill. It killed the hard, sharp, brilliant soul in Simone Weil.

". . . I have a body/and I cannot escape from it. . . . /It is written on the table of destiny that I am stuck here in human form." Anne Sexton looked to an alien God to rescue her from herself. A "masculine" theology puts God almost entirely out of reach—far away and out there. A "feminine" theology allows us to know something of God in the very stuff of nature. To believe in incarnation is to know God as "embodied." Sexton couldn't find the God inside her, the God so close as to be familiar. She killed herself.

And it is true, we must die. And generally we are cowards about death. Our intellectualism is a trick to sleep us through our deaths, rather than feel death's sting. The Briar Rose in us would rather go limp all over, pass out. She would rather die than *feel* death. She will use her brain, or chase after power, rather than feel. She tried to talk the Handless Maiden into getting a job or going back to school instead of weeping around. But the Handless Maiden had the gift of tears. Her living tears carried her through until her feeling hands grew back.

We need to die an infinite number of times to practice that final act of a Great Death. We wave goodbye to our dear friend at the airport. We paper the bathroom with our rejection slips: the death of possibilities. We close off the day in our night prayers and die to controlling everything around us. We die when we discover that marriage isn't the romantic ideal we thought we could design. We die when we send the people we love to live their own lives. Unrequited love, longing, loneliness, loss, physical infirmities, old age—we die and the whole creation groans and travails together with us.

> I Dye Alive . . .
> I live but such a life as ever dyes;
>   I dye, but such a death as never endes;
> My death to end my dying life denyes,
>   And life my living death no whitt amends.
> Thus still I dye, yet still I do revive;
>   My living death by dying life is fedd;
> Grace more than nature keeps my hart alive,
>   Whose idle hopes and vague desires are deade.

Not where I breath, but where I love, I live;
    Not where I love, but where I am, I die;
The life I wish, must future glory give,
    The deaths I feele in present daungers lye.
(From Robert Southwell, martyred in 1594 at
age 24. Quoted in R. H. Blyth, *Zen in English
Literature and Oriental Classics*.)

Our knowledge—no, our *experience*—of death teaches us
about life. Our experience of life teaches us about death. And
when we waken to the death that we are meant to experience,
we will also waken to life—we will finally taste what it is to
live in "eternity's glad sunrise."

Chapter 28

THE TOWER AS
RELIGIOUS FORMATION

The Cult

Even as we try to free ourselves from the prison of cultic and cultural impositions on the feminine—trying to escape what the contemplative monk Thomas Merton called the undramatic, absurd obscurity of religious contemplation—we displace what was religion and religious form. And with that we create a huge religious vacuum. The vacuum sucks in a thousand substitutions—neurotic behaviors, symptoms, superstitions, "religious behaviors" meant to quiet the need without engaging it. New cults stand ready to replace old ones.

Cults appeal directly to the religious vacuum in our culture; and women, who have been afraid to live outside of their intelligence, or who were raised with little religious form, are especially vulnerable to them. Cults move in where the defenses are weakest or where the need is greatest. They offer archetypes: the power of the group, of rituals, music, or magic stones. They return the power of story through the Bible or Eastern wisdoms or "messages from other lives." They provide "spiritual directors" and spiritual or occult forms of communication with the unconscious. They provide the comfort of answers where one does not risk a question.

Being touched where she has been asleep and bonding to others through emotional experiences have a powerful effect on the woman who has been a stranger to her own inner world. Suddenly, mysterious messages are heard—but are taken literally. Brave seekers, lonely women, grandmothers, widows at loose ends, are drawn in and are, in turn, fleeced of their earthly possessions by the cult which has convinced them to "give everything to God."

The Mystic's Tower

> In practice the way to contemplation is an absurdity so obscure that it is no longer even dramatic. There is nothing left in it that can be grasped and cherished as heroic or even unusual. And so, for a contemplative there is a supreme value in the ordinary routine of work and poverty and hardship and monotony that characterize the lives of all the poor and uninteresting and forgotten people in the world. (*Thomas Merton.*)

A mystic's vision, then, of ultimate liberation from the tower's confinement is to reenvision the tower as that which informs with grace and freedom our most ordinary tasks and actions. The freedom in autonomy is not doing what you like. It is liking what you do. It is to see that all that we have labeled as "drudgery" is also the way to the contemplation of Mystery. The poor, the forgotten, the uninteresting, the nonpowerful, the dirt under our feet—this poor body that we have taken for granted or neglected and despised is exactly the housing of our spiritual transformation. *Here* all dwell free.

"Masculine spirituality" has led many away from the God under our feet. ". . . I have a body/and I cannot escape from it . . . I am stuck here in human form," lamented Anne Sexton. Then the agony becomes looking to that which is only beyond you—to be rescued one day from yourself. But the mystic, Meister Eckhart, knew better:

Earth cannot escape heaven, flee it by going up, or flee it by going down, heaven still invades the earth, energizes it, makes it sacred.

Or Dame Julian, again:

God does not despise creation, nor does God disdain to serve us in the simplest function that belongs to our bodies in nature. . . . As the body is clothed in cloth and the muscles in the skin and the bones in the muscles and the heart in the chest, so are we, body and soul, clothed in the Goodness of God and enclosed.

Women's spirituality, but especially feminine spirituality, has been asleep and out of touch for a very long time because masculine spirituality sent us all looking beyond ourselves—beyond our human experience, the ground under our feet, our absurd obscurity, our poverty and monotony, our very bodies—to hope for a salvation which might only come from a distant beyond to wake and rescue us.

I gave a lecture to a class of university students recently and in groping around for an example of the awakening experience of a most ordinary chore—perhaps one that put us in touch with one of the elements of nature—I seized on the chore of cleaning their cars.

"I could imagine," I began, "that those of you who have cars might also be feeling vaguely guilty at the moment for their condition. The need to clean the car nibbles at one from behind. It is an annoying task. It's a waste of time. You've got better things to do.

"But imagine, now, that you decided to approach the task with open eyes and arms, that is, without ambivalence. You put on your old shoes and your old clothes, gather up pails of soapy water and clear water. Get all the right rags and sponges together, and cleaners and wax. Haul out the cumbersome vacuum cleaner with its cords and hoses. Then you set to work. First the inside. Straighten the glove compartment. Throw out the candy wrappers and cups. The floor looks worse than the bottom of a bird cage! You feed the vacuum nozzle into the car and flick on the switch and you feel a surge of energy go through your hands and the satisfying suck of the machine. Then the good sounds: the plink and chinkle of sand and grit rushing up into the hose. You wipe down the dash, 'feed it' with that stuff that makes it shine . . . clean windows inside, now outside. Sponge, slop suds—in and out of the pails of water—sloshing, sometimes scraping, a rinse, a wipedown with dry rags. Now you rub in buttery polish and rub up a gloss. . . ."

That certain hush had settled over the hall—the students utterly engrossed. They soaked in every detail, so that by the time I had them turn their backs on the car and return to the house with their rags and pails I wondered, myself, what might happen next.

"You put everything away where it belongs. (There's the mother in me.) Rinse out the rags and hang them to dry—and bump into your roommate in the kitchen. 'Hey,' you say, 'I just had a religious experience—I washed my car!' "

With that the students burst into loud laughter. With a feeling discharge, they concluded—even vicariously—a laughably ordinary task. For some few minutes they had slipped, not into levitation, but down, down into soapsuds and clear water, into muscle action and polish, into a deep, pregnant place, so rich that they couldn't even move. There, the ordinary becomes transformed, transparent. Grace, immanent and transcendent.

> Think of the soul as a vortex or a whirlpool and you will understand how we are to sink eternally from negation to negation into the One. (*Meister Eckhart.*)

That women have a powerful need and ability in the spiritual realm is just as it should be. The shape and power of woman's spirituality is being recognized again and that she "serve time in a tower" as a religious exercise seems to be a time-honored tradition in myths and legends. It seems to tell us something about the psychic and spiritual development of women. The tower as a religious form has, when it is archetypally sound, all the ingredients necessary for a formation toward wholeness. Such formation must be rooted in what is ancient and larger than we are, even while it is profoundly simple and routine. Religious formation is often built of the stones under our feet: "the ordinary routine of work and poverty and hardship and monotony."

We need containment as we grow, as a caterpillar needs a cocoon. Eastern religions provide it. Jewish law and rituals provide it. In Western Christianity, the structure of the sacred liturgy, the cycles of feasts and fasts, Scripture, the structure of marriage as a sacramental way to holiness, the Holy Rule of Benedict, the Ignatian Spiritual Exercises, the spiritual and corporal works of mercy—all these are tower structures of great power—with a measure of monotony—and are particularly formative and safeguarding in a society without edges.

The tower as a spiritual formation, to do its work, must keep us "for a hundred years." Routine and monotony make time crawl. Wordsworth said: "Suffering is permanent, obscure, and dark, and shares the nature of infinity." But the stories and legends tell us that Briar Rose is contained and strengthened in her tower for a hundred years. Zeus enters through the skylight of the tower where the king of Argos has imprisoned his daughter and rains down gold on her. Rapunzel, in her tower, stays long enough to grow a useful head of healthy hair. St. Barbara's imprisonment in her father's tower allows her, too, to grow the long hair of creative ideas, and to become holy and strong.

To feel caught in a tower and trapped may also be the invitation to have a "room of one's own"—a place designed for healing what has been wounded in us. It may have the same properties as the little house over whose door it is written: HERE ALL DWELL FREE. We can learn to love that room of our own, or we can spend our energy trying to enter the "men's room." We can use that room of our own to nourish our deepest feminine nature, or we make a prison of that place when we bang our heads against the walls of desire—of wanting, of need for power or recognition. Not wanting anything, that is the trick.

Enlightenment frees us from the walls of painful desire. But containment will give form to too much liberty. Wordsworth loved the rules that bind a sonnet. He saw their containment as an enclosed chunk of heaven.

Nuns fret not at their convent's narrow room;
And hermits are contented with their cells;
And students with their pensive citadels;
Maids at the wheel, the weaver at his loom
Sit blithe and happy; bees that soar for bloom,
High as the highest Peak of Furness-fells,
Will murmur by the hour in fox-glove bells;
In truth, the prison, unto which we doom
Ourselves, no prison is; and hence for me,
In sundry moods, 'twas pastime to be bound
Within the Sonnet's scanty plot of ground;
Pleased if some Souls (for such there needs must be)
Who have felt the weight of too much liberty,
Should find brief solace there, as I have found.
(William Wordsworth, "Nuns Fret Not at Their Convent's Narrow Room.")

Teresa of Avila, the mystic who wrote *Interior Castle*, said of her room: "We can make use only of a single cell—what do we gain by its being very large and well built? What indeed? We have not to spend all our time looking at the walls."

Her books were written at the command of her confessors, and she dreaded writing. At first she thought herself much better off at the spinning wheel. Irked, she said: "For the love of God, let me work at my spinning-wheel and go to choir and perform the duties of the religious life, like the other sisters. I am not meant to write: I have neither the health nor the intelligence for it." And she proceeded to write. The most natural and human and unstuffy, unbounded books, that also happened to be filled with genius and mystical experience—God's self-disclosure, shared.

On a foggy morning in Brantwood, England, poking through John Ruskin's drawings and writings, I came upon this observation, which was his philosophy as much as it is the vocation of any teacher or healer or prophet, or "doctor of the Church," or woman or man waking to a new life:

The greatest thing a human soul ever does in this world is to *see* something, and tell what it *saw* in a plain way. Hundreds of people can talk for one who can think, but thousands can think for one who can see. To see clearly is poetry, prophecy, and religion, all in one.

Von Franz reminds us that, even in the misogynous Catholic Church, there have been many women who assume the role of the priest *through the spirit of their personality,* and though they do not have the title, they have the role. And there is, indeed, an energetic new interest in those women who knew about the unsung priesthood they practiced by right of their baptism: Teresa of Avila, Catherine of Siena, Scholastica, Julian of Norwich, the two Mechthilds and the two Gertruds, Hildegard of Bingen—who called herself the reed through which God blew his song. Of these spinners and writers, these pray-ers and painters and poets, only two have been called doctors of the Church and we are glad for that much—but it is also true that most saints and mystics we may never hear from. For holy work is so often like a sand painting, laid out with care and detail, and, having served, then scatters all its blessings in the wind.

The sand painting is the form that dissipates when it has done its work. The reed is the unstopped container for the song. The tower, when it is a scaffolding to build within, is a right and honorable place in which to be spiritually formed.

Chapter 29

WHEN THE
TIME IS RIPE

Eventually—after about a hundred years or so—one must also be transformed. Briar Rose, in her mystical marriage of healing and wholeness, will leave that tower. The daughter of Argos leaves the prison tower, showered with gold and pregnant with Perseus. Rapunzel hauls in her salvation by the hair of her own head and is freed. Barbara, after developing a deeply spiritual life in the prison of her father's tower, is flung out of it by the hair of her head. The bindings of mutual projections in a marriage burst and the relationship is transformed by a deeper, holier love. "When the time is right," the tower is outgrown. Formation moves to transformation and the old tower is abandoned as an outgrown shell. The old, outdated order is no longer able to meet the conditions of the new life.

When the time is right, roses bloom, briars part, doors open, the king's son happens by. The new opportunity always seems to come at the right moment of maturity and readiness. The answer comes to you. The friend arrives out of the blue. The right partner comes along. The job op-

portunity opens. Walls tumble between east and west. The
windows are flung open to a living theology.

> Come you whom my Father has blessed, take for your her-
> itage the kingdom prepared for you since the formation of
> the world. (*Matt. 25:34*.)

The Prince, Humanly Speaking

> *Then the youth said, "You can speak to me of dreadful thorns
> and death by sticking, and yet I will not be afraid. I will go and
> see the beautiful Briar Rose." The old man's efforts to dissuade the
> youth were of no avail. The young man would not listen to the old
> man's words.*
> *But by this time the fated hundred years had just come to an end.
> The day had come when Briar Rose was to wake again. When the
> King's son approached the thorny hedge, it was covered in nothing
> but beautiful, fragrant roses. These parted from each other of their
> own accord and so let the young man pass unhurt.*

Hundreds of Kings' sons have hung themselves up on her
briars, but only one arrives who is "not afraid." Is it *because* he
is not afraid that the thorns part of their own accord? Or *because*
the thorns part, he need not be afraid? I expect that both are
true. Loving and being loved are both the possibility and the
cure when the spell is broken. "Perfect love casts out fear."
Maybe the frog from the beginning of our story has finally

turned into a man? A man conquers his mother complex by entering a man's world. He sheds his ambivalence, he makes decisions and takes a stand and is not held back by the warnings or the viewpoint of his "old man" or of the many generations that went before him. But to be clever or well educated, to be "successful," to have brawn and swagger and daring and worldly skills among men still do not make him a real man.

He too has to wake up to his own feeling and know his full worth. Or he will be halfway up the tower and his mom will call him home again. (If he looks anything like the Disney image of that mincing California beach boy in Superman's cape, I know she will.)

For the prince is more likely to be charmingly flat-footed, he may be bald and have a middle-aged spread, he may have a shirt pocket filled with pens, but on the inside there is nothing flat-footed about him. He knows how to deal with and express his negative feelings as well as his positive ones. Roses or thorns, he can handle them. It is his own energy and sense of liberation that has him clambering up this tower—he's not doing this because his mom told him to be a good scout. He has the brawny masculinity that makes him strong of heart. He is stronger than the barbed fortress towering before him.

Where all his predecessors have fallen in defeat, where the old man warns that all is useless just because *he* has given up, where there is no longer any living memory of hope but only a legacy of failure, yet he is not afraid. Not this time: because he's probably in his middle years by now and all his predecessors were actually he, himself, in his more immature attempts at relationship—or his immature attempts to gain a relationship with the feminine side of himself. He bears the scars of all the attempts that went before.

So the time is right for him too—he is ready to understand what's going on here. He trusts he can work out the combination to entry. He knows that this barrage of words or this stony silence or this thorny exterior is first a need to be heard and understood. He is fully open to that. Perhaps what none of the princes before him understood was how to interpret a confused appeal to be "seen through" and won over. He will not allow himself to become lacerated on the thorns of her defensive manner, nor wither, nor rave, nor slash. He only has to be willing—to die for her!

It takes strength and virtue (a word related to manly) not to react in kind but to function out of patient, gentle, empathic relatedness. Paradoxically, he must be manly enough to be more feminine than she is! The hero's task is to woo and wake and win what is vulnerable in the other *by offering what is vulnerable in himself.* He has gotten this far because he has a good strong ego. But now he must sacrifice his dearest ego and die to it. With that, the thorns will part and the roses bloom.

Perhaps there was a pruning hook, that tool of symmetry and art, that sharp tool of self-criticism and comparison that cuts through intellection and knows, finally, with the knowledge of the heart? Perhaps the many who climbed the tower before him were ill equipped and not sure what it was they sought, and this prince, for whom the thorns part, already brings that which he seeks?

Time Ripened, Culturally-Morally-Religiously

Julian of Norwich said in her *Revelation of Divine Love,* "To seek God without already having Him is of all things the most impossible." For however could this moment of marriage and unity come into existence except with vision and the grace of God? And are, perhaps, the poor dead suitors and all the rest of the men and women in history heroes, too, for having paved the way and worked for a value and died in an attempt to awaken the kingdom to equality and justice? To hasten the ripening of time?

> If they come for the innocent without stepping over our bodies, cursed be our religion and our life. (*Dorothy Day, Catholic pacifist.*)
> We will go before God to be judged, and God will ask us, "Where are your wounds?" And we will say, "We have no wounds." And God will ask, "Was there nothing worth fighting for?" (*Allan Boesak, anti-apartheid activist.*)

Time Ripens with Every Incarnation

The prophet precedes the people through the twisted, thorny vines we still grapple with in our culture. For we are still confused about how heaven and earth are different. And how they are equal. And how they can "marry."

The Christian mystery of the incarnation is that very concept revealed. In the marriage of heaven to earth, the two great opposites unite. God the heavenly Father has through His Spirit impregnated Mary, woman of this earth. Through that mystery, our humanity is made Godlike and God is expressed through what is thoroughly human. All creation is made worthy and perfected through God's presence within it. Material things, earthly matter, the feminine, all are made valuable and equal in this act.

With that, matter is given its rightful place, alongside God: matter is equal in value to the godly, a marriage partner to the divine, a womb of the godly, *but not a God*.

Culturally, morally, religiously, the thick and twisted briars have been growing and entangling us for "a hundred years" because of our lack of experience and belief in the value of our earthly matter as different from but equal to God. We lose track of God when we leave the divine so far out in space that we will never be able to touch something of the Spirit or allow the Spirit to touch our earthly experience. "To seek God without already having Him is of all things the most impossible." Thus, impatient and hungry for something which we've long forgotten, we press matter into being our god. That twisted misperception is the aberration of materialism. We require material things to supply us with ultimate salvation and happiness—and we find that we worship things: some golden calf of the week.

In the Christmas season when the archetypal human need to find God immanent and transcendent floods us, we cannot wait until "the time is ripe" for the revelation of God-with-us. Perhaps that God is not the one we want? Or maybe He will never come? So we go out and buy some god—anything to fill the cavern of our holy need. And on December 26, we sent it back: wrong color, wrong size. Wrong god.

"To seek God without already having Him is of all things the most impossible."

And there is a further thorny twist we become entangled in: when we aren't worshiping the things we crave and want, we also hate matter! We tread the earth and abuse her and think ill of "dirt" and "manure." We rape her forests and poison her seas. We reject huge segments of humanity—all those who cannot vote and have no power, and we make them the lowly, downtrodden and oppressed of our communities. We treat people as we treat the "dirt under our feet." We hate matter. Or we worship her!

But for God's purposes, in the mystery of the incarnation, matter is not too humble and not too high. Matter is worthy *mater*. Woman is fully equal. Mary will bear His Son. Straw and animals, peasant-shepherds and barnyard smells, all that we so quickly think of as worthless or inferior is exactly the setting of God's self-disclosure among us. Until we can awake and *experience* matter as matter, and God as ineffable Mystery, and the two values as equal and married partners, we will not be able to experience God-with-us. The holy in the ordinary.

"To seek God without already having Him is of all things the most impossible."

Chapter 30

THE
AWAKENING

Until we part the tangled, twisted, reversed properties of God and matter—personally, culturally, historically—we'll probably arrange, unwittingly, to suffer one last dreadful pain before we finally get the point. R. H. Blyth cites the following passage and calls it "God's kiss."

> Lord, thy most pointed pleasure take
> And stab my spirit broad awake;
> Or, Lord, if too obdurate I,
> Choose thou, before my spirit die,
> A piercing pain, a killing sin,
> And to my dead heart run them in! (R. L. Stevenson.)

Whatever grace or pain it takes to change an ancient, overgrown system, our fairy tale certainly becomes especially spare and mysterious here. I expect the moment was outrageous and that there were no words to tell it. And so the solution sounds lame, foolish, even infuriating to our ears. No brave deeds? No slain dragons? No trumpets? No fireworks or rolling thunder? Just roses and a kiss? Of course. Words fail and only the kiss remains. It is the ultimate response.

For the thorns, now blooming with roses, part of their own accord, and after the prince enters they close again behind him. He creeps through the rooms of the sleeping castle, he finds and climbs the tower stairs. He comes upon the little room and, seeing the princess as astonishingly beautiful, he loves her and gives her a kiss. Perhaps because of that brave prince . . . perhaps because he loves her . . . perhaps because of his kiss . . . or perhaps simply because at this moment the hundred years are over—in that same instant, *Briar Rose opens her eyes, wakes, and looks at him without fear and with clear eyes.*

> The eye with which I see God is the same eye with which God sees me. (*Meister Eckhart.*)

The union of human sexuality points beyond itself, to every place in our human experience where spiritual and material factors intersect. This is open-eyed consciousness, an embrace of one's own self in all its fullness. In the flesh, we make real the fullness of time. In the marriage of opposites—of masculine and feminine, of heaven and earth, of white and black, of rich and poor—the impossible is made possible and, indeed, salvific. We can see something of the great Mystery without fear and with clear eyes because we have accepted whatever had been forgotten, rejected or ignored as poor, as wounded, as strange, as other.

> He raises the poor from the dust . . . and has exalted the lowly. (*Magnificat.*)

To love what is most repellent in ourselves, to embrace what is dark and frightful and strange, to invite to the party what we don't think we have a plate for, to love as God loves, is to love God in what we least expected to find as holy and divine. Eye has not seen, ear has not heard, nor has it entered our hearts to conceive of the joy of such union of earth to heaven, of self to Self.

The energy and passion of romantic love are continually recycled, sharpened, deepened, translated, transmuted, transformed through our continued personal development.

Maybe it makes sense that the fairy tale is suddenly thin and halting and speechless because what happens now cannot be spelled out, if for no other reason than that we are still learning the words for it—no, still learning to love. And to love as God loves—that love which makes all things equal.

> Love seeketh not itself to please,
> Nor for itself hath any care,
> But for another gives its ease
> And builds a Heaven in Hell's despair.
> (William Blake, *The Clod and the Pebble.*)

> Reflection may make consciousness, but love makes soul.
> (James Hillman, *Lectures on Jung's Typology.*)

With a small turn of the kaleidoscope, an ordinary moment becomes holy. Or we discover that all moments are holy, thorns and roses are all of a piece. This is a moment for the collective awakening of every feminine value. The spell has run its course. Women and the feminine values of receptivity and darkness, earth and moonlight, need no longer interface with the outside world with touchy, hurt feelings or with a touch-me-if-you-dare attitude.

Justice and Peace kiss. Sun and Moon fly down the staircase hand in hand. Masculine and feminine spread through the kingdom as equal powers with different gifts and wake all things to life. Perfect love is a matter of life and death. It is the larger love that contains them both.

The transformation brings about a real world again. When the kingdom wakes up, is it business as usual? Is everything again as it always was? After a transformation everything is exactly as it was, only now it is shot through and shining with Mystery—not just epiphany but diaphany.

"In my Father's house, there are many mansions." But the keys to these can be found only on earth.

All the ordinary things of the kingdom, from the dogs in the yard to the cooks in the kitchen to the fly on the wall, wake and we, in turn, wake to them all as charged, infused with divinity. Heaven and earth, life and death, are a single reality.

> Then I saw a new heaven and a new earth; the first heaven and the first earth had disappeared . . . I heard a loud voice call from the throne . . . "There will be no more death, and no more mourning or sadness . . . Behold, I make all things new." (Revelation 21:1–5.)

Part III

A NEW CREATION

Chapter 31

TELLING OUR OWN STORY

By considering the fairy tales, "The Handless Maiden" and "Briar Rose," we have looked at the healing cycle of two mythic heroes—women whose fates wounded them, and who, through a chosen suffering or through the evolution of a hidden interiority, became autonomous, healed and whole. Thus liberated, each returns to her own realm to function once more out of a renewed vision. Though we looked at only two stories from the rich store of myth and tales available to us, we often found ourselves explained back to ourselves. Certainly we came upon a new view of the healing process of feminine value for our time and culture.

Jung would say that mythic stories explain the archetypal dramas that represent us from the bottom up and unbeknownst to us. They demonstrate to us how our society functions just as they explain our personal mythology.

Jung made the discovery of "his story" paramount in his life: "I asked myself, 'What is the myth you are living?' and found that I did not know 'my' myth, and I regarded this as the task of tasks. . . . I simply had to know what unconscious or preconscious myth was forming me."

Until we know the story that is our own, it will continue to haunt us. Until we wake up to its meaning and the power that archetypes bring to bear on us, we are compelled to repeat its cycles in our lives. Speaking collectively, history, as Santayana put it, for those who do not remember it, is condemned to repeat itself.

The Handless Maiden stopped a cycle of dependencies and is heroic, not for the wounds that fate inflicted on her, but for what she ultimately did with her fate. Whatever the fate or myth, personally or culturally, that forms us, we could not have come away from these stories without having learned that our own experience, too, is not simply what happens to us but what we do with what happens to us.

Our responsibility, then, is to find and know the story that is our own. We then reach out to grapple with it, *choosing* to suffer the conflicts that pull us back into our fate and forward to our true selves. As we become healed and autonomous, we reenter our community and our history, offering our gifts to benefit all and taking our place as cocreators of our personal and communal destinies. All three of these tasks, though developmental in nature, are not necessarily done in stair-step order but cycle around and around, deeper and deeper, as we grow in consciousness and responsibility. All these steps are necessary to being fully alive, feeling, empathic, altruistic adults with a deep sense of the Holy Other as present in the ordinary tasks that make up our days.

Many philosophies, theologies, methods and theories as well as many writers from C. G. Jung to Madonna Kolbenschlag, Sam Keen, David Feinstein and Stanley Krippner challenge individuals to make sense of growing in consciousness, wholeness and transformation through the conceptual paradigm of the Socratic thesis, antithesis and synthesis.*

* Kolbenschlag applies Kierkegaard and Paul Tillich's heteronomy, autonomy and theonomy as a "life map" for the spiritual formation of women and does it with masterful clarity and insight. For a detailed and expanded system of theories, therapies, stages, stories and practical exercises, I recommend Feinstein and

I set forth the same paradigm here, but in its roughest outline, and offer some simple exercises, or considerations, which can be undertaken alone or—better yet—shared with someone you trust to help you on your own journey.

As you read this chapter, you may wish to skim the exercises it contains until you have the leisure, the privacy or the companionship to undertake doing them seriously. But even reading the exercises may trigger insights and questions that you will want to mull over as you go on reading to the conclusion of the book.

Thesis

The thesis is the personal myth into which we are born. It is the personal or historical myth that we must recognize as the fate that we were given. (Sometimes for better, sometimes for worse.) We had no say about the color of our hair, our ethnicity, the names we were given, the nicknames we were called, the traits in us that were encouraged or rejected, the illnesses we suffered or the losses we were compelled to endure. These make up our myth.

And this is the story we will eventually come to recognize as indeed an influence on who we are but as no longer useful, or no longer of service in our coming to adulthood.

The garden of Eden was such a mythic inheritance to Adam and Eve. Each of us knows such an Eden and "remembers" it, though often unconsciously, as the womb of our mother where every need was attended to without question. Perhaps our Eden was an ideal period in childhood when we were carefree, innocent, loved and happy. Such were Briar Rose's first fifteen years of life.

The thesis or myth that we inherited may also have painful and negative realities: poverty, war, physical infirmities, deaths,

---

Krippner's book: *Personal Mythology: Using Ritual, Dreams, and Imagination to Discover Your Inner Story* (Los Angeles: Jeremy P. Tarcher, 1988). Of several books on the subject written by Sam Keen is one he wrote together with Anne Valley-Fox: *Your Mythic Journey* (Los Angeles: Jeremy P. Tarcher, 1973).

issues of psychological survival. Through no fault of our own, or of the family we were born into, we may have inherited a deep spiritual and psychological wound. The Handless Maiden must give up her hands to save her father. Briar Rose will learn to know the curse that came upon her because her father didn't have enough golden plates. If we don't go back and seek out the mythic story that is forming us, then we are compelled to repeat it. We will come to think that what we see through our distorted vision of the objective world is the only view. We are caught in the spell and we repeat our myth unwittingly: we marry partners like our parents. Or we divorce our partners just as our parents divorced. Or we discipline our children just as we were disciplined. We treat the sick and the poor just as we were treated. To know our own story is to find that the pull of gravity into our past is stronger than we thought. To ignore our story is to lose the opportunity to recognize the causes of our woundedness and the inspiration to grab hold of our fate and take responsibility for our own healing process.

- In recalling your personal myth, consider your earliest memories.
  Smells
  Tastes
  Feelings
  Who held you?
  Do you remember your bed?
  Your clothes?
  Your house or garden?
  Your important toys and pets?

- In what role were you cast by your family?
  What did they call you?
  What traits did they see in you and encourage?
  What traits did they see in you and deplore?
  What did your friends call you?
  What were you known for in grammar school among your friends?

What were the rules of home, school or church that you were required to keep?
How did you understand the rules at that time and how were they enforced?

- Draw pictures of these things as you remember them.
- Share your story with a friend.

- Try to remember a myth or fairy tale that you learned as a child. Without looking it up to refresh your memory, write it down as well as you can remember it. Fill it with all the details you can recall.

- Did you have trouble remembering how the story started—how it progressed—how it finished?

- Take this story as you remembered it and compare it, now, with the original story.
  Were you close?
  How had you changed things in your memory?

- How does the story, as you remembered it, match the story of your own life to this point?
- What do your perceived additions or corrections to this story tell you about your own stuck places or resolutions, relationships and desires? This exercise was one that Bruno Bettelheim sometimes used with his students.

- Another interesting exercise is to rewrite the story of your early years as though it were a fairy tale, removing it from your personal parents and history. Ask, rather:
  What garden or kingdom were you born into?
  What role were you to play in this kingdom?
  What were its joys?
  What were its rules?
  What magic food did you eat?
  What taboo did you break?
  Which god was not honored?

Who cast a spell on you?
What was the spell?
Did you pay a price?

This is the period of our enchantment—the time that we
want, on some level, to keep "true" forever. Our enchantment,
whether it was bliss or curse, is often the place where we become
mired in stagnation. We say, "Well, it's true! It's not a myth,
that's what really happened! My aunt beat me with a wooden
spoon every time she didn't like what was going on." If we
say it's "true," then we carry the image of ourselves as the poor
victim who can never change because we lived with a wicked
aunt. There we stagnate. It is almost as if you said, "It's true:
when I was young, Santa Claus came to my house once a year
and brought me wonderful gifts! But when I was six he quit
coming. From there on in, my parents tried to fool me into
believing he still came." We break that stagnation, however,
when we say, "I know something about jealous aunts, jealous
witches. I know something about the archetype of rage and
revenge because I've been there." Or, "I know something about
the archetype of giving gifts in secret and never being found
out." Then you look at your fate as an adult who has created
a connection between a personal fate and the mysteries of the
soul.

Antithesis

In the realm of antithesis, we begin to create the myth that
opposes our personal myth, the anti-myth. We may have been
sent from the garden of Eden because we broke a taboo and
are required to live outside the garden to make a life for ourselves in pain and sweat and hard labor. We have lost our
childlike innocence. How we long to go back to those good
old days in Eden's garden! A cartoon shows an Earthling wandering Mars who comes upon a Martian Eve handing a Martian
Adam an apple; the Earthling rushes between them, shouting,
"No! Don't! Stop! Let me explain!"

Or we are deeply and secretly still sad because Santa Claus

doesn't come anymore and it was "only" our parents who tried to fool us. What's worse, we can't be fooled anymore. Now Christmas never works. We are disenchanted.

THE ADOLESCENT ANTI-MYTH

In adolescence we try to get away from the gravity pull of our original myth. We change the color of our hair and wear clothes that irritate our parents. Or we quit taking piano lessons or going to church because we saw it as a parental thing or an authority issue. Maybe we rejected—or were rejected by—our old dreams, our heritage, our ethnicity, our country—our original fate. We have lost our innocence. This is our anti-myth.

The Handless Maiden leaves the chalk circle of her family and enters the moated garden of her King. There she tries to create her own life. She will not be handless any longer; rather, with silver hands she forgets or suppresses the fate that made her. With silver hands, she can fake it for a while. She tries to be a goddess of sterling gestures, self-determination and responsibility. Briar Rose, with her feminine values on hold, functions as a prickly, correct, upright tower of idealisms and righteous convictions.

- In considering your opposing myth, try to remember the ways in which you were rebellious or independent or idealistic.

- How did your adolescence express your determination not to be the person that others forced you to be through their rules and expectations?

- How were your actions, perhaps, more reactionary or unrealistic than truly autonomous?
  Who were your friends?
  What did they call you?
  What were your hobbies?
  What did your bedroom look like?
  What did you wear?
  Where did you seek warmth and understanding?

Who were your heroes?

What was your dream?

How did you see the world?

After whom did you model yourself?

What was the experience of your disenchantment?

Very likely, our development into autonomy took place amid constant conflict and was filled with anxiety, depressions, guilt and scruples. This is the stage where we want to believe that what happened to us as small children should be both retained *and* rejected. We want the care of our parents and the comforts of home *and* we want to be free of our parents and make our own way. We may want to blame our lives on an aunt for beating us *and* we want to think that we are our own person, building our own life. We may choose the directives offered us by the popular culture in opposition to the directives offered us by home or school or church.

- Write a few pages of diary as though you were the adolescent you once were.

THE ANTI-MYTH OF MIDLIFE

Autonomy, in our culture, seldom comes to completion in adolescence. It takes at least "seven years and seven years," or even "one hundred years." We often find that what we went to sleep on in our adolescence finally wakes up for further consideration in the middle years of our life. The Handless Maiden who kept house and had babies will suddenly need to pursue her unlived life of education or career. The Briar Rose who lived her life in the world and defended herself and her independence will suddenly want to give up that variety of freedom and have babies and perhaps even stay home with them.

The collective value may also drive us to try to do it all: run six miles before dawn, return and make breakfast for the family, dash off to the office to deliver the report and proposal, write the grant, have the power lunch, meet with our committee, dash home—stopping at the grocery store on the way—to make supper, have an intelligent and pleasant conversation with our spouse, listen to the children and help them with their homework, make cookies for the children's class picnic, throw a load in the washing machine, and, of course, be dynamite in bed. A man in these times has equal expectations. The dictates of culture and the latest collective values may become our own without our even noticing.

There are, I suppose, those who can achieve it but many find that autonomy, even after midlife, constantly conflicts with what we *think* life should be and what we *think* we should be able to do. Autonomy—individuality, self-sufficiency, freedom—is often considered by people, and by ideologies and cultures, to be the end goal. But we are never fully autonomous in that sense and can only be dissatisfied at our failure. We feel that we must be responsible for everyone around us. We think that we must fix everything that goes wrong. We protect, rescue and control. We are concerned only with solutions, with answers, with "the bottom line," with performance, with details and with "being right." With the Handless Maiden, we manipulate and expect others to live up to our expectations. We want solutions that cover a vast area and that will reverse history without painful waiting. We like to make our changes from the top down. We think that we must be God. And we do a very poor imitation.

Then we wonder why we feel always so tired, so anxious and afraid. This is the time when disenchantment occurs. We long for the old days when life was simple even while we are determined to make the changes our parents didn't dare to undertake. We can no longer be the person that fate made us and we can't quite make real what society, or our tough expectations, say we should be. We are torn with Hamlet: to be or not to be? We may fall into a depression or suffer a crisis. This is the period that we can prolong forever, or we can see it as our expulsion from a fruitless way and an invitation "into the woods" for our incubation.

- Write or tell the story of your striving for autonomy with its successes and frustrations. In what ways have you taken hold of your own life?

- Find a fairy tale that seems like your story and rewrite it as a short story (in the manner that the story of *Romeo and Juliet* is retold in the musical *West Side Story*).

- Knowing what you do about the myth that formed you and the anti-myth you have been trying to create, write your story as a fairy tale or complete or rewrite the fairy tale you began above as you told the story of your childhood.

- How do you "play God" and try to make changes from the top down?

- Are you often discouraged at the enormity of the problems in this world?

- How have you, as a woman, hoped for men to rescue you on some level? How have you hoped the masculine system would save the culture? How do you blame men or the masculine system for the situation you find yourself in? Have you come to discover the masculine element within you? How does it manifest itself in your life? When does he control you? When does he guide you? Can you give some examples? How feminine do you feel? How do you gather strength in your femininity? Do you think that being feminine rules out being autonomous?

- As a man, how have you hoped that women might rescue you or complete you? How have you blamed them for the situation you find yourself in? What is your attitude and experience with the women's movement? What has it done for you? What are your hopes for it? Have you come to discover the feminine within you? How does she manifest herself in your life as a guide and inspiration? As a witch? How "manly" do you feel? How do you gain strength in your masculinity? Do you think that "hairy-chested" manliness and tenderness cancel each other out?

- How do you resist the change that you need to make?

- In what ways do you go "into the woods" for healing and renewal?

Synthesis

In conceiving a unifying vision of how we were defined and who we are meant to be, we must first bring together the truths of our old myth and our opposing myth and accept something of their conflicting positions, allowing them to overlap. Both realities have contributed to who we are.

John Shea tells of a rite that Native American Hopis perform. The children are gathered in the great earthen kiva as they have always done, year after year, on the feast of the Kachinas. They await the dancing gods as they descend from the mountains and listen to hear the Kachinas approaching with their calling and singing. As the Kachinas draw nearer, they are invited to enter through the hole at the top of the kiva as they have always done, year after year, on this feast. They always come to tell their secret stories, frighten the children with their masks, dance their dances and give their gifts and blessings.

Then one day the children, now become adolescents, gather in the kiva and await the gods. Singing, chanting, bearing their gifts, the children hear the gods approach. They enter the kiva and descend into their midst, but the Kachinas are not dressed in their special robes and masks. The young people see for the first time that the Kachinas are their fathers and uncles and older brothers! Without explanation, the ceremony proceeds as it always has. Then the Kachinas ascend again and disperse.

Thus, disenchanted, the adolescents are wordlessly given a profound religious choice. The revelation shatters a naive faith and they can be distressed and disappointed at having been misled all these years and regret their lost innocence and thrust away the Kachinas as childish. Or they can see this as an invitation into adulthood. They can understand from this ceremony that to be an adult in the community is to play a part in the godly work of the Kachinas. To carry their messages, tell their stories and give their gifts is to make human and incarnational the work of the gods. To emerge out of the hole of the kiva now is an invitation for them to be reborn into adulthood.

To become an adult, then, means that we must go through a disenchantment and enter an initiation, a conversion or a transformation. Our individuality is no longer the central issue of our myth, for to be disenchanted is to move beyond self-sufficiency to self-transcendence. We are invited to the experience of mystery, of transcendence, of faith, of a spirituality or sacramentality which imbues all life with meaning. We are not independent. We are interdependent. Willfulness and power, rebellion and self-centeredness give way to the will of One who is Mystery.

Both the Handless Maiden and Briar Rose because of their woundedness lost out on the experience of living—life passed them by. But after their transformations they gained the meaning of life. Most particularly the Handless Maiden gained the religious meaning of life. Thus oriented to divine mystery, all that is undertaken is colored with meaning. Here one is no longer torn between conflicting realities—handless/silver-handed, goddess/witch, baby/God, passive/aggressive—but is a human cocreator with divine Mystery in the building of a new Eden. As human, as vulnerable and imperfect, we drop our poor imitations of God and thereby become truly Godlike.

The new Eden is now understood as the kingdom of God. It is our privilege as beings—fully human—to help in creating that kingdom. We no longer feel responsible *for* others but are responsible *to* others. We try to be empathic, compassionate, encouraging, generous, honest, sensitive, attentive. We relate, person to person, and make our changes in small, slow ways, from the bottom up. We attend to feelings, our own and others', and we can confront another without devastating or hedging. If we share our own reality, others can become responsible for themselves and their own actions. And we can come to find the religious experience in the simple actions of our lives, actions performed with care and consciousness. We know the earth under our feet to be holy and worthy of respect. We trust. We are free. The feminine value has been integrated—married—to the masculine value.

- Design a simple ritual to help mark some of the major transitions in your day.

- What are some of the ordinary chores and duties that are part of your daily life? How might you transform some of them into the "art of doing," to give back meaning and new energy?

- Describe the difference in feelings you have when you do a particular chore "dutifully" and when you do it with a sense of artfulness.

- How is the work you do now your fate, your choice, or your vocation?

- How does the work you do now relate to the person you were once? Is this the work everyone expected you to do? Is it the work you expected to do? How is the work you do an "art of doing"?

- How is your work helping or hindering you as you try to become the person you think you are meant to be?

- Consider the relationships that need your special attention. Where are you able to achieve empathy?

- What are your contributions to the greater community that arise out of your own understanding of your woundedness and your talent to heal?

- How would you describe those small ways in which you help to shape the new myth in which we all share?

- How have you begun to bring feminine values into your understanding of the "new creation"?

- Consider the role we all play in forming the new creation
  in current politics
  in issues of social justice

in tending to family or community values
in protecting the earth as our common ground
in sharing the holiness in the ordinary with those around us.

The synthesis of old myth and new myth, brought into confrontation and understood, allows us the freedom to live life as we were always meant to live it. In freedom we don't so much do what we love as love what we do. We will no longer be compelled to repeat old conflicts, projecting our inner truths on the world out there, thus wreaking havoc in home, neighborhood, country, culture or natural environment.

The marriage of opposites becomes the marriage of feminine and masculine as a drama of the inner world. Black and white join, merge and do *not* make gray; in synthesis is born a new myth which has all the colors of the rainbow. Conflicts are not resolved so much as in union we know all things and persons to be indispensable to one another. Here, we experience life and relationships as sacramental and holy, the ordinary as the container of the religious experience.

Chapter 32

FORMING
A NEW CREATION

Three Circles Overlapping

In your mind's eye, place three identical circles so that two overlap side by side and form, between them, an almond shape. Place the third under them and allow it to merge the same amount with the two circles above it. The overlapping circles form a three-petaled "flower" where they merge. Name the circles in turn, from the left:

- Thesis/Enchantment/Stagnation
- Antithesis/Disenchantment/Incubation
- Synthesis/Transformation/Initiation

Isolate the almond shape which points upright and has the bowed line that intersects it. This shape, called the *mandorla* in medieval Christian iconography, is the halo which surrounds only the holiest of figures. Most often it is the form where the "Christ in Judgement" is enthroned. Sometimes the throne itself is the intersecting arc represented as a rainbow.

When Christ in the *mandorla* is depicted, as he is over many Romanesque and Gothic church entries, you will see him, carved in stone relief, enthroned and reigning over the tumult of the final judgment day—the high point in a drama of apocalyptic proportions. The great day of leveling has arrived. The tension is electric. Below him, avenging angels blow their trumpets to the four corners of the earth. And each soul, stricken with terror, scrambles forth from a grave, to respond according to her or his own fate. Each soul is to be weighed on the divine scales of justice. Sometimes a demon pulls down his side of the scale, hoping to tip the balance and win a soul for his own fiery kingdom below.

Thus sorted out, to the left hand of the Christ in majesty are sent the damned—the lustful, the proud and powerful. These damned are stuffed like so many vegetables into what looks like a fearsome food processor: the gaping, toothy maw of hell, from whence they are spat out to a lower level, a hell of endless agony.

To the Lord's right hand, the blessed saved, reaching and crawling, shoving and pushing, are lifted through the doors of heaven to rest, finally, on the bosom of Abraham, to live a life of never ending bliss.

Left and right, good and bad, sheep and goats, the great division is a graphic drama on the cathedral tympanum. And, in scanning the scene, it seems that Christ reigns over all as fierce Judge and Prime Divider. Certainly one cannot read here a Christ who is Emmanuel/God-with-us. He seems a God-against-us! He seems the final witness to our spiritual schizophrenia if not the ultimate cause of all divisions. What is more, his final judgment leaves us split apart and divided for all eternity.

I spent considerable time in my youth looking at those medieval images. I'm sure that, at least once, I followed the images down from the top—down from Christ's seat of judgment, through heaven and hell, through the tensions between opposites that I would come to know so concretely as the fate of our human condition, and there, much farther down, dividing the great portals themselves and at eye level, I saw the tree of Knowledge of Good and Evil with Adam and Eve at either side.

A Medieval Theology Stood on Its Head

Today, if I could go back to that spot, older and a little wiser for knowing something about life's heavens and hells, I imagine that down here where any one of us stands eye to eye with Adam and Eve we might *reverse* the way in which we have always viewed that great and final moment. What if we should read this story in stone from the bottom up? Perhaps, indeed, it was always meant to be read in reverse? For here, at the grass-roots level, the whole issue begins to take on a personal meaning. Here, where we stand on a par with Adam and Eve, we know how we have followed our own cravings for the fruit of Knowledge of Good and Evil, of right and wrong, of up and down, of left and right.

Because we are human, we have been free to choose one side over the other. And we must choose. And, having chosen, we pay a price for each choice. But often, because we have been tempted to think ourselves "like to God," we have judged one side to be better than the other—and, having chosen and having judged, we have created those dynamics in which one factor is ever in tension with the other. How often we tip the scales and lose our balance between black and white, left and right, liberal and conservative, feminine and masculine, woman and man, this answer and that one. As married people and lovers, we get caught in wounding, futile arguments. As neighbors, we rage from opposite political positions. Righteousness and rage, for instance, are hurled between those who are "pro-life" and those who are "pro-choice," each side lacerating the other in the name of moral rectitude. Between East and West, North and South, wars are waged and powers are wrested away so that some are to become the winners over the others who must lose. We despair that such factions will ever be able to come to any accord.

It is this same futile tension that seems to be depicted here in this medieval drama. It comes when one side is certain that it is all good and the other side is judged as evil. It comes when we have slashed in halves all that was once One and Simple. There is no possibility of reconciliation when our thinking is merely black and white. Personally and collectively, we create our own hell.

But, paradoxically, because we are human and have been given the gift of free choice, we ourselves have helped to set in motion a process that is also imbued with promise—a process we can only hope will finally make all things "contract into a span" and be as "One Thing on the breast of God." It is through this divisive valley that we make our dangerous and painful human journey—back to the scales to catch our balance and back again to our ultimate unity and harmony with the Christ of majesty and peace, the Christ who redeems.

> O happy fault, O necessary sin of Adam,
> which gained for us so great a Redeemer!

To follow the image of the tree of knowledge from the ground upward and through the traumas of fate and counterfate and the terrible tensions that spin themselves out in the way we live our lives is also an invitation to go beyond the scales of balance and bring about the true marriage of opposites. For just as we can create our hells, we can, with the grace of God, work to bring about heaven. We bring closer the fullness of time and we taste of heaven when, casting aside all judgment and righteousness and every attitude that smacks of our poor imitations of God, we approach the other humbly and humanly. "There is nothing either good or bad," said Shakespeare, "but thinking makes it so." Thus emptied of our ego plots and preconceptions, we approach in empathy and compassion. There where we are weakest we are best able to bear another's burdens and share another's joys—not obliterating who we are, not merely in grudging compromise but, rather, first trying to know to our very bones the fears and feelings that the other bears, to bring the other exactly what is needed. Approaching thus, we meet and touch and our circles, so to speak, overlap a piece and become one—there where we are willing to join the other in openness and vulnerability. In this place where we have become one, we know our wounds and share in the woundedness of the other. In vulnerability we heal and are healed. Through our imperfection we take part in healing a broken and divided world. And in that very human experience of breakthrough and communion we come to know the other and at the same time to have a taste of the divine—of our redemption—of God-*with*-us. Here experience and meaning are of a piece. The Christ in the *mandorla* from this vantage now reigns as fierce and passionate Unifier and unifying experience.

> Come . . . take for your heritage the kingdom prepared for you since the foundation of the world. For I was hungry and you gave me food; I was thirsty and you gave me drink; I was a stranger and you made me welcome; naked and you

clothed me; sick and you visited me . . . . in prison and you came to see me . . . As often as you did it for one of my least ones, you did it for me." (Matthew 25:34–36, 10.)

In the aureole that contains the image of the holy and unifying—in the ellipse intersected with a rainbow—all divisions are healed, all inequities made equal, all oppositions are married and bring forth a new and greater truth.

The rainbow that appears between storm and sunshine is the place of peace that we know sometimes—even now and can know any day—when we stand in the right place at the right time, allowing two opposite realities to meet and merge and bless each other and bring to birth what is new and salvific. Storm and sunshine are not "resolved" but necessary to one another for the rainbow's appearance. "Rainbows" of such grace cannot be carved for all time in stone. But all of us have come to know that moments of transcendence glow and grow, and sometimes even gather to a greatness beyond every hope. The power of mystery and the experience of such grace can be diaphanous—like a rainbow's light which, poured over everything familiar, transforms all for a time, dyeing it all in a new light, soaking it with meaning. And then, like the rainbow grace that it is, it will begin to weaken and fade out. But the very human experience which was just drenched in grace remains with us and lends us the wisdom and the hope to take part again and again in the creation of such an "end time"—such a moment/place/experience which is imbued with holiness and wholeness. For the "final day," in the real order of things, is a fullness which has not yet happened once and for all—but happens in bits and glimpses wherever we give up our power struggles and reach out to the opposite side to overarch our differences and bring about the marriage of a "new heaven and a new earth." Then comes the rainbow seal of peace. As humans and as cocreators with the divine, we are necessary to the creation of the new story and are committed to bringing it to its own reality.

"When half-gods go, The gods arrive."

In the symmetry of this image is reflected the symmetrical expressions of all people everywhere through analogous symbols of a psychic and holy power. In dances and games, in the Native American medicine wheel, even in the symmetry of a fairy tale, in the rose window of the West or the round mandala of the East, from star quilt to sand painting, the energy of wholeness is expressed. In the stylized patterns of ritual and ceremony and in the "art of doing" we are brought to the great unknowable mystery as within reach and knowable in ordinary actions and persons and nature. Our part in the destiny of the fullness of time—of peace over brokenness—is creaturely and human—it is not royal or divine. And yet, basic to our being human and expressive of wholeness, there is a creative and divine center in each of us—that place of great creative energy where dualities inform each other and contradictions are transcended. Only where we allow ourselves to be fully human can God meet us, and here we encounter our true selves, as if for the first time. Here all dwell free.

Part IV

RELATED STORIES

Chapter 33

A DREAM

One day, after hearing the story of the Handless Maiden at a workshop I was conducting, a very beautiful woman well on in years took me aside and said that she had had a dream which she had never forgotten. She spent a lifetime writing down her dreams and remembers this one of some fifty years ago when she was working with the well-known analyst, Fritz Kunkel. She offered to go home and write the dream for me and send it by mail.

This is her dream:

I was a girl without arms. Whether I had been born that way or whether my armlessness was due to some other cause I don't now remember. My dream-mother (unlike my real mother) was a very aggressive, domineering sort of woman. She was ashamed of my armlessness and attempted to keep me hidden as much as possible. I could do nothing for myself—I had to be fed, bathed, bathroomed and cared for in every way. She felt that she did all this out of her great love for me. I, on the other hand, felt unloved and imprisoned. And one day I simply ran away.

Then the focus of the dream changed to the mother who was trying desperately to find me. Rewards offered for information. Appeals to the police of the country. But she finally had to give up. I could not be found. She goes about her life without me—a very active life with the chief accent on socializing—dinner parties, bridge parties.

And then again the dream shifts to me. I am now married to a somewhat rough-looking man, a fisherman, I believe. Uneducated and none too particular about his appearance. We live on a boat—a fishing boat—on a river. We have a baby. And I have been fitted with two prosthetic arms—silver in color. I go to see my mother, carrying my baby. She is very relieved to see me, but disapproves of my caring for a baby when I have no real arms. I tell of my husband and how we live and she disapproves even more. Yet I sense that beneath her conventional disapproval she is actually proud of what I have done with my life. I leave her then, returning to my husband and the boat on which we live. She returns to the bridge game which I had interrupted.

I woke then, and I can remember that the dream had left me feeling happy. It is interesting that at the time I had never so much as heard of the story of the "handless maiden." Please tell the handless maidens of the world that you can live to a ripe old age without knowing how to do any practical thing.

This woman, however, though severely hearing-impaired, was able to drive herself to my lecture and wire me for sound. She is an active practitioner of yoga, a reader for the blind, a gentle, warm, wise woman and a mediator of meaning to whom one is irresistibly drawn. It is right that her dream mother went on to complete a bridge game—the game of wholeness.

Chapter 34

THE
UNFORTUNATE LOVERS

Once upon a time in days long ago, it was still clear to all
Earth's people that the Sun and the Moon were destined to
love one another. For the Sun is a shining, unconquerable
hero and his love, the Moon, a woman of incomparable
beauty. Though they love one another with a mighty love,
it is equally clear that they are afflicted with a fate imposed
on them by a mysterious power which will never allow
them to joyfully fulfill their love. For as soon as the Moon
becomes full and is her most glorious and beautiful self, the
Sun loves her and yearns for her with a great longing. And,
being separated from each other by a great distance, they
move to pursue one another. But even as they travel across
the sky to be near one another, the Moon begins to wane
and fade and, when her bridegroom finally reaches her, she
disappears altogether and is swallowed up into the kingdom
of death.

So great is the Sun's pain and sorrow over the loss of his
beloved that he descends into the underworld to rescue the
captive Moon. The Sun addresses the powers of darkness
and persuades them to release the Moon. The Sun is allowed

to lead his Moon back into the sky and the Moon follows behind him. Finally, as she grows and swells to be ripe and full and beautiful again, the mysterious forces work their powers over the ill-fated pair once more. And so it is that the pursuit of their love swells and fades, dies and revives, in an endless cycle of repetition.

Chapter 35

THE TWO
ROYAL CHILDREN

There once were two royal children
Who loved one another so much.
But the two could not meet one another.
Dark oceans would not let them touch.

"Beloved, please, could you swim over?
Swim over the sea to me.
Three candles I'll set out to flicker
And light up your passage to see.

A dark Fate did o'er hear their plotting,
And while she pretended to sleep,
She snuffed out the three little candles
And the bonny youth drowned in the deep.

It was on a fine Sunday morning
When the people felt joyful and glad;
Not so the King's lovely daughter,
Whose eyes were so dark and sad.

"Oh, Mother, my darling Mother,
My head it does so pain me,
I would love for to go out a-walking
Along the darkling green sea."

"Oh, daughter, my sweetest daughter,
You must not go out alone.
Go wake up your youngest sister
So that she with you might go."

"Oh, Mother, darling Mother,
My sister is yet but a child.
She stops to pluck on the pathway
Every blossom and flow'r that grows wild."

The mother went off to church.
The daughter went to the strand
And she searched and looked till she found
A poor old fisherman.

"Oh, fisherman, my good fisher,
If you would like a reward,
Throw out your nets on the water
And haul in my darling love."

He threw out his nets on the water
And they sank to the ocean floor
And he dragged and he fished till he found him,
The beautiful youth—the King's son.

She folded him in an embrace.
She kissed him on the mouth.
"Little lips, if you could but speak now,
My broken heart would be healed."

So what did she take from her brow
But her shining and royal crown.
"Receive this, my noble fisherman.
It is your well-earned reward."

What took she from her finger?
A ring that shone gold-red.
"Receive this, my noble fisherman,
And buy for your children some bread."

She gathered the youth in her mantle
And draped the cloak round them both
And threw herself into the waters.
As she called adieu to them all.

With that, one heard the bells tolling.
There was wailing and mourning all round:
Here lie the two royal children.
The two royal children are drowned.
(From a German folk song: *Es waren zwei Königskinder*.)

Chapter 36

SUN AND MOON

Once upon a time the great Spirit Father lived in a beautiful garden at the foot of the World Tree. His daughter was the Moon, a creature more beautiful than can be told, and his greatest pride and joy. She was the apple of his eye. She was, perhaps, the golden apple of this World Tree. She was his every and only joy and he loved her above all else. But some dreadful fate over which the two have no control is visited upon this pair. The father, to save himself from an overpowering possession of darkness, is called upon to stunt or subdue the brilliance of his beautiful Moon-daughter. By his own hand he must cut off the radiantly silver, far-reaching beams of light that stream forth from her. Thus wounded and sadly mutilated, the Moon-daughter sets out to wander across the sky, bent under the weight of her own stunted arms, which are tied to her back. She becomes a declining, fading crescent, growing ever weaker and paler—until she finally sinks in total exhaustion out of our sight into the west. There at the depth of her tragic exhaustion—in a secret place out of our view—she comes miraculously upon the World Tree once more in a gardenlike paradise. From this tree she takes nourishment and gains new strength. In this garden she also comes to meet her bridegroom, the Sun King—the true owner and keeper of this garden. The Moon and her heavenly bridegroom, the Sun, celebrate their sacred nuptials.

The fruit of their joyous union is a son: the small, bright sickle of the fast-growing New Moon.

But their blessed luck does not seem to hold out, for promptly the Sun and the Moon appear to grow more and more distant again. The Sun, it is said, has been called away to duty in a far-off land. And from his distant place it is he himself who now issues the order—not just to stunt his own wife—he orders the death of his beautiful Moon-queen and their child. (When the Queen is the Greek mourning mother Niobe—she is "all tears," as Shakespeare described her. When the little Moon-child is the fruit of an incestuous relationship, as in an Indian myth, he is named The Howler—the inconsolate one. Thus it was said in many sun and moon myths that rain or the dew that fell in the night came from the moon and were its tears.)

Through the skillfully arranged deceptions of heaven's queen, however, it is not the Moon herself who is put to death but her horned likeness in the body of a hind—a deer (or a white cow in some stories). It is the hind that wanes and fades in the eastern skies. With her eyes and her tongue cut out, as the King had decreed should be done to his wife, the hind sinks blindly, silently, without complaint into the silence of the blackest night.

And now, in a renewed round of flight and frantic searching, the Sun will cross the sky—this time, indeed, to save the little Moon-boy who is their son and, in finding him, he finds his Queen the Moon, again alive, healed and fully regenerated. In a place of mystery on the other side of darkness the Sun and Moon fall into embrace and are reconciled once more. Their love, which was doomed to die, is also destined to regenerate.

Thus, traced into the very sky over our heads, we mortals have been witness from the beginning of time to the cyclic drama that ever reflects our common human experience and ever renews our common human hope: the hope that one day Sun and Moon—night and day, masculine and feminine, life and death, every opposite—might meet in their resplendent wholeness and, with hands and healing, bless one another and embrace, never to be separated again.*

* Variations of Sun and Moon myths abound in every culture, and two of them, "The Unfortunate Lovers" and "Sun and Moon," are mentioned in *Das Mädchen ohne Hände: Grimms Märchen Tiefenpsychologisch Gedeutet* by Eugen Drewermann. (Olten and Freiburg im Breisgau, Germany: Walter-Verlag, 1981.)

Chapter 37

A RECOUNTING OF THE MYTH OF DEMETER AND PERSEPHONE

One day Persephone is playing in the fields with her girl-friends. She strays from the ever watchful eye of her mother and basks in all that is girlish and feminine. She is blind to everything but this happy, carefree celebration of her individualism and independence. As she plays in the fields, she happens upon a beautiful flower—a narcissus—and in the very act of plucking it for her own, the earth is violently split open and she is sucked down into hell. There she becomes the captive of Hades, who is king of this underworld. It is there that the beautiful Persephone becomes his joyless, silent, ice-cold queen.

Here in the kingdom of the dead there is a garden where rustling poplars and weeping willows grow. But there are no flowers. There is no bird song. There is only one tree in the whole realm of Hades that bears fruit: a little pomegranate tree. Persephone in her sadness refuses to eat. Most especially, she will not eat of the pomegranates with which the gardener of the underworld tempts her. She refuses to touch the food of the dead. And her heart becomes colder and colder.

On earth, her mother, Demeter, who is the goddess of the harvest, is desolate over the loss of her daughter and in a fit of rage freezes the fruitful earth with a vast winter death. With that, all that blooms and grows on the earth withers up in frost. Crops die. Animals die. Finally, even the people begin to die.

The gods beg Demeter to bless the earth again, but she cries out to Zeus that she will never again make the earth green until he commands Hades to return her daughter to her. Indeed, Zeus could never let the earth perish, so he sends a messenger to Hades commanding that Persephone be returned to her mother.

Hades must obey Zeus. And just as Persephone is about to leave Hades to return home to her mother, she does a fateful thing: absent-mindedly she eats some seeds of the pomegranate, which turn her fate—and ours. She has tasted of the fruit of the dead. Now there is hell to pay. Now she is obliged to return to dark Hades.

While her mother, radiant with renewed beauty and joy, rushes to meet her daughter, the fields and flowers bloom again and the grain ripens. Persephone, however, must admit that she has tasted of the fruit of the dead and must return to the dark underworld. But Zeus decrees that mother and daughter should not be parted forever; rather, Persephone will spend only a part of each year with hell's king—the "king of the silent dead." For each seed eaten, she must spend one month with Hades. The other part of the year she may spend with her mother.

And so it is that Persephone fades out of life and returns with each springtime. The earth's cycles of extroverted life and introverted conception and fertility reflect the mother-daughter relationship above ground and the dark and silent seasons of the underworld.

Chapter 38

THE ARMLESS MAIDEN:
A RUSSIAN FAIRY TALE

In a certain kingdom, not in our land, there lived a wealthy merchant; he had two children, a son and a daughter. The father and mother died. The brother said to the sister: "Let us leave this town, little sister; I will rent a shop and trade, and find lodgings for you; we will live together." They went to another province. When they came there, the brother inscribed himself in the merchants' guild, and rented a shop of woven cloths. The brother decided to marry and took a sorceress to wife. One day he went to trade in his shop and said to his sister: "Keep order in the house, sister." The wife felt offended because he said this to his sister. To revenge herself she broke all the furniture and when her husband came back she met him and said: "See what a sister you have; she has broken all the furniture in the house." "Too bad, but we can get some new things," said the husband.

The next day when leaving for his shop he said farewell to his wife and his sister and said to his sister: "Please, little sister, see to it that everything in the house is kept as well as possible." The wife bided her time, went to the stables, and cut off the head of her husband's favorite horse with a saber. She awaited him on the porch. "See what a sister you have," she said. "She has cut off the head of your favorite horse." "Ah, let the dogs eat what is theirs," answered the husband.

On the third day the husband again went to his shop, said farewell, and said to his sister: "Please look after my wife, so that she does not hurt herself or the baby, if by chance she gives birth to one." When the wife gave birth to her child, she cut off his head. When her husband came home he found her sitting and lamenting over her baby. "See what a sister you have! No sooner had I given birth to my baby than she cut off his head with a saber." The husband did not say anything; he wept bitter tears and turned away.

Night came. At the stroke of midnight he rose and said: "Little sister, make ready; we are going to mass." She said: "My beloved brother, I do not think it is a holiday today." "Yes, my sister, it is a holiday; let us go." "It is still too early to go, brother," she said. "No," he answered, "young maidens always take a long time to get ready." The sister began to dress; she was very slow and reluctant. Her brother said: "Hurry, sister, get dressed." "Please," she said, "it is still early, brother." "No, little sister, it is not early, it is high time to be gone."

When the sister was ready they sat in a carriage and set out for mass. They drove for a long time or a short time. Finally they came to a wood. The sister said: "What wood is this?" He answered: "This is the hedge around the church." The carriage caught in a bush. The brother said: "Get out, little sister, disentangle the carriage." "Ah, my beloved brother, I cannot do that, I will dirty my dress." "I will buy you a new dress, sister, a better one than this." She got down from the carriage, began to disentangle it, and her brother cut off her arms to the elbows, struck his horse with the whip, and drove away.

The little sister was left alone; she burst into tears and began to walk in the woods. She walked and walked, a long time or a short time; she was all scratched, but could not find a path leading out of the woods. Finally, after several years, she found a path. She came to a market town and stood beneath the window of the wealthiest merchant to beg for alms. This merchant had a son, an only one, who was the apple of his father's eye. He fell in love with the beggar woman and said: "Dear father and mother, marry me." "To whom shall we marry you?" "To this beggar woman." "Ah, my dear child, do not the merchants of our town have lovely daughters?" "Please marry me to her," he said. "If you do not, I will do something to myself." They were distressed, because he was their only son, their life's treasure. They gathered all the merchants and clerics and asked them to judge the matter: should they marry their son to the beggar woman or not? The priest said: "Such must be his fate, and God gives your son his sanction to marry the beggar woman."

So the son lived with her for a year and then another year. At the end of that time he went to another province, where her brother had his shop. When taking his leave he said: "Dear father and mother, do not abandon my wife; as soon as she gives birth to a child, write to me that very hour." Two or three months after the son left, his wife gave birth to a child; his arms were golden up to the elbows, his sides were studded with stars, there was a bright moon on his forehead and a radiant sun near his heart. The grandparents were overjoyed and at once wrote their beloved son a letter. They dispatched an old man with this note in all haste. Meanwhile the wicked sister-in-law had learned about all this and invited the old messenger into her house: "Come in, little father," she said, "and take a rest." "No, I have no time, I am bringing an urgent message." "Come in, little father, take a rest, have something to eat."

She sat him down to dinner, took his bag, found the letter in it, read it, tore it into little pieces, and wrote another letter instead: "Your wife," it said, "has given birth to a half dog and half bear that she conceived with beasts in the woods." The old messenger came to the merchant's son and handed him the letter; he read it and burst into tears. He wrote in answer, asking that his son be not molested till he returned. "When I come back," he said, "I will see what kind of baby it is." The sorceress again invited the old messenger into her house. "Come in, sit down, take a rest," she said. Again she charmed him with talk, stole the letter he carried, read it, tore it up, and instead ordered that her sister-in-law be driven out the moment the letter was received. The old messenger brought this letter; the father and mother read it and were grieved. "Why does he cause us so much trouble?" they said. "We married him to the girl, and now he does not want his wife!" They pitied not so much the wife as the babe. So they gave their blessing to her and the babe, tied the babe to her breast, and sent her away.

She went, shedding bitter tears. She walked, for a long time or a short time, all in the open field, and there was no wood or village anywhere. She came to a dale and was very thirsty. She looked to the right and saw a well. She wanted to drink from it but was afraid to stoop, lest she drop her baby. Then she fancied that the water came closer. She stooped to drink and her baby fell into the well. She began to walk around the well, weeping, and wondering how to get her child out of the well. An old man came up to her and said: "Why are you weeping, you slave of God?" "How can I help weeping? I stooped over the well to drink water and my baby fell into it." "Bend down and take him out." "No, little father, I cannot; I have no hands, only stumps." "Do as I tell you. Take your baby." She went to the well, stretched out her arms, and God helped, for suddenly she had her hands, all whole. She bent down, pulled her baby out, and began to give thanks to God, bowing to all four sides.

She said her prayers, went on farther, and came to the house where her brother and husband were staying, and asked for shelter. Her husband said: "Brother, let the beggar woman in; beggar women can tell stories and recount real happenings." The wicked sister-in-law said: "We have no room for visitors, we are overcrowded." "Please, brother, let her come; there is nothing I like better than to hear beggar women tell tales." They let her in. She sat on the stove with her baby. Her husband said: "Now, little dove, tell us a tale—any kind of story."

She said: "I do not know any tales or stories, but I can tell the truth. Listen, here is a true happening that I can recount to you." And she began: "In a certain kingdom, not in our land, lived a wealthy merchant; he had two children, a son and a daughter. The father and mother died. The brother said to the sister: 'Let us leave this town, little sister.' And they came to another province. The brother inscribed himself in the merchants' guild and took a shop of woven cloth. He decided to marry and took a sorceress to wife." At this point the sister-in-law muttered: "Why does she bore us with her stories, that hag?" But the husband said: "Go on, go on, little mother, I love such stories more than anything!"

"And so," the beggar woman went on, "the brother went to trade in his shop and said to his sister: 'Keep order in the house, sister.' The wife felt offended because he had said this to his sister and out of spite broke all the furniture." And then she went on to tell how her brother took her to mass and cut off her hands, how she gave birth to a baby, how her sister-in-law lured the old messenger—and again the sister-in-law interrupted her, crying: "What gibberish she is telling!" But the husband said: "Brother, order your wife to keep quiet; it is a wonderful story, is it not?"

She came to the point when her husband wrote to his parents ordering that the baby be left in peace until his return, and the sister-in-law mumbled: "What nonsense!" Then she reached the point when she came to their house as a beggar woman, and the sister-in-law mumbled: "What is this old bitch gibbering about!" And the husband said: "Brother, order her to keep quiet; why does she interrupt all the time?" Finally she came to the point in the story when she was let in and began to tell the truth instead of a story. And then she pointed at them and said: "This is my husband, this is my brother, and this is my sister-in-law."

Then her husband jumped up to her on the stove and said: "Now, my dear, show me the baby. Let me see whether my father and mother wrote me the truth." They took the baby, removed its swaddling clothes—and the whole room was illumined! "So it is true that she did not tell us just a tale; here is my wife, and here is my son—golden up to the elbows—his sides studded with stars, a bright moon on his forehead, and a radiant sun near his heart!"

The brother took the best mare from his stable, tied his wife to its tail, and let it run in the open field. The mare dragged her on the ground until she brought back only her braid; the rest was strewn on the field. Then they harnessed three horses and went home to the young husband's father and mother; they began to live happily and to prosper. I was there and drank mead and wine; it ran down my mustache, but did not go into my mouth.

Chapter 39

THE ONE-HANDED GIRL:
A SWAHILI TALE

An old couple once lived in a hut under a grove of palm trees, and they had one son and one daughter. They were all very happy together for many years, and then the father became very ill, and felt he was going to die. He called his children to the place where he lay on the floor—for no one had any beds in that country—and said to his son, "I have no herds of cattle to leave you—only the few things there are in the house—for I am a poor man, as you know. But choose: will you have my blessing or my property?"

"Your property, certainly," answered the son, and his father nodded.

"And you?" asked the old man of the girl, who stood by her brother.

"I will have blessing," she answered, and her father gave her much blessing.

That night he died, and his wife and son and daughter mourned for him seven days, and gave him a burial according to the custom of his people. But hardly was the time of mourning over, than the mother was attacked by a disease which was common in that country.

"I am going away from you," she said to her children, in a faint voice; "but first, my son, choose which you will have: blessing or property."

"Property, certainly," answered the son.

"And you, my daughter?"

"I will have blessing," said the girl; and her mother gave her much blessing, and that night she died.

When the days of mourning were ended, the brother bade his sister put outside the hut all that belonged to his father and his mother. So the girl put them out, and he took them away, save only a small pot and a vessel in which she could clean her corn. But she had no corn to clean.

She sat at home, sad and hungry, when a neighbour knocked at the door.

"My pot has cracked in the fire, lend me yours to cook my supper in, and I will give you a handful of corn in return."

And the girl was glad, and that night she was able to have supper herself, and next day another woman borrowed her pot, and then another and another, for never were known so many accidents as befell the village pots at that time. She soon grew quite fat with all the corn she earned with the help of her pot, and then one evening she picked up a pumpkin seed in a corner, and planted it near her well, and it sprang up, and gave her many pumpkins.

At last it happened that a youth from her village passed through the place where the girl's brother was, and the two met and talked.

"What news is there of my sister?" asked the young man, with whom things had gone badly, for he was idle.

"She is fat and well-liked," replied the youth, "for the women borrow her mortar to clean their corn, and borrow her pot to cook it in, and for all this they give her more food than she can eat." And he went his way.

Now the brother was filled with envy at the words of the man, and he set out at once, and before dawn he had reached the hut, and saw the pot and the mortar were standing outside. He slung them over his shoulders and departed, pleased with his own cleverness; but when his sister awoke and sought for the pot to cook her corn for breakfast, she could find it nowhere. At length she said to herself,

"Well, some thief must have stolen them while I slept. I will go and see if any of my pumpkins are ripe." And indeed they were, and so many that the tree was almost broken by the weight of them. So she ate what she wanted and took the others to the village, and gave them in exchange for corn, and the women said that no pumpkins were as sweet as these, and that she was to bring every day all that she had. In this way she earned more than she needed for herself, and soon was able to get another mortar and cooking pot in exchange for her corn. Then she thought she was quite rich.

Unluckily someone else thought so too, and this was her brother's wife, who had heard all about the pumpkin tree, and sent her slave with a handful of grain to buy her a pumpkin. At first the girl told him that so few were left that she could not spare any; but when she found that he belonged to her brother, she changed her mind, and went out to the tree and gathered the largest and the ripest that was there.

"Take this one," she said to the slave, "and carry it back to your mistress, but tell her to keep the corn, as the pumpkin is a gift."

The brother's wife was overjoyed at the sight of the fruit, and when she tasted it, she declared it was the nicest she had ever eaten. Indeed, all night she thought of nothing else, and early in the morning she called another slave (for she was a rich woman) and had him go and ask for another pumpkin. But the girl, who had just been out to look at her tree, told him that they were all eaten, so he went back empty-handed to his mistress.

In the evening her husband returned from hunting a long way off, and found his wife in tears.

"What is the matter?" asked he.

"I sent a slave with some grain to your sister to buy some pumpkins, but she would not sell me any, and told me there were none, though I know she lets other people buy them."

"Well, never mind now—go to sleep," said he, "and to-morrow I will go and pull up the pumpkin tree, and that will punish her for treating you so badly."

So before sunrise he got up and set out for his sister's house, and found her cleaning some corn.

"Why did you refuse to sell my wife a pumpkin yesterday when she wanted one?" he asked.

"The old ones are finished, and the new ones are not yet come," answered the girl. "When her slave arrived two days ago, there were only four left; but I gave him one, and would take no corn for it."

"I do not believe you: you have sold them all to other people. I shall go and cut down the pumpkin," cried her brother in a rage.

"If you cut down the pumpkin you shall cut off my hand with it," exclaimed the girl, running up to her tree and catching hold of it. But her brother followed, and with one blow cut off the pumpkin and her hand too.

Then he went into the house and took away everything he could find, and sold the house to a friend of his who had long wished to have it, and his sister had no home to go to.

Meanwhile she had bathed her arm carefully, and bound on it some healing leaves that grew nearby, and wrapped a cloth round the leaves, and went to hide in the forest, that her brother might not find her again.

For seven days she wandered about, eating only the fruit that hung from the trees above her, and every night she climbed up and tucked herself safely among the creepers which bound together the big branches, so that neither lions nor tigers nor panthers might get at her.

When she woke up on the seventh morning she saw from her perch smoke coming up from a little town on the edge of the forest. The sight of the huts made her feel more lonely and helpless than before. She longed desperately for a draught of milk from a gourd, for there were no streams in that part, and she was very thirsty, but how was she to earn anything with only one hand? And at this thought her courage failed, and she began to cry bitterly.

It happened that the king's son had come out from the town very early to shoot birds, and when the sun grew hot he felt tired.

"I will lie here and rest under this tree," he said to his attendants. "You can go and shoot instead, and I will just have this slave to stay with me!" Away they went, and the young man fell asleep, and slept long. Suddenly he was awakened by something wet and salty falling on his face.

"What is that? Is it raining?" he said to his slave. "Go and look."

"No, master, it is not raining," answered the slave.

"Then climb up the tree and see what it is," and the slave climbed up, and came back and told his master that a beautiful girl was sitting up there, and that it must have been her tears which had fallen on the face of the king's son.

"Why was she crying?" inquired the prince.

"I cannot tell—I did not dare to ask her; but perhaps she would tell you." And the master, greatly wondering, climbed up the tree.

"What is the matter with you?" said he gently, and, as she only sobbed louder, he continued:

"Are you a woman, or a spirit of the woods?"

"I am a woman," she answered slowly, wiping her eyes with a leaf of the creeper that hung about her.

"Then why do you cry?" he persisted.

"I have many things to cry for," she replied, "more than you could ever guess."

"Come home with me," said the prince; "it is not very far. Come home to my father and mother. I am a king's son."

"Then why are you here?" she said, opening her eyes and staring at him.

"Once every month I and my friends shoot birds in the

forest," he answered, "but I was tired and bade them leave me to rest. And you—what are you doing up in this tree?"

At that she began to cry again, and told the king's son all that had befallen her since the death of her mother.

"I cannot come down with you, for I do not like anyone to see me," she ended with a sob.

"Oh! I will manage all that," said the king's son, and swinging himself to a lower branch, he bade his slave go quickly into the town, and bring back with him four strong men and a curtained litter. When the man was gone, the girl climbed down, and hid herself on the ground in some bushes. Very soon the slave returned with the litter, which was placed on the ground close to the bushes where the girl lay.

"Now go, all of you, and call my attendants, for I do not wish to stay here any longer," he said to the men, and as soon as they were out of sight he bade the girl get into the litter, and fasten the curtains tightly. Then he got in on the other side, and waited till his attendants came up.

"What is the matter, O son of a king?" asked they, breathless with running.

"I think I am ill; I am cold," he said, and signing to the bearers, he drew the curtains, and was carried through the forest right inside his own house.

"Tell my father and mother that I have a fever, and want some gruel," said he, "and bid them send it quickly."

So the slave hastened to the king's palace and gave his message, which troubled both the king and the queen greatly. A pot of hot gruel was instantly prepared, and carried over to the sick man, and as soon as the council which was sitting was over, the king and his ministers went to pay him a visit, bearing a message from the queen that she would follow a little later.

Now the prince had pretended to be ill in order to soften his parents' hearts, and the next day he declared he felt better, and, getting into his litter, was carried to the palace in state, drums being beaten all along the road.

He dismounted at the foot of the steps and walked up, a great parasol being held over his head by a slave. Then he entered the cool, dark room where his father and mother were sitting, and said to them:

"I saw a girl yesterday in the forest whom I wish to marry, and, unknown to my attendants, I brought her back to my house in a litter. Give me your consent, I beg, for no other woman pleases me as well, even though she has but one hand!"

Of course the king and queen would have preferred a daughter-in-law with two hands, and one who could have brought riches with her, but they could not bear to say "No" to their son, so they told him it should be as he chose, and that the wedding feast should be prepared immediately.

The girl could scarcely believe her good fortune, and, in gratitude for all the kindness shown her, was so useful and pleasant to her husband's parents that they soon loved her.

By and by a baby was born to her, and soon after that the prince was sent on a journey by his father to visit some of the distant towns of the kingdom, and to set right things that had gone wrong.

No sooner had he started than the girl's brother, who had wasted all the riches his wife had brought him in recklessness and folly, and was now very poor, chanced to come into the town, and as he passed he heard a man say, "Do you know that the king's son has married a woman who has lost one of her hands?" On hearing these words the brother stopped and asked, "Where did he find such a woman?"

"In the forest," answered the man, and the cruel brother guessed at once it must be his sister.

A great rage took possession of his soul as he thought of the girl whom he had tried to ruin being after all so much better off than himself, and he vowed that he would work her ill. Therefore that very afternoon he made his way to the palace and asked to see the king.

When he was admitted to his presence, he knelt down and touched the ground with his forehead, and the king bade him stand up and tell wherefore he had come.

"By the kindness of your heart have you been deceived, O king," said he. "Your son has married a girl who has lost a hand. Do you know why she has lost it? She was a witch, and has wedded three husbands, and each husband she has put to death with her arts. Then the people of the town cut off her hand, and turned her into the forest. And what I say is true, for her town is my town also."

The king listened, and his face grew dark. Unluckily he had a hasty temper, and did not stop to reason, and, instead of sending to the town, and discovering people who knew his daughter-in-law and could have told him how hard she had worked and how poor she had been, he believed all the brother's lying words, and made the queen believe them too. Together they took counsel what they should do, and in the end they decided that they also would put her out of the town. But this did not content the brother.

"Kill her," he said. "It is no more than she deserves for daring to marry the king's son. Then she can do no more hurt to anyone."

"We cannot kill her," answered they; "if we did, our son would assuredly kill us. Let us do as the others did, and put her out of the town." And with this the envious brother was forced to be content.

The poor girl loved her husband very much, but just then the baby was more to her than all else in the world, and as long as she had him with her, she did not very much mind anything. So, taking her son on her arm, and hanging a little earthen pot for cooking round her neck, she left her house with its great peacock fans and slaves and seats of ivory, and plunged into the forest.

For a while she walked, not knowing whither she went, then by and by she grew tired, and sat under a tree to rest and to hush her baby to sleep. Suddenly she raised her eyes, and saw a snake wriggling from under the bushes towards her.

"I am a dead woman," she said to herself, and stayed quite still, for indeed she was too frightened to move. In another minute the snake had reached her side, and to her surprise he spoke.

"Open your earthen pot, and let me go in. Save me from sun, and I will save you from rain," and she opened the pot, and when the snake had slipped in, she put on the cover. Soon she beheld another snake coming after the other one, and when it had reached her it stopped and said, "Did you see a small grey snake pass this way just now?"

"Yes," she answered, "it was going very quickly."

"Ah, I must hurry and catch it up," replied the second snake, and it hastened on.

When it was out of sight, a voice from the pot said:

"Uncover me," and she lifted the lid, and the little grey snake slid rapidly to the ground.

"I am safe now," he said. "But tell me, where are you going?"

"I cannot tell you, for I do not know," she answered. "I am just wandering in the wood."

"Follow me, and let us go home together," said the snake, and the girl followed him through the forest and along the green paths, till they came to a great lake, where they stopped to rest.

"The sun is hot," said the snake, "and you have walked far. Take your baby and bathe in that cool place where the boughs of the tree stretch far over the water."

"Yes, I will," answered she, and they went in. The baby splashed and crowed with delight, and then he gave a spring and fell right in, down, down, down, and his mother could not find him, though she searched all among the reeds.

Full of terror, she made her way back to the bank, and called to the snake, "My baby is gone!—he is drowned, and never shall I see him again."

"Go in once more," said the snake, "and feel everywhere,

even among the trees that have their roots in the water, lest perhaps he may be held fast there."

Swiftly she went back and felt everywhere with her whole hand, even putting her fingers into the tiniest crannies, where a crab could hardly have taken shelter.

"No, he is not here," she cried. "How am I to live without him?" But the snake took no notice, and only answered, "Put in your other arm too."

"What is the use of that" she asked, "when it has no hand to feel with?" but all the same she did as she was bid, and in an instant the wounded arm touched something round and soft, lying between two stones in a clump of reeds.

"My baby, my baby!" she shouted, and lifted him up, merry and laughing, and not a bit hurt or frightened.

"Have you found him this time?" asked the snake.

"Yes, oh, yes!" she answered, "and, why—why—I have got my hand back again!" and from sheer joy she burst into tears.

The snake let her weep for a little while, and then he said—

"Now we will journey on to my family, and we will all repay you for the kindness you showed to me."

"You have done more than enough in giving me back my hand," replied the girl; but the snake only smiled.

"Be quick, lest the sun should set," he answered, and began to wriggle along so fast that the girl could hardly follow him.

By and by they arrived at the house in a tree where the snake lived, when he was not travelling with his father and mother. And he told them all his adventures, and how he had escaped from his enemy. The father and mother snake could not do enough to show their gratitude. They made their guest lie down on a hammock woven of the strong creepers which hung from bough to bough, till she was quite rested after her wanderings, while they watched the baby and gave him milk to drink from the coconuts which they persuaded their friends the monkeys to crack for them. They even managed to carry small fruit tied up in their tails for the baby's mother, who felt at last that she was safe and at peace. Not that she forgot her husband, for she often thought of him and longed to show him her son, and in the night she would sometimes lie awake and wonder where he was.

In this manner many weeks passed by.

And what was the prince doing?

Well, he had fallen very ill when he was on the furthest border of the kingdom, and he was nursed by some kind people who did not know who he was, so that the king and queen heard nothing about him. When he was better he made his way slowly home again, and into his father's palace, where he found a strange man standing behind the throne with the peacock's feathers. This was his wife's brother, whom the king had taken into high favour, though, of course, the prince was quite ignorant of what had happened.

For a moment the king and queen stared at their son, as if he had been unknown to them; he had grown so thin and weak during his illness that his shoulders were bowed like those of an old man.

"Have you forgotten me so soon?" he asked.

At the sound of his voice they gave a cry and ran towards him, and poured out questions as to what had happened, and why he looked like that. But the prince did not answer any of them.

"How is my wife?" he said. There was a pause.

Then the queen replied:

"She is dead."

"*Dead!*" he repeated, stepping a little backwards. "And my child?"

"He is dead too."

The young man stood silent. Then he said, "Show me their graves."

At these words the king, who had been feeling rather uncomfortable, took heart again, for had he not prepared two beautiful tombs for his son to see, so that he might never, never guess what had been done to his wife? All these months the king and queen had been telling each other how good and merciful they had been not to take her brother's advice and to put her to death. But now, this somehow did not seem so certain.

Then the king led the way to the courtyard just behind the palace, and through the gate into a beautiful garden where stood two splendid tombs in a green space under the trees. The prince advanced alone, and, resting his head against the stone, he burst into tears. His father and mother stood silently behind with a curious pang in their souls which they did not quite understand. Could it be that they were ashamed of themselves?

But after a while the prince turned round, and walking past them into the palace he bade the slaves bring him mourning. For seven days no one saw him, but at the end of them he went out hunting, and helped his father rule his people as before. Only no one dared to speak to him of his wife and son.

At last one morning, after the girl had been lying awake all night thinking of her husband, she said to her friend the snake:

"You have all shown me much kindness, but now I am well again, and want to go home and hear some news of my husband, and if he still mourns for me!" Now the heart of the snake was sad at her words, but he only said:

"Yes, thus it must be; go and bid farewell to my father and mother, but if they offer you a present, see that you take nothing but my father's ring and my mother's casket."

So she went to the parent snakes, who wept bitterly at the thought of losing her, and offered her gold and jewels as much as she could carry in remembrance of them. But the girl shook her head and pushed the shining heap away from her.

"I shall never forget you, never," she said in a broken voice, "but the only tokens I will accept from you are that little ring and this old casket."

The two snakes looked at each other in dismay. The ring and the casket were the only things they did not want her to have. Then after a short pause they spoke.

"Why do you want the ring and casket so much? Who has told you of them?"

"Oh, nobody; it is just my fancy," answered she. But the old snakes shook their heads and replied:

"Not so; it is our son who told you, and, as he said, so it must be. If you need food, or clothes, or a house, tell the ring and it will find them for you. And if you are unhappy or in danger, tell the casket and it will set things right." Then they both gave her their blessing, and she picked up her baby and went her way.

She walked for a long time, till at length she came near the town where her husband and his father dwelt. Here she stopped under a grove of palm trees, and told the ring that she wanted a house.

"It is ready, mistress," whispered a queer little voice which made her jump, and, looking behind her, she saw a lovely palace made of the finest woods, and a row of slaves with tall fans bowing before the door. Glad indeed was she to enter, for she was very tired, and, after eating a good supper of fruit and milk which she found in one of the rooms, she flung herself down on a pile of cushions and went to sleep with her baby beside her.

Here she stayed quietly, and every day the baby grew taller and stronger, and very soon he could run about and even talk. Of course the neighbours had a great deal to say about the house which had been built so quickly—so very quickly—on the outskirts of the town, and invented all kinds of stories about the rich lady who lived in it. And by and by, when the king returned with his son from the wars, some of these tales reached his ears.

"It is really very odd about that house under the palms," he said to the queen; "I must find out something of the lady whom no one ever sees. I daresay it is not a lady at all, but a gang of conspirators who want to get possession of my throne. To-morrow I shall take my son and my chief ministers and insist on getting inside."

Soon after sunrise next day the prince's wife was standing on a little hill behind the house, when she saw a cloud of dust coming through the town. A moment afterwards she heard faintly the roll of the drums that announced the king's presence, and saw a crowd of people approaching the grove of palms. Her heart beat fast. Could her husband be among them? In any case they must not discover her there; so just bidding the ring prepare some food for them, she ran inside, and bound a veil of golden gauze round her head and face. Then, taking the child's hand, she went to the door and waited.

In a few minutes the whole procession came up, and she stepped forward and begged them to come in and rest.

"Willingly," answered the king; "go first, and we will follow you."

They followed her into a long dark room, in which was a table covered with gold cups and baskets filled with dates and coconuts and all kinds of ripe yellow fruits, and the king and the prince sat upon cushions and were served by slaves, while the ministers, among whom she recognised her own brother, stood behind.

"Ah, I owe all my misery to him," she said to herself. "From the first he has hated me," but outwardly she showed nothing. And when the king asked her what news there was in the town she only answered:

"You have ridden far; eat first, and drink, for you must be hungry and thirsty, and then I will tell you my news."

"You speak sense," answered the king, and silence prevailed for some time longer. Then he said:

"Now, lady, I have finished, and am refreshed, therefore tell me, I pray you, who you are, and whence you come? But, first, be seated."

She bowed her head and sat down on a big scarlet cushion, drawing her little boy, who was asleep in a corner, onto her knee, and began to tell the story of her life. As her brother listened, he would fain have left the house and hidden himself in the forest, but it was his duty to wave the fan of peacock's feathers over the king's head to keep off the flies, and he knew he would be seized by the royal guards if he tried to desert his post. He must stay where he was, there was no help for it, and luckily for him the king was too much interested in the tale to notice that the fan had ceased moving, and that flies were dancing right on the top of his thick curly hair.

The story went on, but the storyteller never once looked at the prince, even through her veil, though he on his side never moved his eyes from her. When she reached the part where she had sat weeping in the tree, the king's son could restrain himself no longer.

"It is my wife," he cried, springing to where she sat with the sleeping child in her lap. "They have lied to me, and you are not dead after all, nor the boy either! But what has happened? Why did they lie to me? And why did you leave my house where you were safe?" And he turned and looked fiercely at his father.

"Let me finish my tale first, and then you will know," answered she, throwing back her veil, and she told how her brother had come to the palace and accused her of being a witch, and had tried to persuade the king to slay her. "But he would not do that," she continued softly, "and after all, if I had stayed on in your house, I should never have met the snake, nor have got my hand back again. So let us forget all about it, and be happy once more, for see! our son is growing quite a big boy."

"And what shall be done to your brother?" asked the king, who was glad to think that someone had acted in this matter worse than himself.

"Put him out of the town," answered she.

BIBLIOGRAPHY

As this book itself is not a work of scholarship, nor is scholarship appropriate to its purpose, the book lists that follow are not meant to be complete or exhaustive—they are far from that. Rather, they are more a selection of writings that came my way by fate or grace and that have had a role to play in my own development, in the development of this book, or that seem of value for those who would like to read something more on or around the subject.

Primary Materials

that contributed to the development of this book.

Franz, Marie-Louise von. *Problems of the Feminine in Fairytales*. Zurich and New York: Spring Publications, 1972. Dr. von Franz, under the mentorship of C. G. Jung, first began her analytical work with fairy tales when she was in her late teens. Her work in the field is seminal, vast and creative. I found her books and her courses at the Jung Institute in Zurich to be astonishingly valuable and informing. But I also found the intensity and concentration of her information and wisdom to be as rich and compressed as a broth cube. And so I built my own work on her "bouillon cube" as one might build a soup, adding water very slowly, stirring it up and expanding it with offerings from my own garden in their seasons. Readers will find the countless fairy tales von Franz illuminates in her several books on the subject to be absorbing. Basic Jungian theory is a helpful prerequisite.

Grimm, Ludwig Karl. *Grimm's Fairy Tales: Complete Edition.* Translated by Margaret Hunt and James Stern, illustrated by Josef Scharl. (New York: Pantheon Books, 1944, and Random House, 1972.) This is the book my parents gave me when I was a child. Even then I knew it was a serious collection for its size alone and for its handsome binding and colored line drawings. But after 830 pages of stories there appeared a section called: "Folkloristic Commentary." This meant it was a *really* serious book: one, obviously, I would never need outgrow. Ultimately this serious commentary was my introduction to that student of myth and fairy tale whom today so many of us have come to know and respect: Joseph Campbell. This entire collection is now in print again, albeit paperbound and without its color. But Campbell's commentary is still there and as lively as ever.

Guterman, Norbert, editor and translator. *Russian Fairy Tales.* Illustrated by A. Alexeiff. (New York: Pantheon Books, 1945, and Random House, 1973.) There are nearly two hundred fairy tales in this book, Russian treasures saved up before they disappeared. Eudora Welty wrote of these in 1945 as ". . . rambunctious, full-blooded and temperamental . . . tense with action, magical and human . . . gorgeous." And this you can verify in the Russian fairy tale included as chapter 38 of this book: "The Armless Maiden." This book and its Grimm's counterpart mentioned just preceding are my two favorites for reading to children (circa age six and upward). Children benefit most from *hearing* fairy tales told them—and in their stark, unpolished form, unspoiled by the addition of "morals." (The interpretation of a fairy tale is appropriate only for adults.)

Lang, Andrew. *The Lilac Fairy Book.* (New York: Dover Publications, 1965.) This is one in a series of books for children of fairy tales collected from around the world, and in it I found the Swahili version, "The One-Handed Girl," included here as chapter 39 of this book. Dover has provided, with this series, a broad collection of tales at affordable price.

Secondary Studies

Books with critical interpretations of fairy tales and literature, studies, speculation and meditation on the nature of humankind and the religious search.

Bellah, Robert N., Richard Madsen, William M. Sullivan, Ann Swidler, and Steven M. Tipton. *Habits of the Heart: Individualism and Commitment in American Life*. (San Francisco: Harper and Row, 1985.) The best possible sociological examination of our Western myth, a.k.a. the American Dream, and the moral dilemma such dreams are made of.

Bettelheim, Bruno. *The Uses of Enchantment: The Meaning and Importance of Fairy Tales*. (New York: Alfred A. Knopf, 1977.) An engagingly written, popularly received and psychoanalytically oriented work on fairy tales. It gives readers permission to return fairy tales to the young as a source of pleasure and emotional and moral sustenance—even if they are scary. The Freudian orientation leaves the explications within the realm of early development and, indeed, more within the nature of enchantment than in the later developmental task of disenchantment and the processes of the second half of life. A book to encourage the reading of fairy tales to children and to gain insight on the tasks and emotional development of childhood.

Birkhäuser-Oeri, Sibylle. *The Mother: Archetypal Image in Fairy Tales*. (Toronto: Inner City Books, 1988.) Unconscious processes are compared with mythic images in fairy tales to bring clarity to what is obscure, chiefly the pervasive influence of the mother complex, positive and negative. This little book, because of its Jungian approach, cuts through superficialities and drops directly to that deep dimension at the heart of folk literature—that level which other studies seem only to skate over.

Bly, Robert. *Iron John: A Book About Men*. (Reading, MA: Addison-Wesley, 1990.) As I was putting together my book, I made a point of not reading Bly's work on the fairy tale, "Iron Hans," so as not to be unduly influenced by his approach or observations. But knowing enough of both that fairy tale and Bly's work with men and the issues of growing to mature masculinity, it seems only right that I include his work in this bibliography. If Bly can urge men to grow up to a manliness which is mature and decisive first, and feeling and caring as well, then the world and its women can only be the better off for it. For the coy, furtive man will only meet up with the sharp, prickly woman. And neither of them will be his or her true, best self. Both will only be in complicity with the "patriarchy" exactly as we know it now.

Blyth, R. H. *Zen in English Literature and Oriental Classics*. (New York: E. P. Dutton, 1960.) This book offers a connection with the spirit of Zen Buddhism which infuses the best of the world's literature. The book primes the reader with that spirit and equips one to discover the Zen in every work of art (fairy tales too) and art in every experience.

Chinen, Allan B. *In the Ever After: Fairy Tales and the Second Half of Life*. (Wilmette, IL: Chiron Publications, 1989.) A psychiatrist who cares especially about adult development and aging offers stories from around the world. Warmly and wisely he unfolds them and returns them to those who have no models to grow old by and who fear aging in a difficult world.

Dieckmann, Hans. *Twice-Told Tales: The Psychological Use of Fairy Tales*. (Wilmette, IL: Chiron Publications, 1979.) In the foreword by Bruno Bettelheim I learned that he had his graduate students in psychology retell a fairy tale as they recalled it and reflect on why this particular tale was especially significant for them, how it became altered in their memory of it and what the distortion could reveal about the problems they grappled with in their own lives. Hans Dieckmann, a German psychiatrist and Jungian analyst, reveals, through case histories, the fairy tales that people live—that is, the mythic construct that has "cast a spell" on a person and causes him to be trapped in a life grown desolate. He uses fairy tales to illustrate the stages of psychological development.

Doyle, Brendan. *Meditations with Julian of Norwich*. (Santa Fe: Bear and Company, 1983.) Dame Julian, fourteenth-century poet, mystic and anchorite, is translated here and presented in a light arrangement for meditation and learning. The book catches enough of Julian's passion and poignancy and her understanding of "God-within-us" that the reader will be compelled to go further and seek out more serious presentations of her writings.

Eliade, Mircea. *Rites and Symbols of Initiation*. (New York: Harper Torchbooks, 1958.) Only one selection from a multitude of books by the late historian of religions which might relate to our subject and inspire the reader. Even while flooding us with data and scholarly interpretation, Eliade has always managed to be profound, insightful and aware that every longing is essentially a religious one. Rebirth is one such longing and Eliade discloses it for the religious transfiguration it means to be despite its frequently secular, unconscious expressions. One can trace in Eliade's study the journey of the heroes in our stories.

Feinstein, David, and Stanley Krippner. *Personal Mythology: Using Ritual, Dreams, and Imagination to Discover Your Inner Story*. (Los Angeles: Jeremy P. Tarcher, 1988.) An extensive and detailed program designed to bring to consciousness what has been an unconscious personal or imposed mythology with help toward gaining influence over personal patterns that block healing and transformation. The authors look further than do most authors of self-help books—beyond becoming simply an "independent individual" toward becoming a responsible participant in the creation of a global society.

Fox, Matthew. *Meditations with Meister Eckhart*. (Santa Fe: Bear and Company, 1983.) Fox has brought the mystics and their prophetic teachings out from the hidden places where they were lost with scholars and theologians and made them available and even popular with ordinary mortals. This series of books is a good introduction to the mystics for beginners, though Eckhart-made-simple may happily lead many readers to look for Eckhart in all his richness and wisdom: "[The] spirit seeks to be broken through by God. God leads this spirit into a desert, into the wilderness and solitude of the divinity where God is pure unity and where God gushes up within himself."

Franz, Marie-Louise von. *Shadow and Evil in Fairytales*. (Zurich and New York: Spring Publications, 1974.) How what we don't know hurts us and hurts the whole of society around us.

———— and James Hillman. *Lectures on Jung's Typology*. (Zurich and New York: Spring Publications, 1971.) Useful in understanding typology. Brilliant in its description of our cultural lack of feeling value and our distortion of feelings.

Gilligan, Carol. *In a Different Voice: Psychological Theory and Woman's Development*. (Cambridge, MA: Harvard University Press, 1982.) Harvard psychologist Gilligan (first using the voice of scholarship and controlled studies, but then the voice of story and myth) shows how the voices of genders *differ* in moral strength and the ethic of care in relationship. Once we know in how many ways genders differ and are ready to celebrate our differences, we can begin to honor our differences equally: equal rights for different voices. But the characteristics of the female personality are but an important step in the direction of knowing the *nature of the feminine* as it is found in *both genders* and the consequence of leaving that archetype in the unconscious world.

Hall, Nor. *The Moon and the Virgin: Reflections on the Archetypal Feminine*. (New York: Harper and Row, 1980.) "I refer to myths and fairy tales as essential psychic facts. . . ." And the author proceeds to demonstrate through intelligent and lyrical writing a feminine way of knowing as she unfolds stories and graciously puts flesh on the abstract bones of archetypal concepts. The book is an adventure inward.

Haughton, Rosemary. *Tales from Eternity: The World of Fairytales and the Spiritual Search*. (New York: Seabury, 1973.) Fairy tales reopened and presented as a guide to finding our place historically and spiritually. The author, a respected theologian always on the cutting edge, is here again uncommonly wise, articulate and original.

Johnson, Robert. *She: Understanding Feminine Psychology*. (New York: Harper and Row Perennial Library, 1977.) The Greek myth of Eros and Psyche examined as a story about the developmental tasks of a woman becoming whole.

Jung, Carl Gustav. *Memories, Dreams and Reflections*. (New York: Pantheon, 1961.) Perhaps, if one had to choose for a neophyte only one of Jung's prolific writings as an introduction to his life and work, this would be the book to choose. It steeps the reader in Jung's world and experience and thoroughly engages and expands the outer limits of the reader's consciousness. This may be the best way to learn and understand basic Jungian theory.

Kolbenschlag, Madonna. *Kiss Sleeping Beauty Good-Bye*. (New York: Doubleday, 1979.) A book somewhat long on shattering the old stories and short on seeing myths and fairy tales as descriptive of universal human inclinations with their own warning systems and instructions for spiritual healing. But still it is a richly thorough book full of heady, impatient energy for "world making" among women.

Lorenz, Konrad. *The Waning of Humaneness*. (Boston: Little, Brown, 1987.) That brilliant animal behaviorist had, perhaps, even more to say about human behavior. All of his books are wonderful reading, but in this, his last work, he airs his final warnings and makes his urgent pleas for us to discover and live up to the dignity of humanness. He shows us how only the "domesticated animals" become irresponsible and immoral. He offers insight, wisdom and suggestions for the education of the young and the healing of our society.

Luke, Helen M. *Woman Earth and Spirit*. (New York: Crossroad, 1984.) Using Scripture, myth, folklore and the poetry of Charles

Williams, the author, a student of Jung, seeks to reconnect us to images and symbols of the feminine. A small, rich, wise book.

Mornell, Pierre. *Passive Men, Wild Women.* (New York: Ballantine Books, 1979.) Essentially this book describes how the differing developmental tasks that take men and women on opposite courses affect their relationships and their struggles to meet and understand each other's needs.

Nelson, Gertrud Mueller. *To Dance with God.* (New York/Mahwah: Paulist Press, 1986.) A discussion on the nature and need for ritual and celebration to return meaning to our human experiences. Ritual is essentially the truth of myth enacted and celebration is at its best when we celebrate our archetypal moments of transition and transformation. One section reexamines rituals, especially Christian rituals in their liturgical cycle, and probes for their deepest meaning. Thus restored and reintroduced, they become useful again and healing. For individuals and for groups as they celebrate their personal and collective seasons and cycles.

Opie, Iona and Peter. *The Classic Fairy Tales.* (London: Oxford University Press, 1974.) This collection is brought together to show that the "magic in tales lies in people and creatures being shown to be what they really are." The authors' introduction alone is worth the price of the book for its explication of transformation as the process of *dis*enchantment and a revelation of Cinderella as a Christ figure. The book also has a good bibliography for background information.

Shea, John. *Stories of God.* (Chicago: Thomas More Press, 1978.) The author unfolds and translates the meaning of the Gospel. Dry doctrine and abstract Christian message are transposed to meaning and the symbolic world of revelation and Mystery. Shea's story about the Hopi ceremony of disenchantment gave fresh insight on the process of transformation and our invitation to choose our adulthood.

Ulanov, Ann Belford. *The Feminine in Jungian Psychology and in Christian Theology.* (Evanston: Northwestern University Press: 1971.) A professor of psychiatry and religion as well as a practicing therapist, the author writes with admirable clarity and scholarly thoroughness. And for all that, this book also manages to be utterly engaging and freeing. Her chapter entitled, "Descriptions of the Feminine," untangles the knots of modern confusion about the nature of the feminine that so hinder our understanding of women and divide the women's movement.

———— and Barry Ulanov. *Cinderella and Her Sisters, the Envied and the Envying*. (Philadelphia: Westminster Press, 1983.)

Woodman, Marion. *The Owl was a Baker's Daughter: Obesity, Anorexia Nervosa, and the Repressed Feminine* (Toronto: Inner City Books, 1980). An excellent psychological study of bodily symptoms as symbols of the woundedness and repression of the feminine nature in our selves and in our culture.

Recording

Page, Christopher, director. *A Feather on the Breath of God: Sequences and Hymns by Abbess Hildegard of Bingen*. (London: Hyperion Records.) This recording allows us to hear and feel and experience the words and music of one of the most interesting and original of mystics. The experience may transport you.

About the Author

GERTRUD MUELLER NELSON was born in Germany and grew up in St. Paul, Minnesota. She studied printmaking in Cologne and has a background in Montessori education. She attended the C. G. Jung Institute in Zurich. Her work as an artist and illustrator is known internationally and she writes and lectures on myth and ritual. Her first book, *To Dance with God,* has brought her a large and devoted audience. Mueller Nelson and her husband live in California. They have three grown children.